I0025142

Bajju Christian Conversion in the Middle Belt of Nigeria

SIL International®
Publications in Ethnography
47

The Publications in Ethnography series focuses on cultural studies of minority peoples of various parts of the world. While most volumes are authored by members of SIL International® who have done ethnographic research in a minority language, suitable works by others will also occasionally form part of the series.

Series Editor
Susan McQuay

Managing Editor
Eric Kindberg

Content Staff
Becky Quick, Volume Editor
Dirk Kievit, Copy Editor
Carol Brinneman, Copy Editor
Newton Frank, Copy Editor
Gene Burnham, Proofreader

Production Staff
Lois Gourley, Production Director
Judy Benjamin, Compositor
Barbara Alber, Graphic Designer, Cover Photographer

About the cover: Clay pot drums (*bakinkyim*) like this one are used by women to provide the rhythm for songs sung in church.

The images by A. J. N. Tremearne (1877–1915), figures 6.2 and 6.3, are thought to be in the public domain. They are from *The Tailed Headhunters of Nigeria*, originally published in 1912.

Bajju Christian Conversion in the Middle Belt of Nigeria

Carol V. McKinney

SIL International®
Dallas, Texas

© 2019 by SIL International®
Library of Congress Catalog No: 2018953730
ISBN: 978-1-55671-398-9
ISSN: 0-0895-9897

All rights reserved

No part of this publication may be reproduced, stored in a retrieval system, or transmitted in any form or by any means—electronic, mechanical, photocopy, recording, or otherwise—without the express permission of SIL International®. However, short passages, generally understood to be within the limits of fair use, may be quoted without permission.

Data and materials collected by researchers in an era before documentation of permission was standardized may be included in this publication. SIL makes diligent efforts to identify and acknowledge sources and to obtain appropriate permissions wherever possible, acting in good faith and on the best information available at the time of publication.

Copies of this and other publications of SIL International® may be obtained through distributors such as Amazon, Barnes & Noble, other worldwide distributors and, for select volumes, publications.sil.org:

SIL International® Publications
7500 W. Camp Wisdom Road
Dallas, Texas 75236-5629 USA

General inquiry: publications_intl@sil.org
Pending order inquiry: sales@sil.org

Contents

Figures

Maps

Tables

Preface

The ethnohistory of the Bajju adoption of Christianity is a story that needs to be told. It is one example of a continent-wide movement to Christianity that continues today. The Christian church is growing the most rapidly in Sub-Saharan Africa than in any other place in the world. Because of this and because little is known of ethnic groups in southern Kaduna State, this book provides an important window to what has happened and continues to occur there.

This book contains Bajju historical, colonial, and more recently collected data. It is a companion volume to *Baranzan's People: An Ethnohistory of the Bajju of the Middle Belt of Nigeria,* also published 2019. My husband, Norris, and I began our fieldwork among the Bajju in 1968, and together we worked on their language and culture until 2010 when my husband died. I have continued working with them off and on until the present. Hence this book represents a long relationship enjoyed with the Bajju. We began learning Jju, the language spoken by the Bajju, while living in Zaria. On December 26, 1968, we moved to Unguwar Rimi,[1] the "Village of the Kapok Tree," in the southern Bajju area in the Middle Belt of Nigeria. While there we immersed ourselves in their language and culture. We lived there until 1976, except for

---

[1]Gunn (1956) termed Unguwar Rimi, Tunwar Tagwai. This earlier name for Unguwar Rimi reflects an event in which Tagwai, a Hausa warrior, when in this area in the precolonial period was killed by the Bajju in their interethnic warfare. Hausa warriors came each dry season to raid this area for slaves and plunder. The Bajju vigorously resisted.

1971, which we spent in the US. We also spent time in Jos where our children attended school. We returned to Nigeria again in 1983–1984 when I conducted my doctoral research; and we have continued to be in occasional contact with the Bajju since then. Norris was there again in 1986, and I spent one month there in 2010.

Our field trips were sponsored by Wycliffe Bible Translators, SIL International, the Sociology Department of Ahmadu Bello University, the Nigerian Bible Translation Trust, and Bajju friends. My husband and I were grateful for the generosity of these organizations and I once again wish to express our appreciation to them. Our work in Nigeria would have been impossible without the continual hospitality and help we received. I would also like to thank the staff of the National Archives in Kaduna, who allowed me access to archival material that dealt with the colonial era.

There are numerous unnamed Bajju who willingly assisted in this project and who allowed us to join in their activities and responded with patience to our many inquiries. I wish to express my special thanks to His Royal Highness Nuhu Bature, the chief of the Bajju, who values the Bajju highly and who shared with us many of his insights about his people.

I appreciate the hospitality and assistance I received from numerous individuals, including Dr. and Mrs. Abashiya Ahuwan, Rev. and Mrs. John Ashcraft, and Rev. Dr. and Mrs. Chidawa Kaburuk each of whom opened their homes and received me as a member of their households during 1983 and 1984. Rev. Dr. and Mrs. Chidawa Kaburuk also hosted Elinor Abbot and me in November 2010. I am grateful for the help of Rev. Dr. Sam Waje Kunhiyop, who, while pursuing his own thesis research, teamed up with me in the study of Bajju religious change. I also thank Haruna Karick, who worked together with me in several ventures. He wrote the stories for the Jju primers. He later assisted me with data collection, particularly in administering the interview schedule both in 1984 and 2009.

My thinking and writing have been influenced profoundly by numerous invaluable comments on drafts of this manuscript made at various stages of its development, including by Carolyn Sargent, the late Dennis Cordell, William Pulte, Barbara Moore, and John and Pat Hanne. Among the Bajju I thank Phillip Allahmagani, D. K. Allahmagani, Dr. John and Martha Adive, the late Rev. Dr. Musa Asake, Yabo Bayai, Rev. Dr. Sam Waje Kunhiyop, Rev. Dr. Chidawa and Kande Kaburuk, Iliya and Asabar Ahuwan, Bulus, the late Elisha Sambo, Yabo Yashim, and numerous other Bajju. I would also like to thank Mike Cahill, Marilyn Gregerson, Eric Kindberg, Sue McQuay, and Becky Quick of Global Publishing Services for their generous work on this manuscript. Special thanks go to my late husband, Norris, who accompanied me on my field trips, shared with me the joys and frustrations of fieldwork, and gave me immeasurable support during the writing of my books. I thank our children Mark, Eric, Susan, and Christy who shared their mother with their Bajju colleagues as

I undertook this project. I also wish to thank Elinor Abbot who accompanied me to the Bajju area for the month of November 2010.

A note on Jju

The Bajju, formerly termed the Kaje, speak Jju, a member of the Central Platoid group of languages within the Benue Congo language family (Bendor-Samuel, ed. 1989:364). It resembles several other languages (often called dialects) spoken in southern Kaduna State. Hausa, the language of wider communication in the area, belongs to the Chadic branch of the Afro-Asiatic language family, a language family quite different from the language family Jju comes from and as such is quite dissimilar to it.

In the sociolinguistic environment of this area, it is almost inevitable that spelling of the language of wider communication influences previously unwritten minority languages. While a CVCV consonant-vowel pattern is characteristic of Hausa, Jju has consonant clusters, and a nearly complete set of fortis and lenis consonants that sometimes require two or three letters in the practical orthography to spell a single consonant. Further, there is palatalization and labialization in Jju that is not present in Hausa (for example, *kpukpwei* 'a thick bean soup', *kyang* 'thing'). The alphabet used for transcribing spoken Jju in this book is that of Jju spelling which was approved by the Nigerian National Language Center in the early 1990s. It leaves out the extra *i*'s and *u*'s that the Bajju often insert because of the influence of Hausa. For example, I write the term for 'father' as *a̱ttyi* rather than *a̱tiyi*.[2] This spelling approximates Jju pronunciation more closely than does the spelling influenced by the spelling of Hausa.

A note on references

There are two reference sections in this book. The first group of archival references includes letters, manuscripts, and reports that were found in the National Archives in Kaduna (NAK). They are labeled NAK or ZARPROF, which stands for Zaria Province. All other author and date references are found in the reference list at the end of the book.

---

[2] Jju distinguishes between [a] and [ə], the latter of which is represented in the practical orthography by "a̱." The high central vowel [ɨ] is written as "u̱."

Abbreviations

C&S	Cherubim and Seraphim Church
CMS	Church Mission Society, the Anglican missionary society
CRI	Christian Religious Instruction
ECWA	Evangelical Church of West Africa, the denomination founded by SIM, now the Evangelical Church Winning All
H.	Hausa language
J.	Jju language (Kaje)
N.A.	Native Authority
NAK	National Archives in Kaduna
NLFA	New Life for All
SIM	Sudan Interior Mission, now known as SIM (Serving in Mission)
SUM	Sudan United Mission
TEE	Theological Education by Extension
UNA	United Native African Church, now the First African Church Mission Inc.
WAFF	West African Frontier Force
ZARPROF	Zaria Province

1

Bajju Christian Conversion

Introduction

The center of world Christianity has shifted from the northern hemisphere to the southern one. This shift is particularly evident in Sub-Saharan Africa where Christianity is spreading rapidly, as seen in this quotation from Sanneh.

> In 1900, Christianity's center of gravity was emphatically in the North Atlantic, with Europe and North America together accounting for 82 percent of the world's Christians. A hundred years later, the picture has changed dramatically, with the southern hemisphere emerging as the new center of gravity. Today only about 35 percent of the world's Christians live in the North Atlantic region. (Sanneh 2012:231)

In 1900 there were approximately 8,736,000 Christians in Sub-Saharan Africa. This number continues to increase such that in mid-2011 there were 486,695,000 Christians in all of Africa (Johnson, Barrett, and Crossing 2012:28–29), with a Christian population growth of 2.68% per year (Barrett, Kurian, and Johnson 2001:13). Why is this conversion occurring?

This book looks at some answers to this question for the Bajju, the largest ethnic group in southern Kaduna State[1] in the Middle Belt of Nigeria, West Africa. This change occurred within a fifty-five-year time period (1929–1984). Why did they move from having no Christians to having almost one hundred percent identify with Christianity? Though most of their traditional Bajju religious practices have disappeared, my data indicate that many of the Bajju traditional religious beliefs remain and are held by Christian converts.

This book presents an ethnohistorical picture of Bajju Christian conversion, beginning with a brief discussion of their precolonial culture, including their religion, next the Hausa-Fulani context in the precolonial era, followed by the colonial era, the missionary context, and more recent times. For a theological analysis of Bajju religious conversion see Kunhiyop 2005.

All of the ethnic groups in southern Kaduna State have experienced rapid religious and cultural change by adopting Christianity. They have lived within the same political structure, experienced economic changes, and in general, dealt with rapid culture change as a result of colonialism, missionization, education, and globalization. Their movement to Christianity is remarkable, with most churches full every Sunday. Numerous people from this area have attended Bible schools, Christian theological seminaries, teachers' colleges, secondary schools, advanced teachers' colleges, universities, and other institutions of higher learning.

Bible translation is progressing in several of the local languages. For example, the Bajju now have the New Testament (NT) in their language, with the Old Testament (OT) translation in progress. Their northern neighbors, the Atyap, now have their New Testament translation. Translations are also in progress in Gwong, Hyam,[2] Gorok, and the desire is growing for Christian Scriptures in many other indigenous languages in southern Kaduna State and elsewhere in Nigeria. Sanneh states that "Christianity is a form of indigenous empowerment by virtue of vernacular translation" (2012:217). Developing a written form of an oral language contributes to the preservation of a language and culture.

Personally, my husband and I began working on the Jju language in 1968; our family moved to the Bajju area in December 1968. We lived in the teachers' quarters across the road from the senior primary school in Unguwar Rimi, the Village of the Kapok Tree, for a number of years. During this time we analyzed their language, together with Bajju speakers proposed an alphabet for their language, and with a Bajju team translated the New Testament into Jju. Throughout that time we observed Christianity spreading rapidly. Since the language used in Christian contexts is Hausa,

[1] This area has been referred to as Southern Zaria, a term that dates from the precolonial and colonial periods.
[2] Hyam is the language spoken by the Ham (Jaba) people.

I wondered, How much of the Christian message do they understand? Why are they converting? And how many of their traditional religious beliefs are they retaining? This book is the result of my investigation into these questions.

The following section relates how some of the first Bajju became Christians. It makes clear the fact that the Bajju "went out and brought Christianity home."

The first Bajju Christians

Christianity among the Bajju began in the southern Bajju area. Oral history relates that Dogo, Mutum, and Bakut, three sons of Bitiyong, converted to Christianity in December 1929; others had also converted, for example, some Bajju at Arikawan. Dogo and Mutum had drunk palm wine one dry season afternoon. As they were returning home to Unguwar Rimi, Dogo fell down while near the Atacap[3] River, and his brothers had to help him up. Dogo, a spirit medium in the *bvori*[4] spirit-possession cult, often had visions in which he foresaw the future and predicted what would happen. In this instance, while Dogo was down he had a vision in which he received a message that he should ask his brother Bakut where he had been learning to read. Further, in the vision the voice told him not to drink palm wine or any other alcoholic beverage from that day forward, and that he should go to Kagoro where he would be told what to do. His obedience to this vision was tested the very next day during festivities surrounding the naming ceremony of his daughter. Those who served palm wine placed a pot of this brew in his hut as usual. When he told them to take it away, the local people at first thought that his refusal was because he had had a recent experience with a *bvori* spirit. As a leader in the men's secret organization, the *abvoi*, Dogo drank heavily; it was not like him to refuse palm wine. However, gradually they came to realize that some change had happened in him.

Dogo continued to pursue the message he received in the vision by seeking out those who were learning to read. His brother Bakut took him to the nearby village of Arikawan where he found Dadi, Yakusak, and Abvoi[5] learning to read. Dadi surprised Dogo because Dadi had difficulty speaking (perhaps this was from stuttering, though oral history does not specify the nature of his speech problem; it simply relates that he had trouble with his

---

[3] The Atacap River is known as the Kogum River in Hausa.

[4] *Bvori* is pronounced *bori* in Hausa, the language of wider communication. Bori is the name of a village in northern Benin where this spirit-possession cult is practiced and possibly originated. The word *bori* is now used throughout the Hausa area to refer to a spirit-possession cult (see Besmer 1983).

[5] Whether Dadi, Yakusak, and Abvoi were Christians before Dogo and his brothers, we simply do not know as the oral tradition does not tell us. We do know that they went to Kagoro before the three brothers as evidenced by their learning to read.

tongue). How could this man who had difficulty speaking learn to read? Dogo reasoned that if this man could learn to read, he could too.

Soon after this, Dogo, together with his brothers Mutum and Bakut, attended church at Kagoro, a village approximately twelve miles from their home village of Unguwar Rimi.[6] They were amazed to see Agorok people in church wearing clothes similar to those of the Hausa, when most Agorok and Bajju men still wore skins and women wore leaves. There these three brothers heard about Christianity from Tom and Grace Archibald, a Scottish missionary couple, who served with Sudan Interior Mission (SIM) and who had opened the mission station at Kagoro in April 1927. At Kagoro the brothers learned about Jesus Christ, and in particular they learned that Christians who associated with SIM did not drink alcoholic beverages, did not participate in *abvoi,* and did not have more than one wife.

That day the three brothers decided to follow Christ. Following the service while trekking the twelve miles home, they talked among themselves about what they would do now that they were Christians. For example, Dogo had four wives, Mutum had two, and Bakut had four. Which wife should each man keep, leaving the others with no husband? They decided that any woman who wanted to stay with them for the sake of her children could do so, but she would no longer be a wife. They also wondered what to do about their positions in the men's society.

The next day the brothers declared their newfound faith to the people at Unguwar Rimi. They also revealed the secrets of the men's secret organization openly, including to women and children, something that they had sworn never to do when they were initiated. Since Dogo had been a leader within the men's secret organization, he and his brothers knew that this act had the threatened consequences of death within the *abvoi* shrine. Shock and outrage spread throughout the Bajju area following this action, and the elders quickly decided that these brothers had to die. However, Bitiyong, their father, restrained the others from carrying out this sentence. While he failed to understand his sons' actions, he trusted them.

Dogo and his brothers joined the reading class held by the Archibalds at Kagoro. Dogo became the first Bajju evangelist. In this capacity he traveled throughout the Bajju area, both on his own and together with Rev. Archibald, evangelizing his people. He suffered much for his faith. On one occasion the chief of the nearby village of Afana accused the Christians of failing to pay their taxes. The white colonial official, the Madaki Jema'a who resided in Unguwar Rimi, accepted the allegations that Dogo and the Christians had failed to pay their taxes. He put Dogo into wooden stocks with his hands and feet bound and had him beaten until his back bled. This took place on market day in the market in the center of town. The

---

[6] Unguwar Rimi is the Hausa name for this village. In Jju it is termed Angbakpat, the "Village of the Hausa."

Christians prayed earnestly for Dogo and about their situation. Later at the trial, the Christians produced their tax receipts, and consequently the judge dismissed the case. The colonial administrator persisted in his allegations, to which Dogo responded, "I leave you with God." That colonial administrator was removed from office, and, as a result, felt quite defeated, having lost face in this showdown with the new believers. The chief of Afana, who had brought the accusations, died the day of the trial. After that the Christians experienced greater freedom; they considered it a power encounter between the colonial administration, traditional society, and Christianity.

During the early days of Dogo's conversion, he often invited Christians home following church services, to feed them. This was especially appreciated during the hungry season, the time between when food from the previous harvest had been exhausted and new crops were planted but were not yet ready for harvest. During this time many people were reduced to eating chaff.

Mutum became the treasurer of the local church he attended. Since he was illiterate, he had others record the weekly offering in his notebook. At his death the record was found to be accurate even down to the last penny!

The conversions of Dogo, Mutum, Bakut, and others such as those at Arikawan began a movement to Christianity among the Bajju that has radically changed—and continues to change—the people in southern Kaduna State. Similar conversions to Christianity have also occurred among most of the other groups in southern Kaduna, such as among the Ham, Agorok, Atyap, Asholio, Gwong, Yeskwa, Adara, Kanikom, Angan, and Bakulu. Churches are now centers of daily activities, and most villages have one or more churches (see Appendix A for Bajju villages with Christian churches).

The dates when the early Christians converted at various villages are as follows:

1. 1929 Unguwar Rimi
2. 1930 Madakiya
3. 1931 Katssik, Azaru, Kurmin Bi, Zonkwa
4. 1932 Kamarum
5. 1934 Abet

African traditional religions and religious change

Ray (1976) discusses study of African traditional religions[7] in terms of three periods. The first is represented by eighteenth and nineteenth

---

[7] By African traditional religions I refer to a host of indigenous beliefs and practices held by different ethnic groups. This phrase is not meant to imply that these religions were static, for beliefs and practices have changed as general cultural change has occurred in these cultures. Rather I use the term in contrast to Christianity, Islam, and other major religious systems. While the term animism has been used, I object to it as it does not include the variety of religious phenomena that the term African

century accounts written by travelers, missionaries, and colonial agents. The second period, which began in the late nineteenth century, resulted in more objective and systematic field studies by trained anthropologists. In the third period African authors have written a number of philosophically and theologically orientated studies. Ray also states that more recently researchers have combined anthropological and historical perspectives to provide more adequate models of religious change. This study does precisely this in combining both ethnographic and historical perspectives on Bajju religious change.

Evans-Pritchard (1976, originally published 1937) contributes significantly to our understanding of the internal logic of indigenous African religious structures through his investigation of Azande witchcraft, magic, and sorcery. Witchcraft beliefs enable the Azande of the Central African Republic, Democratic Republic of the Congo, and South Sudan to explain evil, misfortune, illness, and death through identifying the perceived sources of those problems. The goal of the Azande is to handle situations where witchcraft is suspected in order to restore harmony in interpersonal relations. An individual suspected or accused of witchcraft is asked to "cool" his witchcraft substance, an activity his spirit and witchcraft substance may have performed even without his knowledge (1976:41–42). This belief system works towards the maintenance of conformity to societal norms. Evans-Pritchard's work is relevant to the Bajju as they too have witchcraft beliefs, though the way they handle the confrontation of a suspected person differs from that of the Azande.

In discussing African indigenous religions, Mbiti states that in Africa, "religion permeates into all the departments of life so fully that it is not easy or possible always to isolate it" (1969:1). During the colonial era in order for British colonial administrators to understand African cultures, they requested that researchers first study the political systems of African peoples to enable them to govern, then their economy, social organization, and lastly their art and religion; however, when researchers sought to carry out studies in this order, religion rose to the top as of primary importance for understanding African societies.

Turaki asserts that African traditional religion is not a "cognitively oriented system" with esoteric doctrines, and strict rules or regulations. Rather, it is a very existential and experiential religion that is "more felt than understood" and is thus very powerful (2006:19). This assertion enables us to see where the Bajju are coming from in their religious beliefs and practices, including in their adoption and practice of Christianity.

Religion continues to be extremely important in African life. For example, Elizabeth Ohene, a Ghanaian reporter recently wrote, "It is generally agreed that religion is the most active sector of the economy in most African

---

traditional religion does. Further, animism does not imply belief in God, an afterlife, reincarnation, etc., which are often found in different African traditional religions.

countries. Certainly in Ghana the growth of churches far outpaces growth in any other sector" (Ohene 2011).

British colonial administrators employed cultural anthropologists within the colonial administration to carry out this agenda. For example, Meek (1931) and others who were ethnographically trained produced fairly good descriptions. However, anthropologists occupied an ambiguous and thankless position within the colonial administration. For example, if there was a disturbance in a particular area, an anthropologist was often sent to investigate the causes of the problem. By the time the anthropologist submitted his findings, the disturbance had subsided. Colonial administrators read the reports and found them interesting; however, rarely did the anthropologists' findings translate into public policy. This became obvious to me as I read in the National Archives in Kaduna.

Religious conversion

In investigating Bajju people's adoption of Christianity, it is important to understand religious conversion itself. It is a complex process, which results in changes of consciousness, social belonging, and identity, as well as one's beliefs. What is involved relates to the cultural and historical context, including factors such as beliefs and practices of the indigenous religion, oppression, a political climate that allows or encourages it, economic benefits for the convert, and the social context of conversion. It seldom occurs simply based on a moment of insight or inspiration, though that too occurs.

Religious conversion is a change of identification and allegiance from one religious system to another. It involves a change in mental attitudes and physical setting. It is a turning from indigenous religious practices and turning to Christianity. However, it does not necessarily repudiate indigenous beliefs, but tends to add to them. Horton writes that it is a change from a local microscopic religious system to a macroscopic one, such as Christianity or Islam. He asserts that it often occurs because change is in the wind anyway with local missionary change agents filling the roles of catalysts for change (Horton 1971:104). When religious change occurs, it involves a further expansion of people's knowledge of the Supreme Being. Further, he writes that acceptance of either Christianity or Islam is as much a local response to other factors in the modern situation as it is to the activities of missionaries.

Conversion often occurs in contexts of oppression in which one social class or ethnic group oppresses another; oppression includes factors such as lack of political representation, economic deprivations, psychological distress, poverty, war and interethnic terrorism, and alienation. Bajju conversion occurred in the context of their subordination to two Hausa-Fulani emirates, those of Zazzau and Jema'a, and British colonialism and its aftermath. Therefore it is relevant to ask: Were the emirates and the colonial presence oppressive of the Bajju? How did their presence impact the Bajju and in particular their religion? Had they been exploited by the Hausa and/or the British? Did the Bajju have political representation during the colonial era? What attitudes and subsequent policies did the colonial administration implement that impacted the Bajju such that they turned to Christianity?

The Bajju see Christianity as a religion that they reached out and brought home to their area. Sanneh asserts that local Christian converts, such as Dogo, Bakut, Mutum, Dadi, Yakusak, and Abvoi, have often played a much greater role in the expansion of Christianity than have missionaries (Sanneh 1983:xii). Local Christians, as insiders to their cultures, are able to model Christianity to others in ways that are appropriate and meaningful within their cultural context. They contextualize Christianity in ways that missionaries as outsiders have difficulty doing.

From a Bajju perspective Christianity brought an expansion of their knowledge of God (*Kaza*). As one Cherubim and Seraphim pastor stated, "Before Christianity came, we knew God existed, now we know him" (United Native African Senior Apostle Lekot, personal interview, Zonkwa 1983; translation is mine).

An understanding of factors that affected Bajju conversion involves study first of their pre-Christian precolonial culture, their relationship to Zazzau and Jema'a Emirates, colonial policies and practices that impacted the Bajju and other cultures in Southern Zaria, the activities of missionaries and education, and finally the results of those factors in the lives of individual Bajju and the corporate life of their communities.

In the last chapter I chart comparisons between Bajju traditional religion and culture and that of Christianity. My purpose in doing so is to ascertain how many of their traditional religious beliefs have been retained by Bajju Christians. I also want to see where their traditional religious beliefs have been modified or are no longer held as a result of Christianity.

The issue of language use also enters into the picture of Bajju conversion. As stated earlier, Hausa is the language of the church while Jju is largely the language of the home. While knowledge of Hausa is increasing in the area, it is important to ask whether use of the language of wider communication has hindered understanding of the basic Christian message. In my research in 1983–1984 I found that clearly it hindered an understanding of Christianity, particularly for females who were forty years of age and older who comprised a linguistically neglected segment within the Christian church. Their grasp of Hausa was limited or even nonexistent, so the use of Hausa in the church did not allow them to understand the Christian message.

In the next chapter I examine Bajju traditional culture and specifically their religious beliefs. This provides a basis for later addressing whether or not these beliefs have been retained, modified, or abandoned by Bajju Christians.

2

Bajju Traditional Culture

Introduction

The Bajju traditionally were horticulturalists growing guinea corn, millet, yams, cocoa yams, a variety of leaves, onions, tomatoes, and various fruits—mangoes, guavas, citrus, pawpaw, pineapple, etc. They appreciated having large families, particularly sons, as the more sons a man has, the more land he can farm. All farming was done by hand using traditional hoes.

Traditionally the Bajju were ruled by elders, with elders at the family level, village level, the sectional level, and the entire Bajju level. Once a year the elders of the five sections met together at Dibyyi to decide on matters that affected the entire ethnic group. They could also meet together if some matter came up that affected everyone—for example, an epidemic, warfare, or murder—or to deal with any issues that were not handled adequately at a lower level.

God and spirits

The Bajju believe in God, *Kaza*,[1] who is the Creator of humans and the universe. He is the one to whom final appeal is made; as for example, in the event of illness when all other remedies have been tried but to no avail, one can always appeal to God. God is just and man's final judge; consequently

---

[1] The word *kaza (kadza)* means 'God, up, north, tall, and above'.

God punishes an individual who wrongs another individual. God is all-present, all-knowing, and eternal. He is the Creator, though the Bajju do not have a story that tells how he created the world. God gives only good things such as children, good hunting and crops, wealth, health, and blessings; thus death, illness, natural disasters, misfortunes, and evil do not originate with God, other than for an individual who deserves punishment for his offenses. For example, if a man swears falsely on the drum, the death that results comes from God. Swearing on a drum was usually done for boundary disputes between two people or groups of people, as between the Bajju and the Fulani cattle herders. Prior to the coming of Christianity, while the Bajju had knowledge of God, he was not worshipped.

Most deaths are thought to be unnatural; they are usually attributed to *nkut*, the inherent spiritual power within individuals that can harm others in the spiritual realm resulting in physical illness, death, evil, or misfortune. *Nkut* is the Bajju term for witchcraft, such as Evans-Pritchard (1937) wrote about among the Azande.

The Bajju also believe in a number of spirits that inhabit the world around them. For example, the Bajju believe in small invisible spirits, known as *nạtenyrang* (*kạtenyrang*, sing.), which inhabit the bush in the Bajju territory. Some assert that the *nạtenyrang* are people who have been reincarnated as spirits. These spirits are thought to be either black or white. They are short in stature with big heads (Kunhiyop 1988:12). If black they have an evil nature, and if white they have a good nature and bring fortune and goodness to people. They have their own chief, known as *ạgwam kạtenyrang*. They inhabit their own villages that resemble those of the Bajju, complete with round huts, paths, and roads. Their villages may be either in among the Bajju or out in the bush away from them. They are known to surround their compounds with thorn bushes; consequently, one way that the Bajju recognize that a site either is or was inhabited by *nạtenyrang* is by the presence of thorn bushes.

If an individual offends one of these spirits, he may become ill with a fever, mental illness, or epilepsy. Since these spirits are short in stature, the illnesses they cause are often associated with one's legs, such as paralysis or sores on one's legs. The Bajju traditionally dealt with that type of situation by making a payment of beans (*jok*) that they left near the place where these spirits are believed to live. The individual might also take some money and leave it for the spirits. Usually the diviner told the individual how much he or she should leave to appease them.

Most people lack the capacity to see *nạtenyrang* and their villages because these spirits are invisible; however, some people with spiritual vision, such as a diviner (*ạbvok*), could see them. One former diviner told me that she washed her face daily with a special medicine to enable her to see within the spiritual realm. However, for most people, to see *nạtenyrang* implied that sickness would result. Diviners were like the village doctors.

People would go to them to inquire why someone was ill or why someone had died. In order to tell them, the diviners would often go into trances in which the spirits would come to them to tell them why.

When humans move into an area, *nₐtenyrang* may move to other sites as they do not like noise or light. After they have abandoned their villages for other sites, anyone is able to see the ruins of their villages. Some evidence of these abandoned villages includes small round mud walls, pot shards, and thorn bushes. The mud walls of such abandoned *nₐtenyrang* houses are valued as medicine. People come to Kajju from as far away as Zaria in order to obtain this type of medicine, which when mixed with water and herbs can be rubbed on a person's affected legs and also drunk.

Another category of spirits are water spirits, the *bₐconcong* (*ₐconcong*, sing.), also known as the *gₐjimale*, who live in clear still water, as well as in the bush, in trees, or in caves. A water spirit may come out of the water to seduce its victim by transforming itself into a beautiful woman and appear thus to a man, or as a handsome man to a woman, or as a snake. While *gₐjimale* can transform themselves, one can identify them because they cannot transform their toes, which are like those of horse hooves (Kunhiyop 1988:14). The *gₐjimale* are also thought to be serpents that live under mountains.[2]

A third category of spirits are very tall spirits, the *bₐninyet* (*ₐninyet*, sing.), who are so tall that they reach high into the sky, so that an individual cannot see its head. These spirits appear late at night or early in the morning, between 3 to 6 a.m., when some people set out on journeys. While some state that they are harmful to humans, others say that if a person sees one and admits to others to having seen one, that individual will die. One source stated that they are a type of *nₐtenyrang*, though others put them in a class by themselves. *Bₐninyet* may speak to people when they meet them.

By contrast, Kunhiyop states that the *bₐninyet* are harmless (1993:71). He asserts that if an individual goes to the dwelling of an *ₐninyet*, that spirit will not hurt him or her. He states further that the *bₐninyet* have their dwellings among human beings.

One Christian Bajju man reported seeing an *ₐninyet* early one morning. When he saw it, he closed his eyes and prayed; when he opened them again, the spirit had vanished, thus proving to him that the power of the Holy Spirit is stronger than that of the *bₐninyet*.

Elderly Bajju also spoke of the mother of God to whom final appeal can be made. If someone does something really bad to you, a person who is bigger and stronger than you, you can always appeal to the mother of God. You could strongly say, "You will meet with the mother of God," and mothers can be quite stern in dealing with those under them. Today the concept of

---

[2] The Kuteb of Nigeria also believe in a giant dragon or snake that lives under mountains. When mud slides occur, they are believed to be caused by the dragon or snake moving (Rob Koops, pers. comm., 1984).

the mother of God has largely died out. We only encountered knowledge of it from elderly Bajju.

The largest and most important category of spirits is the spirits of the departed (*ạbvoi*, sing., *bạbvoi*, pl.). They occupy a central position within Bajju daily life. The Bajju believe spirits inhabit the underground ancestral spirit world (*bạnyet yabyen* or *bạnyeyabyen*, with *ạyabyen* referring to the underground world). After the introduction of the *ạbvoi* society, the two categories of spirits, *bạnyet yabyen* and *bạbvoi*, tended to merge. Elderly male ancestors comprise most of the *ạbvoi*; however, though rarely, respected elderly women could also become ancestral spirits within the family.

Spirits of deceased infants, children, women, and men who had no progeny are believed to be reincarnated. The Bajju concept of reincarnation is not based on merit, unlike in Hinduism. Rather a person who has not fulfilled his or her functions in life before death is reincarnated. A human can be reincarnated as a bird, an animal, or another human being, whether male or female. This helps to explain the close relationship between animals and humans.

Infants born around the time of the recent death of another person are often seen as the reincarnated spirit of that person. The child is given a name that reflects this reincarnation, such as *Ạbrok*, meaning 'he has returned'. If the Bajju see a shooting star at night, it indicates that a person is being reincarnated.

A person's functions in life include being married, having children, managing his often polygynous household well, and becoming a respected elder. If these goals were fulfilled, at death a man's spirit was believed to enter the spirit world that resides under the ground. After a man's death and burial, his widow(s) had to walk carefully on the ground in order not to disturb the recently deceased. He entered the world of the living dead or the ancestors. Each evening, for approximately a month after death, his spirit was believed to return to eat food that was set out for him. In the morning, the children of the household were given that food to finish eating.

Spirit-possession cult

The Bajju borrowed the spirit-possession cult from people who lived to the north. It was known as the *bvori* cult. The Hausa refer to it as *Bori*, which is the name of a village in northern Benin where this cult may have originated. One older woman I talked with told of the spirit entering her body, often causing her to fall down, sometimes into the fire. She spoke of knowing what was happening to others within the village even without anyone coming to tell her. It was the spirits who told her. Later once she became a Christian, she continued to be very aware of the spirits. I have seen her stand up in church to ask people to pray for her as the spirits were bothering her again.

Oaths

Law and order were traditionally maintained through the direction of the elders and through oaths. An oath is "a promise or affirmation, usually calling on a divine authority to punish the oath taker in case of perjury" (Winick 1977:387). Winick further states that an oath for some people is like a self-curse with almost magical potency. It is a solemn promise in which an individual attests that his or her statement is true or that he or she is determined to keep a promise. Often an oath includes some statement of the possible consequences if the individual's statement is found to be untrue or if the individual does not keep his or her promise. The Bajju used oaths extensively, and some continue to do so. Swearing and oath-taking served to discourage individuals from behavior disruptive of society.

There are two verbs in Jju that relate to oaths, *sshi* and *sswa*. *Sshi* translates as 'to swear', while *sswa* translates as 'to take an oath' (*sswa nak*, 'to take an oath' or literally 'to drink an oath'). They form a continuum, with swearing used for less serious issues and taking an oath for more serious ones. Because they form a continuum, these two activities are considered together. Oaths are sworn on items in frequent use by the one who swears. There are oaths for men, oaths for women, and oaths for both men and women.

Repentance and retracting oaths

After taking oaths, some decide to retract their oaths. When an individual, either on his behalf or that of a lineal ancestor, desires to retract words or actions that are untrue or that have negative consequences to him or for the Bajju, that individual may repent. To do so is termed "to drink ashes" or "to take an oath on ashes (*sswa bạtwak*)." The person takes a small amount of ashes into his mouth, swears that he repents of his former words, then spits them out into a small hole in the ground he has dug, covers the hole to indicate that the words he or his lineal ancestor had spoken are spit out, buried, and no longer effective. Next he takes a small amount of ashes into his mouth and swallows it, indicating a blessing. The Bajju assert that God finds the ashes that were spit out and forgives the individual. Ashes symbolize coolness of what was formerly hot. The Bajju identify anger with heat, and forgiveness and absence of anger with coolness. In addition to taking an oath of repentance after confession of an offense, an individual could be fined. This fine could be a black goat, or a red cock, or hen.

Sswa bạtwak is used in the event of one having sworn an oath, then finding that he has to retract that oath. For example, if a man swore that he would not move his house for any reason, but then found it necessary to move his house, the *sswa bạtwak* ritual is necessary. It can also be used in other instances. For example, if a woman is in the process of giving birth but is having difficulty, she may be asked to *sswa bạtwak*, to confess the number of men she has had sexual relations with. After doing so, she would then be able to successfully deliver her infant.

Witchcraft

The Bajju believe that people are born with an inherited, inherent capacity to harm others in the spiritual realm that can result in evil, physical illness, misfortune, unexpected occurrences, and even death. This belief is termed *nkut* in Jju. For example, if a driver turns left at an intersection and his car is hit by another car, it must have been caused by someone practicing witchcraft against him (McKinney 2018; Gunn 1956). Lots of other cars also turned left at the same intersection, but none of them were hit. The question arises as to why his car was hit and not some other car. It helps to explain the intersection of time and event. It explains the ultimate cause of an occurrence. While there is recognition of the immediate cause, it is usually the ultimate cause that is more important.

There are various ways to identify a witch. Usually the person accused does not follow regular conventions of behavior. For example, he or she may look intently at someone, an action that only a witch would do. He or she might be jealous, contentious, angry, or always stirring up trouble. When someone becomes ill or dies, the person who displays these negative behaviors and attitudes is likely to be accused of causing the problem. He or she may be beaten and sent home to his or her relatives. Often it is elderly women who are so accused. They may have swelling in their ankles, something that is not seen as natural. It is a sign of a witch.

Dreams

The Bajju believe that the ancestors appear to them in dreams and visions in order to communicate their messages to the living. It is only those dreams that come from the ancestors that the Bajju pay careful attention to. For example, one woman left her husband after their two sons had died. His relatives had urged her to leave as they felt that his witchcraft had caused the deaths of their sons. However, once back in her home village she had a dream from a recently deceased Christian ancestor who told her to return to her husband. That ancestor told her that if she did not do so, she would not see God when she died. So she returned to her husband.

Values

The Bajju value extending hospitality to guests and visitors. Traditionally, they were known to be very kind at home but very wicked out in the bush. When a person comes to a compound, the host or hostess should give their guest a gift, whether a gift of food to eat or something to take home.

The Bajju also value many children and large extended families. One's identity is tied to one's family. Hence individualism is not valued, while one's identity revolves around the people who are part of one's family.

Marriage

Marriage is highly valued among the Bajju as it is for most ethnic groups in Sub-Saharan Africa. Kunhiyop states, "Marriage is a key cultural value to the Bajju people." They perceive marriage as a "sacred duty which every normal person must perform. Failure to do so means in effect stopping the flow of life through the individual, and hence the diminishing of mankind upon the earth" (Kunhiyop 2005:71). Traditionally the Bajju practiced monogamy, polygyny (a man having two or more wives), and polyandry (a woman having two or more husbands). In the last form the woman lived with only one of her husbands at a time. Basically, if the bridewealth had not been returned and if she had had a child by a husband, she could return to him, for example, when her next husband died. Since the bridewealth was rarely returned, in effect it was as though there was no divorce. The exception was in the case of barrenness in which a young bride could be returned to her father if she did not have a child to continue the husband's lineage. Having children is that important. The goal of marriage is to have many children. One proverb states *Banyet byyi banyet a hwok shamsham,* "Blessed are those who have people" (Kunhiyop 2005:73).

Traditionally marriage was by capture of the young woman. The husband's family and the bride's family finished negotiations over the bridewealth that was to be paid, and they agreed together when and where the capture was to take place. The only one who did not know was the young woman. Her parents might send her to fetch water from a stream at a specific time, where the young man and his friends would be waiting to capture her. On occasion she was able to escape capture. If so, she knew enough to realize that her parents knew of the capture plot, so she would run to another relative's house. The young men then went to her parents' compound where they waited until the parents found their daughter and gave her to them.

The Bajju stated that "they did not take wives from villages where they married sisters." The "sisters" were women from villages that their village had a marital alliance with. Wives, also termed secondary wives, came from other villages.

The Bajju are patrilineal,[3] meaning that descent is traced through the male line. They also reside patrilocally, with a young man bringing his new bride home to live with him in his father's compound. The new bride is taught how to cook and relate to people in that compound by the groom's

---

[3] See McKinney 1983 for further discussion of Bajju kinship and see McKinney 1992 on Bajju marital patterns.

mother. At the end of an approximately three-month period, his mother puts pots out as a sign that the young woman has learned sufficiently and will now cook for her husband. Children belong to the patrilineage, so in the event of divorce the children remain with their father. The extended family lives together in the father's compound.

When a man dies, his son inherits his father's wives other than his own mother. If there is no son, then the man's brother or other close male relative inherits his wife (wives). If this did not occur, the widow would return to her father's compound and leave her children with her husband's family. Widow inheritance keeps the family together allowing a mother to stay together with her children. When a woman married, she married into the patrilineage. So, when she was inherited, there was not another wedding. Traditionally widow inheritance occurred one month after the death of her husband. The woman had a say in whether or not she wanted to marry a specific brother. One male relative would send her some tobacco and she would ask who sent it. If she agreed to marry that man, she accepted the tobacco. If she did not agree, she rejected it and waited until another brother or other close male relative sent her tobacco and then would decide whether or not she wanted to become the wife of that man.

Sacrifice

The elders met to decide what to do in case of any transgressions that disrupted society and to cleanse the society of the consequences of those transgressions. The penalties they imposed depended upon the seriousness of the offence. For less serious transgressions the elders imposed a fine of a pot of beer and/or a red or white cock; a black cock was unacceptable because black symbolizes impurity or filthiness. Red represents sin, while white symbolizes purity. For more serious offenses, such as adultery and incest, they imposed a fine of a male goat (*kɑrom*). In the case of homicide they sacrificed a horse. Whether they sacrificed a cock or a goat, a blood sacrifice was necessary to cleanse the community.

Offenses that might require a blood sacrifice included sins such as murder, homicide, stealing, adultery, incest, lying, and disrespect of one's parents. The Bajju were aware of right and wrong within their traditional society.

When Christianity came it addressed the issue of sacrifice, namely that Jesus' death was the final sacrifice for the sins of the world. The Bajju felt that they no longer needed to sacrifice animals to cleanse the community. So blood sacrifice of animals is no longer practiced.

Men's secret organization

Among the Bajju the men directed activities within the community through a men's secret ancestral organization, the *ɑbvoi*. This type of society was widespread in Northern Nigeria.[4] It was often referred to as the *dodo* society. Women and uninitiated children were excluded from this society and its secrets. The ạbvoi maintained the myth that it was all-knowing and all-present through various means, for example, engaging a boy to accompany a woman when traveling and then reporting back to the ạbvoi any misdeeds that occurred on the trip. The woman would be disciplined for those misdeeds when she returned home.

Boys were initiated into the ạbvoi society when the men deemed them ready for initiation. In initiation they were figuratively swallowed by the ạbvoi and then vomited out at the end of the initiation. When they first emerged from the ạbvoi shrine, they were told to act as though they were very weak. They were then taken to the river to bathe. Then they poured oil over them, reviving them. They would begin dancing as they returned to the enclosure where their mothers and other relatives waited to welcome them with their new status as men. They were no longer classified with the women and children but joined the initiated men in Bajju society.

---

[4] When I refer to Northern Nigeria I capitalize the word Northern. Today formal regions are no longer governmental units but rather Nigeria has states. When talking about the north of Nigeria, I do not capitalize northern.

3

Precolonial Hausa-Fulani Emirates and the Bajju

The Hausa and Fulani[1] from Zazzau Emirate, with its principal city located in Zaria, claimed Southern Zaria, including the Bajju area, within their territory. Zazzau Emirate was the most extensive of any emirate in northern Nigeria (Palmer 1936:274). By the sixteenth century the influence of this emirate had reached Nupeland. Palmer noted that among the inhabitants of this area, "There were also in the land of Zazzau many places inhabited by barbarians" (Palmer 1936:274). The Bajju no doubt fell into his "barbarian" category.

Prior to the *jihad* or holy war of Usuman ɗan Fodio[2] (1804–1812), the relationship between the pastoral Fulani and the minority ethnic groups of the area, including the Bajju, was mutually beneficial. Their relationships involved mutual respect and cooperation. Fulani paid an annual tribute to these minority ethnic groups for the use of their land for grazing their cattle during the dry season after the local people had harvested their crops. The crop residue left in the fields provided food for the cattle and the cattle

---

[1] The Hausa-Fulani consist of the Hausa (Habe), a sedentary people who are horticulturalists, and the Fulani (Fulbe), who are nomadic and semi-nomadic pastoralists. Today the Bajju continue to relate to the nomadic pastoral Fulani known as the Bororo Fulani, semi-nomadic Fulani pastoralists, and the Fulani *Gidan*, or house Fulani who no longer have cattle, many of whom have intermarried with the Hausa.

[2] Usuman ɗan Fodio is also spelled Uthman ɗan Fodio and Othman ɗan Fodio; after the *jihad* he was known as Sarkin Musulmi (Chief of the Muslims).

left manure that fertilized the fields. For the Bajju this annual tribute usually consisted of a number of head of cattle, which were given to them at Kachichere. This relationship paralleled that which existed between Fulani and the indigenous people of Adamawa as noted by Abubakar, who states that prior to settling and grazing their cattle in an area, the Fulani and the ruler of the area would negotiate. He states, "There would be serious negotiations, sometimes necessitating some form of agreement such as yearly payment of tribute, grazing dues, and herding the non-Fulbe's cattle along with their own" (Abubakar 1977:35).

While one oral source asserted that the Bajju received an annual payment from the Fulani for pasturing their animals on Bajju land after the crops had been harvested, another oral source asserted that this did not happen. He stated that use of their land for Fulani cattle to graze upon the crop residue in the dry season was done free of charge. The Fulani did pay an annual tax (*jungali*)[3] per head of cattle to the emirate; however, this was not paid to the local population.

While the semi-settled Fulani live among the Bajju, they are considered temporary occupants of the land that the Bajju consider theirs. Some of these Fulani have lived among the Bajju for extended time periods, but they do not have any legal rights to live there or pasture their animals. The instances of court cases between Fulani and Bajju usually involve crop damage by Fulani cattle.

This relationship contrasts with that between the Bajju and the representatives of the Hausa-Fulani emirates, a relationship that involved slave raiding, looting of property, and extracting tribute, as well as legitimate trade. In the following section I discuss the relationship between the Bajju and the emirates in the precolonial period.

Zazzau and Jema'a Emirates, and the Bajju in the precolonial period

The *jihad* of Usuman ɗan Fodio, a Fulani Muslim cleric, affected the relationship between the Hausa-Fulani and the Bajju as well as that of other minority ethnic groups in northern Nigeria. That *jihad* began in 1804 and ended in 1812 when al-Kanemi, the leader of the Kanembu near Lake Chad, asserted that they were already Muslims and hence did not need a *jihad* to purify Islam or to impose it on them. The *jihad* resulted in a number of emirates or city-states, all of which gave allegiance to the emirate of Sokoto. These included the emirates of Kebbi, Gwando, Zazzau, Kano, Katsina, and Gobir.

In the *jihad* Usuman ɗan Fodio gave flags or banners of religion to various military commanders as a sign of their authority to wage war in his name. For example, Mallam Usuman from Jema'a sought a flag as his insignia of

---

[3] This tax was abolished in 1976.

office for the new emirate of Jema'a na Daroro. However, Mallam Musa, the emir at Zaria from 1804 to 1821, turned Mallam Usuman back by claiming that the Shehu of Sokoto had given him the southern regions, including the Bajju area. However, Mallam Musa gave a flag to Mallam Usuman. This indicated that Mallam Usuman could wage war for Zazzau Emirate, and as a result Jema'a Emirate became a vassal state of Zazzau Emirate. Jema'a joined Zazzau's other vassal states of Keffi, Doma, Kajuru, Kauru, Lapai, Lafia, and Nassarawa. Non-Hausa and non-Muslim ethnic groups occupied these areas.

While members of the Hausa-Fulani ruling party considered the southern regions as subservient to Zaria, this was not the local perception of their relationship with the emirates. Morrison states concerning this early period that the Bajju when confronting the Hausa-Fulani often sought refuge among the Irigwe,

> Moving south-westward, Zaria appears to have had problems defeating the Kaje[4] [Bajju] and other groups on the lowlands between 1830 and 1850. Thus the Irigwe villages of Miango (Nyango) and Kall on the western edge of the Plateau were affected only indirectly by the incursions of Zaria, receiving refugee immigrants like the Kaje, but never confronting the Hausa directly. (Morrison 1982:142)

When necessary, Bajju refugees fled to the plateau from their land in the southern regions in order to avoid enslavement from the raids conducted by representatives of the emirates each dry season. Morrison further adds that the Bajju who were resident at Miango obtained large horses for the Irigwe that the Irigwe used for military purposes. He states,

> With the Kaje's trade connections, the Irigwe obtained large horses which were used for military purposes to push the Birom—Gyel and Kuru—and the Rukuba farther away from their original areas. For example, the Irigwe attacked and burned parts of Vwang c. 1840. The Irigwe also acted as trading agents for captives that were brought by other ethnic groups in exchange for larger horses. These captives the Irigwe passed on through the Kaje to Zangon Katab, where horses were standard exchange for captives. (Morrison 1982:144)

---

[4] The Bajju were known by outsiders as the Kaje, a word that probably derives from Kajju, meaning the "land of the Bajju." Prior to approximately 1980, if asked one's ethnic identity a Bajju speaker would likely respond "Kaje." However, since approximately 1980 the Bajju prefer to be known as the Bajju rather than the Kaje. Today to use the term Kaje to refer to the Bajju is viewed as pejorative.

Both horses and cowries were used to redeem persons who had been enslaved in northern Nigeria. For example, Mary Smith recorded the biography of Baba, a Hausa woman. Baba told about a raiding party that enslaved fourteen persons from her household (1954:68–70). When people from Baba's household found where those people had been taken and sold into slavery, they began the long process of collecting sufficient money in the form of cowries for their ransom (*fansa*, H.).

Military raids conducted by the Hausa-Fulani had as their primary goals extending the realm of their domination and taking captives, most of whom ended up as slaves. For example, though details are sketchy for the period after the *jihad* of Usuman dan Fodio, oral traditions and archival records provide some understanding of what occurred during that period. In 1835 Emir Abdul Karimi, the Fulani emir at Zaria, conducted a number of raids against the Bajju. In 1849 Emir Mammon Sani,[5] emir of Zazzau, conducted a punitive expedition against the Bajju. During his expedition he maintained a camp at Fadan Kaje (NAK ZARPROF 607). He burned the villages of "Ferma, Sakwot, Gantam, Kurdan, and Kachip" and occupied the district for approximately six weeks before returning to Zaria (NAK K 2985, Kirkpatrick 1914).

According to the *Gazetteers*, during this expedition he divided the Bajju into two spheres of influence, with the southern half under the emir of Jema'a, and the northern half under himself as the emir of Zazzau (Ames 1934:227). Smith reports that Emir Mammon Sani gathered an immense booty of slaves so that by the time of his death he owned nine thousand slaves (Smith 1960:157–158). In one of his slave camps or villages (*rumada*, *rinji* H.), he had over three thousand slaves, some of whom were likely Bajju. The size of a family's slave village was an indication of a person's wealth. While most of the slaves ended up purchased locally among the Hausa and Fulani, some entered the trans-Saharan slave trade. For example, camel caravans brought salt and other products from the Sahara and North Africa to Kano and Katsina, and in turn purchased slaves as well as grain, leather, cloth, gold, and other products from farther south to transport across the Sahara.

Olive Temple records a later attempt to bring about Bajju submission to Zazzau Emirate. In this instance in 1858 Emir Audu of Zazzau led a raid against them (Temple 1922:194). According to her account this raid finally broke the "recalcitrant" Bajju.

Under Emir Abdullahi (1863–1873) taxation increased. Tatumare, a Bakulu convert to Islam, became the military officer (*kuyambana*, H., literally 'the one responsible for worthless people') in charge of a heavily armed cavalry (*lidifi*, H.), which sought to extract payment of tribute from Southern Zaria (Smith 1960:170). Because of his intimate knowledge of the area he was able to secure more regular payment of tribute from various ethnic groups.

---

[5] Also spelled Emir Mohman Sani.

Abdullahi's successor, Emir Abubakar (1873–1876), added the office of treasurer (*ma'aji*, H.) for south-central Zaria. From the perspective of the emirates, he had jurisdiction over the Bakulu (Ikulu), Angan (Kamantan), Ham (Jaba), and other neighboring ethnic groups (Smith 1960:174). However, Abubakar led only one expedition into Southern Zaria before his death in 1876.

Efforts to extract tribute intensified under Emir Abdullahi (1876–1881). His successor, Emir Sambo (1881–1890), attacked the Adara (Kadara), Agorok (Kagoro), and Gwari, though with little success. He appointed Yawa, one of his slaves, to the position of Sarkin Yamma, the slave raiding chief, for the west and the area along the trade routes to the south and southwest of Zaria. He was stationed together with a cavalry unit at Kachia for purposes of slave raiding, protecting the southern boundary of the emirate, and policing the caravan route through Southern Zaria. According to Smith, this force increased in size and power (Smith 1960:186). By the 1890s the cavalry at Kachia possessed firearms, then available through the Royal Niger Company at Lokoja. Yero (1890–1897) succeeded Sambo as emir of Zazzau. He engaged in extensive slave raiding in Southern Zaria and led attacks against the Pitti and Rukuba on the western edge of the Jos Plateau (Smith 1960:192).

Emir Kwassau (1897–1903) succeeded Yero as emir of Zazzau. During his reign the Atyap rebelled and refused to pay the one hundred slaves requested by Zazzau Emirate. Emir Kwassau therefore undertook one expedition in which he stated that he would take no slaves; he would only kill his enemies. After that punitive campaign, no Hausa traders dared enter the area for two years for fear of reprisals. The Kaduna River was said to have run red with blood (NAK ZARPROF 607, 1932). Bajju remember the reign of Kwassau as particularly brutal.

Bajju and emirates interaction

The relationship between the emirates of Zazzau and Jema'a and the people of Southern Zaria was marginal in the precolonial era. The Bajju received little benefit from them; rather, these emirates oppressed them. Both historical records and Bajju oral traditions focus on this aspect of the relationship between the emirates and the populace of Southern Zaria. Because of this oppression, both the political and religious structures of the Bajju were under pressure. The Hausa practice of appointing chiefs undermined the authority of the elders, *bagado,* whose authority was replete with supernatural sanctions. By failing to utilize the existing Bajju religio-political structure, the emirates were attacking its functions of maintaining social control and reinforcing the wishes of the ancestors.

The Hausa introduced and tried to control weak secular village chieftaincies. These weak chieftaincies were superimposed upon the traditional religio-political structure. In oral tradition as early as 1850 the Hausa had established such chiefs (*agwam*, sing.; *bagwam*, pl.); however, within the Bajju society these chiefs were subservient to the elders. When first introduced, the position of chief was denigrated as a job that respected members of the community would not undertake. The activities of a chief were to relate to outsiders, particularly to the Hausa-Fulani emirates, collect taxes, and sell slaves. Hausa-Fulani held chiefs responsible for problems they encountered in their contacts with people of Southern Zaria, and especially with the Bajju.

One elderly man, who claimed to be two hundred years old,[6] recalled the Hausa setting up one man as a chief. They bestowed upon him a Hausa gown (*riga*, H.) and other insignia of office. When the Hausa left, they took the new chief's daughter with them. This was completely unacceptable to him as chief, so he organized an attack on the Hausa. He succeeded in getting his daughter back and refused to have anything further to do with the role of chief which the Hausa had bestowed upon him.

Hausa[7] traversed Southern Zaria along a caravan route. The Emir of Zazzau maintained camps (*zango*, H.), as stopping places along the trade route through Southern Zaria. For example, there were camps at Kachia, Ashafa (on the east side of Fadan Kamantan), Madauchi, Kachichere, Zangon Katab,[8] and Kagoro. The emir of Zazzau had walled camps constructed at these locations. They maintained these walled compounds as caravan stops along the trade routes and also in order to protect themselves from the indigenous people. These walled camps served as staging locations for their slave raids, pillaging, and tax and tribute collection in the area. The practice of building their own walled areas conforms to the usual practice of Hausa traders who live outside their home area. They typically have a ward or section of the city where they reside. For example, Cohen described the Hausa quarter of Ibadan where the Hausa traders chose to reside apart from the Yoruba. They lived there because they wanted to maintain their distinctive culture, practice Islam, and continue their monopoly over the lucrative long-distance cattle and kola nut trade (Cohen 1969).

The picture that emerges is that during each dry season emirate representatives conducted slave raids and demanded tribute from the minority ethnic groups throughout the southern regions. Smith states concerning this period,

---

[6] In precolonial times the Bajju counted each dry season as a year and each rainy season as another year. So there were two years to one year within a solar year.

[7] The Hausa are known as traders throughout West Africa, including in the precolonial era.

[8] Zangon Katab later became the seat of the district head during the colonial era, and it remains a Hausa enclave.

The *jihad* was annually renewed in dry-season raids and campaigns designed to extend the Fulani dominions or to intensify the subjugation of non-muhammadan populations already within them. Slavery was the usual fate of captives, and the collection of captives was a major object of these military adventures. For the fifty years following their conquest of Zaria, the Fulani were engaged in somewhat indiscriminate offensive wars. (Smith 1960:96)

The Bajju and other minority ethnic groups in the southern regions feared the Hausa-Fulani slave raids and their efforts to collect slaves, taxes, and tribute. The raiders came suddenly without warning to capture slaves. Smith describes the destructive nature of these raids,

The collection of overdue payments from pagan tribes normally involved the burning of a few towns and the enslavement or execution of considerable numbers of people. The Jaba tribe defeated by Mamman Sani in the 1840s were loath to pay tribute in slaves, and suffered heavily, although preserving their independence. The slave-general stationed at Kacia c. 1885 was charged with the collection of the annual tribute from the Kaje, Kamantan, Ikulu, and neighboring tribes, if necessary by force. (Smith 1960:99–100)

The Bajju sought to defend themselves. For example, in one oral tradition, a Bajju warrior killed a Hausa Fulani warrior named Tagwai[9] with a poisoned arrow as he sat in camp near the village of Sakwak. A number of Bajju children born around this time received the name Tagwai.[10]

The Bajju also recall chasing one Hausa warrior out of Unguwar Rimi and Bakin Kogi. His Bajju opponent sat on horseback challenging the intruder for three days at the boundary between the Kafanchan and Bajju, resulting in the establishment of the present boundary between Bakin Kogi and Kafanchan.

According to Bajju oral tradition, in one raid by the Hausa, some Bajju hid in a cave near Kamrum. However, someone betrayed their hiding place, and then the Hausa set a fire near the mouth of the cave. Two individuals continued walking farther back into the cave, and they eventually found another entrance; however, the rest of the Bajju in the cave perished. The

---

[9] Tagwai Dutse, a Hausa-Fulani emirate official, was stationed at Kachia in the precolonial period. His primary responsibility was to collect taxes, tribute, and slaves from the local population. Whether this is the Tagwai that the Bajju killed or not is speculative at present, though he may have been.

[10] When we lived in Unguwar Rimi in the southern Bajju area, the chief of the village was Akau Tagwai. In the Bajju naming system each person is given a first name, and the second name is the name of his or her father. Thus Akau's father was named Tagwai, no doubt because he was born around the time Tagwai was killed.

Gazetteers record an incident in which there was a cave fire in Southern Zaria, though it is unclear whether or not this is the same one mentioned in the Bajju oral tradition. They describe that cave fire as follows:

> About 1859 when they [the Kagoma] refused to pay trib-
> ute, with the result that Audu, Emir of Zaria, arrived on the
> scene with a large army and attacked the town of Aso which
> is on the top of a rugged hill. The Aso men and women had
> taken refuge in a cave half-way up the hill where they were
> eventually joined by their men-folk, who had found that
> they were outnumbered and that their arrows were of little
> avail against the dane-guns of the Zaria men.
> Audu caused the mouth of the cave to be blocked up
> with fuel and grass and then set fire to it. A large number
> of the Kagomas were suffocated by the smoke, a very few
> escaped and the rest were captured. (Ames 1934:231)

The particular ethnic groups involved in these skirmishes are frequently misidentified in various early accounts, so it is likely that it was the Bajju who died in this cave fire.

In speaking about the role of the Fulani and Hausa in slave raids of this area, the cattle Fulani in some instances joined with the indigenous population in opposing raids from the emirates. Waters-Bayer describes this relationship between cattle Fulani and some of the indigenous people as follows:

> The Kaje and Kamantan did not generally associate the cat-
> tle Fulani with the Hausa/Fulani rulers: as one elderly Kaje
> farmer said, our Fulani and the 'Hausa' attackers must have
> been different peoples. This man explained that the 'Hausa'
> expected the Fulani herders to assist them in attacking the
> Kaje villages; in cases when the Fulani failed to help, the
> 'Hausa' would even attack their rugas [Fulani cattle encamp-
> ments]. Another Kaje elder had heard that the Fulani who
> grazed their cattle on the Abet Plains sometimes used to
> help the Kaje in their battles against the 'Hausa'. (Waters-
> Bayer 1982:13)

While slave raiding and tribute collecting had occurred prior to the *jihad* of Usuman dan Fodio, they intensified following the *jihad*. Hausa emirates, particularly those of Zazzau and its vassal states of Kajuru and Jema'a, considered the Bajju and other ethnic groups in the southern regions their subjects. The *Gazetteers* described the general effects of Hausa-Fulani emirates' penetration of other ethnic groups:

> Its main effect, and possibly its main objective, was the
> payment of tribute by those tribes which were conquered.

Payment was always in kind and usually took the form of corn, horses or slaves; sometimes cloth was substituted for corn and sometimes iron. Slaves were usually demanded only every second or third year and were fixed in number.... Whenever possible, they were obtained, by those who had to pay, from some other tribe or village either by capture or purchase and, if none had been obtained, horses were offered and often accepted instead. The quantity of corn was arbitrary, probably as much as could be wheedled out of the various villages. In addition there were extractions for the benefit of the messengers and representatives of the various Emirs, when visiting or travelling through to other places. (Ames 1934:33)

The tribute Ames mentioned was the *jizya*, H., a payment made in kind or cash by a non-Muslim who resided in Muslim territory and who was protected by a Muslim power. In the case of the southern regions where the Bajju reside, this payment was forcefully extracted from people who did not recognize Muslim sovereignty over them. Indeed, these people needed protection from the emirate officials. Consequently, each time representatives from the emirates came, they had to fight with the local population for any payment.

In theory Muslims could not enslave other Muslims, so they looked to the nearby non-Muslim population as a source of slaves. Adamu states, "the acquisition of slave labour from outside Hausaland is a recurring theme in the history of the Hausa people" (1978:26). The Hausa made little effort to convert these ethnic groups to Islam. If they had done so, their nearby source of slaves would have dried up. Fisher and Fisher also noted this when they stated, "The concentration upon Pagans, and to a much lesser extent Christians, as the eligible candidates for enslavement may have slowed down the spread of Islam" (Fisher and Fisher 1970:26).

Hausa-Fulani emirates extracted slaves annually. The Bajju and other ethnic groups in Southern Zaria lived in the catchment area that contributed slaves to the Hausa city-states, to the trans-Atlantic slave trade, and the trans-Saharan slave trade. Smith states that the vassal state of Jema'a paid Zaria one hundred slaves per year (Smith 1960:157). Zazzau Emirate was so dependent upon slaves as a source of labor that their economic system was characterized as a slave mode of production (Lovejoy 1983:275). In 1860 Sokoto Caliphate had approximately four million slaves (Lovejoy and Hogendorn 1993:1), many of whom came from Southern Zaria.

The Bajju resisted enslavement. They were excellent archers both in warfare and hunting. Further, they had the reputation for being very kind at home and very treacherous in the bush. Until firearms penetrated this area, the Bajju and other minority people had a fighting chance to effectively protect themselves from the emirates' raids. After the introduction of firearms, the indigenous people were no longer able to protect themselves adequately other than through abandoning their villages.

Hausa-Fulani emirate representatives used various means to obtain slaves. These included obtaining slaves by (1) capture during warfare, (2) kidnapping while raiding (*samame,* H.), as for example, by kidnapping people at night when they were taken unaware, (3) stirring loudly while cooking food, thereby attracting people to the area where they were then captured, (4) purchase of persons considered worthless to the Bajju (for example, thieves), (5) purchase of persons captured in the local interethnic warfare, (6) acquisition as tribute, and (7) any other means they found available. Sometimes through bribery they could persuade a Bajju to betray the hiding place of other Bajju.

The above means, which I collected from elderly Bajju, correlate well with the four main ways given by Adamu as means of enslavement used by the Hausa. Those included (1) capture, (2) payment of tribute, (3) purchase, and (4) gifts (Adamu 1979:166). He distinguishes between legal capture, in which a person was taken into slavery in a battle or punitive expedition, and illegal capture that involved kidnapping. From the perspective of those enslaved all of these means were illegal.

Many of the slaves acquired through these raids were taken to Zaria to be sold and used for labor within the Hausa economy. Today it is not unusual to see Hausa in Zaria with facial scars characteristic of ethnic groups in southern Kaduna State. Some are descendants of persons taken into slavery from Southern Zaria.

Other slaves entered the trans-Saharan and trans-Atlantic slave trade. Evidence for this comes from Koelle in his book *Polyglotta Africana* who found a thirty-year-old Ham (Jaba, H.) from Southern Zaria who had been liberated and taken to Freetown (Koelle 1963 reprint, as quoted in Isichei 1982:39). The Ham are the adjacent ethnic group southeast of the Bajju. This Ham individual had been enslaved by the Hausa seven years previously. Slaves walked for as long as three months before reaching the coast where they were sold into the trans-Atlantic slave trade (Manning 1979:126). Few white people came on shore and did not actually capture slaves. The west coast of Africa was known as the white man's grave because white men have no natural resistance to malaria[11] but would die from malaria shortly after coming on shore. Rather, white slavers purchased slaves from African middlemen who sold them to the white slavers on ships.

Following the *jihad* campaigns in the nineteenth century, slave markets emerged. Adamu attributes the shift in marketing of slaves from home sales

---

[11] Early on, people had no idea what caused malaria. The word itself means "bad air," which some assumed caused this deadly illness. When quinine was first used, it was given to help a person recover who was already suffering from malaria. Over time it was discovered that it could prevent malaria. Until then white people avoided spending much time on shore.

to slave markets to three factors: (1) the drying up of the Atlantic slave trade following the abolition of slavery by European and trans-Atlantic powers, (2) the decrease in the number of slaves sold into the trans-Saharan route, and (3) the increase in the number of slaves obtained following the *jihad* campaigns (Adamu 1979:171–172). This increase in slave acquisition resulted in a lower population density in the Middle Belt of Nigeria (Mason 1969). The Middle Belt is the U-shaped portion of Nigeria that lies between the Yoruba and Igbo in the southwest and southeast respectively, and the Hausa-Fulani in the north. It encompasses the region where numerous minority ethnic groups reside. The Bajju are one of hundreds of Middle Belt people.

At the time of the British conquest Temple lists prices of slaves as follows:

> The average prices given were, for an old woman, 8,000 cowries = 4s[12]; for an old man, 10,000 cowries = 5s; for a virgin, 16,000 cowries = 8s; for a young man 20,000 cowries = 10s, prices which compare unfavourably with those which horses would command, i.e., 100,000 cowries = 50s, or even bulls, 20,000 cowries = 10s. (Temple 1922:189)

The Bajju also had slaves who were treated as members of the family. There were certain households known to have had slaves. Further, there were also certain households known to shelter slaves, as for example, if they had been able to escape from their Hausa captors.

The Bajju sought to protect themselves from slave raids by building their settlements in defensive positions on hilltops. From these vantage points they could more easily see approaching raiders and defend themselves. With the cessation of warfare under colonial rule the Bajju moved to the plains, which allowed them to live closer to their farms.

Turaki summarizes the place of the Hausa and Fulani within the emirate system and particularly the place of slavery within the emirates as follows:

> The rich Hausa and Fulani controlled economic activities, guilds, trades, crafts and agriculture. However, slavery was the economic backbone of the Caliphate. The rulers and aristocrats bought and owned slaves in large numbers, keeping the majority for domestic use and exporting the rest. (Turaki 2010:72)

Slavery in Bajju proverbs

An institution that had as central a role as slavery understandably surfaced within Bajju oral traditions, particularly in the following proverbs:

---

[12] Here, *s* represents a shilling.

Akwwa a saai kamyyim ba'.
A slave does not make an appointment. (Bayei 1983:2)

Arabo akpat a pfong byin ba'.
He who is doomed to be taken captive does not heed a warning.
(Bayei 1983:4)

Ayin nu a rop akwwa ni, nu a ni bvwo karet ka byyik i.
He who tied a slave knows how to untie him. (Bayei 1983:5)

In the above proverbs the Bajju looked at the practical aspects of slavery and slave capture. For example, the first proverb asserts that slaves do not make appointments, but rather are at the service of their masters at all times. The second looks at the importance of heeding warnings in order to avoid capture. Finally, the last proverb lets a person know that the captor can also untie the slave and set him free.

Trade and raids

While the Bajju were self-sufficient for most of their subsistence needs, there were some commodities they needed from outside their area. For example, they needed salt, potash, and other commodities that they purchased from traders who traversed their area along a couple of trading routes. For centuries the Hausa have engaged in trade locally as well as long-distance, which led across the Sahara and also to the Atlantic Ocean.

According to Adamu the main caravan route led from Zaria through Zangon Aya, Fantswam (Kafanchan), Barnawa (Kaduna), Kudaru, Zangon Katab, the Kafanchan area, Jangindi, Kwakwasa, and Nunkoro (Adamu 1978:46). From Nunkoro the route continued to the Kwatto market of Panda, Umaisha, and Koton Karfe. Then it crossed the Benue River at Kwatan Tunga and continued on to Wukari. From the market at Panda the Hausa obtained trade items from the sea farther south.

The Bajju frequently raided traders on this route for salt and other commodities. What they stole from the travelers they divided at the home of the ruling elder. According to Temple, the Bajju were "expert highway robbers" (Temple 1922:195).

The emir at Zaria forbade people to rob travelers, but the problem continued. For example, between 1850 and 1870 the Hausa asked Dodo, the chief of Tsoryang, to produce the men who had robbed one caravan. He refused to do so, therefore the Emir of Zazzau held him personally responsible for the robbery. They took him to Zaria and from there to Sokoto. He died while in exile in the north while serving the sentence the Hausa imposed on him.

Jema'a Emirate and the Bajju in the precolonial era

From 1810 onwards the southeastern portion of the Bajju came under the nominal influence of Jema'a Emirate. The founder of this emirate was Mallam Usuman, who began as an advisor and Islamic religious teacher to the Fulani who lived on the Kachichere Plateau in the early 1800s.

About 1810 Mallam Usuman obtained a flag from Mallam Musa, emir of Zazzau (1804–1821) (Smith 1960:141–148) to represent the Fulani who had settled near the Daroro Hills; hence the name of the new settlement was Jema'a na Daroro. The colonial record states concerning his return to the area:

> Mallam Usuman returned with the flag, gown and knife as insignia of office to Jemaa but the Fulani, who wished to live their own lives as herdsmen under their elders, did not appoint an Emir. The gown and flag lay for some time in the house of one of them. At last Mallam Usuman persuaded them to make him their chief. The Fulani, not caring about these things, agreed and installed him and gave him wives, cattle, and slaves to support his position and, too late, the Fulani woke up to the fact that they had exchanged their advisor for a master. Mallam Usuman's visit to Zaria took place about 1810 and he reigned until 1833. (NAK 208, 1918)

According to archival data, during his reign he subdued the Ayu, part of the Numana, the Gwandara, and the Kaje (NAK 208, 1918).

Usuman died in 1837 near Lafia where he was slave raiding together with a Zaria force. His son Abdullahi succeeded him in office. The emirate continued through three other sons. When the British arrived, his grandson, Abdullahi Manchu, was emir. The British found the area in a state of semi-civil war, with Fulani slaves, Kagoma, Bajju, and people from Jagindi opposing the emirate. When the British colonial force arrived, the town of Jema'a na Daroro offered no opposition to the British administration, but the other ethnic groups in the emirate frequently revolted. If these ethnic groups had been peacefully under the rule of the emir of Jema'a, there would not have been this differential reaction of the emirate and the local population to the imposition of the British administration.

The rule of Jema'a Emirate was harsh. Emirate officials forced the indigenous people to plant trees on the boundary between the area claimed by Zazzau Emirate and that of Jema'a. Further, representatives of Jema'a Emirate frequently beat the Bajju. Consequently, the Bajju applied the term *Kpat*, the sound of a slap, to the Hausa language and *Bạkpat* to the Hausa people.

The problem with Jema'a Emirate from the beginning was that the first emir, who received his recognition from Zazzau Emirate, did not have a population base under him. The Fulani among whom he lived did not want him as an emir. Under his continued pressure they finally acquiesced, but soon found that they had a tyrant over them. It was not a Hausa area, hence an emirate established in this area lacked legitimacy among the local people.

Summary

The Zazzau and Jema'a Emirates had a multifaceted relationship with the Bajju and other people of Southern Zaria. Hausa traders traversed this area and sold needed provisions that were not available in the local area. These traders stayed within walled enclaves (*zangon*, H.) that they set up to protect themselves from the local population. Each dry season Hausa-Fulani warriors from the two emirates slave raided the people, taxed them, and extracted any tribute that they could get from the local population. Many were killed during these raids, villages were burned, and general havoc ensued. Slave raids instilled fear and extracted able-bodied men, women, and children from the society, thus reducing the population of the Bajju and other Middle Belt people. The local population of Southern Zaria protected themselves in whatever ways they found available. Where possible the local population developed settlement patterns for defensive purposes in which they built their compounds on hilltops.

This situation resulted in a deep-seated resentment against emirate representatives because of the oppression the people experienced through their encounters with them. Further, the Hausa-Fulani developed a deep prejudice against the pagans (*arna*, H.), whom they looked down upon. Further, the Hausa-Fulani emirate pattern of setting up chiefs undermined the political and religious authority of the ruling elders and put in place a competing political structure between chiefs and ruling village elders.

In general the cultures of the Middle Belt people were under extreme attack from their encounters with emirate representatives. Unfortunately, their oppression continued during the colonial era.

4

The Bajju under Colonialism

Under British colonial penetration in Nigeria, a process of culture change continued, change that was begun during the time of the Hausa-Fulani emirates which slave raided, taxed, and plundered the Bajju and other ethnic groups in Southern Zaria. It was during colonialism that Bajju Christian conversion began. This chapter addresses questions such as: When did the first contact between the Bajju and the British colonists occur and what was the nature of that contact? What happened in the colonial context that affected the Bajju? Did they have any political representation throughout the colonial era and, if so, what representation was there? How did the British colonialists relate to Christian missionaries in this area? These issues are discussed below.

Colonialism established

In 1857 the British occupied Lagos, and soon thereafter established the Protectorate of Southern Nigeria. On January 1, 1900, the British established the Protectorate of Northern Nigeria. On that date the union flag was hoisted over the Royal Niger Company at Lokoja in the presence of Captain (later Lord) Frederick Lugard, the British high commissioner. Initially the British governed their northern and southern protectorates separately. Lugard was appointed governor of the Colony and Protectorate of Southern Nigeria and the governor of the Protectorate of Northern Nigeria. He held both offices with the goal of bringing these two entities together under one administration. He established the capital of Northern Nigeria initially at Zungeru and subsequently moved it to Kaduna; while he resided in the south, his lieutenant governor represented him in the north.

The British colonial administration decided to combine these two protectorates on January 1, 1914, and named this colony the Colony and Protectorate of Nigeria. They had two reasons for doing so. First, the Protectorate of Northern Nigeria was poor, and thus had to have a subsidy from the government of the Protectorate of Southern Nigeria, which had a surplus in its treasury. This helped the British goal that each of its colonies be financially self-sufficient. Second, the British wanted to unite the railway systems of the two protectorates; linking the two governments made this feasible. This linkage facilitated taking commodities from the north to the south for export. According to Crowder and Abdullahi, "The administrations of the Northern and Southern Provinces continue to exercise most of the functions they had under the old Protectorate days. Only the Treasury, Railways, Survey, Judiciary, Military, Posts and Telegraphs and Audit were centralised under the Governor-General" (1979:157).

Nigeria remained under British rule until October 1, 1960. October 1st is now a national holiday that celebrates Nigerian independence.

When the Bajju first encountered white men, they identified them as small white spirits (*ŋatenyrang*). They often told their children that white people would eat them. This created a real fear in the minds of the Bajju towards white people, particularly among children.

The first contact occurred early in 1900 when Colonel Kimball, the commandant of the West African Frontier Force (WAFF), visited the emir of Zaria (Ikime 1977:186). On his way there he burned Remo and Kaje, two towns that obstructed his way to Zaria.

The next mention in the National Archives in Kaduna of interaction between the British WAFF and the Bajju occurred on April 3, 1903. A company under Lieutenant Short engaged the Bajju at Kankada for eight hours. Major Crawley described the battle as follows:

> On leaving ZUNGO'N KATAB (KATAB Dist) we approached KAINKADAN one of the head KAJE [Bajju] towns and here the enemy showed considerable resistance. The town consisted of long straggling villages. I detached Lieut Short with his company to clear the villages south of main ridge on which stands the principal part of the town which I attacked with the rest of the force. Fighting lasted for about 8 hours when the enemy dispersed and fled in all directions. Lieut Bosher did useful work with M/M [Maxim] gun constantly placing a shell among parties of the enemy who had fled to what they considered a safe distance from us and thereby spreading great consternation amongst them. 25 of the enemy were killed and several wounded. 10 prisoners were

captured and the town was burned. Our casualties were 6
wounded 3 horses captured. (NAK SNP 7/2148, 1903)

From Kankada this force continued to Madakiya where the Bajju shot
arrows at the British scouts. By the time the main force arrived, the people
had fled. The British then burned Madakiya. From there the force continued to
Katssik (Kachim) where the people had fled to the nearby hills. The force then
split into three parties, one of which killed eighteen Bajju, and another captured
fifty-nine prisoners. The force regrouped and then marched to Zonkwa. Though
they found that most of the people had fled Zonkwa, they did capture three prisoners and three horses. Fadiya was the last village where they engaged the Bajju
and where the British scouts narrowly escaped an ambush. There they killed two
Bajju at close quarters in the skirmish. Each of these villages where the WAFF
engaged the Bajju was a traditional Bajju village; it was Bajju territory and the
WAFF had little reason to attack them or be in their area.

These early skirmishes with the British and the WAFF paralleled some
of the interactions the Bajju had with representatives of the emirates previously, though without the advantage of the superior weaponry of the
Maxim automatic machine gun. It seems likely that the Bajju correlated
taking prisoners with taking of slaves and the burning of their villages, such
as representatives of the emirates had done earlier.

A second National Archives entry records contact between the Bajju and
colonial forces in September 1903. S. W. Sarota wrote,

> I have the honor to transmit herewith for your information
> copy of a report of Military Operations undertaken by com-
> mand of His Excellency the High Commissioner in the pagan
> countries South-East of Zaria. These operations were deemed
> necessary owing to the blocking of the roads to the South
> and the raiding of caravans and murders of many traders by
> the Gadas and Kaje tribes. (SNP 7 2148/1903)

A third punitive raid against people in this area occurred in 1907, which was
conducted against the Angas, Sura, Kagoro, and Zangon Katab (Annual Reports
1900–1911:644). In 1909 similar patrols occurred against the Gussoro, Montol,
Wurkum, Hill Angas, Ninzam, Attaka, Kagoro, and Mada. The colonial report
states that "the object of the patrol was to visit tribes of Attaka and Kagoro, who
had not yet made their submission, and also to visit Ninzam and Mada, who had
given considerable trouble and were killing people in the surrounding villages
and on the roads" (Annual Reports, 1900–1911:700).

Similarly Lord Lugard wrote,

> All these expeditions (punitive patrols) were most ably
> conducted, and the officers in command were instructed
> to achieve their objects with a minimum of loss of life or
> costly delays. All were accompanied by a political officer

of the province in which they took place, who was careful to explain to the people the reason of the expedition and to impress upon them that a recurrence of lawlessness and the perpetuation of murders and outrages would bring a further chastisement. (ARNN [Annual Report Northern Nigeria], pg. 331, as quoted in Turaki 1982)

Another raid in the Bajju area occurred at Chenccuk where the Bajju killed one of the white British soldiers passing through. The soldiers set fire to all the houses there in retaliation. Meanwhile the Bajju all ran off to hide.

Most of these punitive patrols were in association with collection of taxes. However, peace under the British colonizers had not yet been established, there were no local bureaucratic institutions or taxation systems in place, and the people had no market economy or available currency. While the Hausa may have told the British that they taxed the local population, there was no agreement by the Bajju to pay them anything. Taxation was a means of British domination of the local peoples. Initially the local people were taxed at 5 shillings per year per adult. Often the cost of collecting taxes exceeded the amount collected. From the local people's perspective taxation was an especially hated form of domination.

Indirect Rule

Lugard, who served as British high commissioner of the Protectorate of Northern Nigeria from 1900 to 1907 and again from 1912 to 1914, established Indirect Rule as the British colonial policy for governing its colonies. C. L. Temple, who served with Lugard first as the resident of Bauchi Province and later as lieutenant governor of Northern Nigeria (1914–1917), formulated the policy of Indirect Rule as follows:

> By Indirect Rule I mean a system of administration which leaves in existence the administrative machinery which had been created by the natives themselves; which recognises the existence of Emirs, Chiefs, and native Councils, native Courts of Justice, Muhammadan Courts, Pagan Courts, native Police controlled by a native executive, as real living forces, and not as curious and interesting pageantry; by which European influence is brought to bear on the native indirectly, through his chiefs, and not directly through European officers—political, police, etc., and by which the European keeps himself a good deal in the background, and leaves the mass of native individuals to understand that the orders which come to them emanate from their own Chief rather than from the all-pervading white man. (Temple 1918:30)

Lugard viewed rule by the British Empire as having

> only one mission—for liberty and self-development on no
> standardized lines, so that all may feel that their interests
> and religion are safe under the British flag. Such liberty and
> self-development can be best secured to the native popu-
> lation by leaving them free to manage their own affairs
> through their own rulers, proportionately to their degree of
> advancement, under the guidance of the British staff, and
> subject to the laws and policy of the administration. (Lugard
> 1926:94)

Lugard contrasted Indirect Rule with Direct Rule. He cited the disad-
vantages of Direct Rule as follows: (1) the number of British staff necessary
for Direct Rule is too small compared to the population over which they
would rule; (2) Direct Rule by Europeans would have a disintegrating effect
on tribal authority and institutions; (3) the resulting system would be alien
to them; and (4) social evolutionary change would not then occur through
their own efforts and in their own way (Lugard 1926:214–215). A further
factor mitigating against Direct Rule was expense.

Turaki wrote concerning the policy of Indirect Rule,

> Consistent with these principles, the Indirect Rule estab-
> lished by the British incorporated indigenous socio-political
> institutions from the Muslim emirate system, and Islamic
> religion, culture, values and institutions, into the new colo-
> nial structure. Thus the Islamic political philosophy and
> culture of the Caliphate formed the foundations of both
> indigenous and colonial administration in Northern Nigeria.
> Even though the Muslim rulers were defeated and lost their
> sovereignty, their British colonial masters created a system
> in which they could continue to rule. (2010:115)

As Lugard implemented Indirect Rule in Nigeria, he allowed persons
to hold leadership positions in areas in which they resided, even if they
did not belong to the local ethnic group or were not acceptable to the local
population. For example, in 1913 he allowed the son of the emir of Bauchi
to be appointed as the district head over six "pagan" villages. His rationale
for doing so was that "a ruler should be resident among the people—that
rule was laid down by myself as a cardinal principle in the appointment
of a District Head" (NAK K 4046 SNP 17/8). In other words, Indirect Rule
did not mean that the British allowed every ethnic group to govern itself
according to its own structure and rulers. Thus, Lugard built into British
administration the possibility of inequality between ethnic groups.

Tibenderana points out that the term Indirect Rule was a misnomer. He
states,

> But recent studies on British administration in northern Nigeria have shown that it was not a diarchy ruled jointly by the emirs and the British. It was a British colonial territory ruled and governed by the British alone. The emirs were British assistants and not rulers—if by a ruler we mean one who exercises supreme or sovereign authority. (1983:519)

Perhaps a more accurate description of British administration in Northern Nigeria is the emirate model under British control. The British extended the authority of the emirs throughout Northern Nigeria. For the Bajju and other non-Muslim ethnic groups in Southern Zaria, that included extending the authority of the emirs of Zazzau (Zaria) and Jema'a over them, thereby bypassing the traditional political structures of these ethnic groups. The exceptions were those accorded independent status, namely the A̲gorok (Kagoro), A̲sholio (Moroa), and Ham (Jaba). Though these districts were independent of Zaria Native Authority in terms of local government, they shared with the Native Authority the treasury and the local education committee (Yahaya 1980:14).[1] Thus the ability of ethnic groups accorded independent status to act autonomously was limited.

The application of the emirate model over minority ethnic groups strengthened the emirates at the expense of the local populations who were the sons of the land, the *yan kasa* in Hausa. These horticultural groups are smaller than the Hausa, non-Muslim, and were not easily controlled by the emirates. The colonial presence in this area was very limited. Further, there were no major export cash crops from this area, though over time some did develop such as ginger, citrus fruit, palm wine, hogs, and locust bean cakes. Both citrus trees and the introduction of hogs came through Christian missionary initiatives.

Hannerz states that "No doubt, Christianity, in becoming the strongest religion in Southern Zaria, served at the same time as an organizational and symbolic vehicle for the old opposition of the *yan kasa* to Hausa domination" (1978:4).

Initially the Bajju were divided between two administrative units, namely those of Plateau Province and Zaria Province. The northern part of the Bajju was under the emir of Zazzau and the southern half under Plateau Province governed by Jema'a Emirate. Jema'a Emirate was part of Plateau Province, though it owed its allegiance to the emir of Zazzau. Plateau Province, which was formed in 1926, included the Jos Division, the ethnic groups in the Pankshin area, the Kanam Division, the Shendam Native Administration together with two independent districts. Jema'a Emirate and the Southern Division had their headquarters at Wamba (Ames 1934:47–48). Thus Plateau Province included the southern half of the Bajju.

[1] Two Treasuries were established in 1914; one was for the independent districts and one for the emirate. These were combined into one in 1918 (Ames 1934:44).

There are several reasons why the British bypassed the political structures of the non-Muslim ethnic groups of this area. First, they sought to per-
petuate the prior status each ethnic group had with respect to the emirates
before colonial rule. Often British investigation of that status in the precolonial period was superficial, resulting in some groups being formally placed
under emirate rule when previously there had been no formal control. This
was true in the case of the Bajju. Second, some British colonial administrators accepted theories that postulated stages of socio-cultural evolutionary
development of people and their cultures. They saw the Hausa with their
organized emirate structure, wearing of clothes, and monotheistic Islam as
further evolved than the people who wore skins and leaves. Third, British
colonialists came from a class-conscious society. One administrator compared the emirs to the barons in British society and stated that the peasantry
looks to their barons for protection (NAK: ACC 873 638, 1937). They carried
this class-consciousness over into their administration of Nigeria. Fourth,
the British recognized no leaders among the non-Muslim ethnic groups in
Southern Zaria above the head of the family unit who could exercise political authority (NAK ZARPROF 3456). Such leaders did exist. These traditional leaders combined religious and political power (Yahaya 1980:16),
but they were never recognized during the colonial era.

The concepts of a class-structured society and socio-cultural evolutionary
stages are intertwined. In the philosophical milieu prevalent in some intellectual
circles in Europe at the time of the colonial conquest, some scholars classified
cultures of the world according to socio-cultural evolutionary stages. For example, Sir Edward Tylor (1832–1917) proposed a scheme that ranked cultures
according to three evolutionary stages: the savage, the barbaric, and civilized
life (Tylor 1871). Temple espoused a similar viewpoint when he stated,

> The native is a human being like ourselves, but in a different
> stage of development. Some natives are, even to-day, in the
> stage of our Druidical ancestors, whereas others are in the
> stage which we passed through in about the Middle Ages.
> The whirligig of time has brought us about five hundred to
> a thousand years ahead of them in the process of evolution,
> that is all. (Temple 1918:31)

Temple considered the Hausa-Fulani emirates in the Northern
Provinces of Nigeria and the Yoruba chieftaincies in the Southern
Provinces to be more advanced along the road to civilization than "the
even greater sections of the native community which are more backward"
(Temple 1918:61). When colonialism was established in all the colonies
in Africa, the generally accepted reasons were to advance civilization,
Christianity, and commerce. The fourth "C," which is not usually men-
tioned, was conquest of lands that belonged to indigenous populations.
In Northern Nigeria the British initially sought to suppress slave raiding,

slave sales, and opposition. Slavery itself was not outlawed by the British administration until 1936.

Lugard similarly subscribed to the concept of socio-cultural evolution. He divided cultures into those in the patriarchal stage, the tribal stage, and advanced communities (Lugard 1926:75–76). He stated that those in the patriarchal stage lacked any but the most rudimentary communal organization. In contrast, those in the tribal stage had recognized chiefs and some cohesion for attack and defense. Finally, those in advanced or progressive communities ascribed to a monotheistic religion and had a written language. From Lugard's perspective advanced communities owed that advancement to the adoption of Islam. Lugard further recognized that by the British administration's rule through Muslims, the government "unavoidably encourage[d] the spread of Islam" (Lugard 1926:210). The effects of those colonial decisions to favor one group over another continue today where religion and politics have become intertwined and, for some, radicalized.

Figure 4.1. Muslim prayer place beside the road (Carol McKinney).

Other colonial officials similarly used terms that indicated their belief in socio-cultural evolution. For example, in 1915 Sciortiono, the acting resident of Nassarawa Province, wrote, "The Kaje are primitive pagans" (see NAK 2089, 1915). This type of thinking continued until fairly late into the colonial era. For example, as late as 1941, one resident characterized the Bajju as still being in the family stage of evolution (NAK ZARPROF 3456). People in this stage of evolution were judged incapable of self-rule. Consequently, British administrators felt that "pagans" had to be ruled by those judged to be further along the road to civilization. As Temple stated,

> In the primitive groups it is unavoidable that he [the Resident] interfere more with the tribal institutions than is the case in the more advanced sections. Their habits are more at variance with humanity and reason. So the Resident finds it necessary to interfere, and all such interference weakens the hold of the Chief or elders of the tribe as the case may be. (Temple 1918:70)

Temple felt that ethnic groups in the mountainous districts in the southern part of the Northern Provinces were in a very primitive stage of evolution. In fact, he considered them in a rather curious way when he wrote,

> Generally speaking, they are an entirely robust, well developed race and remarkably free from disease of all sorts. Their healthy, primitive life they lead enables their constitutions to resist the effects of very great excesses in the use of alcohol until late middle or old ages is [sic] reached. (Temple 1918:173)

Such thinking led the British colonial administration to classify the peoples of Northern Nigeria into two categories, pagans and Mohammedans, and to apply different policies to each (see Ballard 1972:1–14). Those classified as "pagans" occupied a position at the bottom of the social class structure. Turaki (1982) has cogently argued that the British institutionalized the inferior status of the non-Muslim ethnic groups in Northern Nigeria.

Figure 4.2. Representatives from Zazzau Emirate in the Bajju area (Norris McKinney).

Colonial administration under two Emirates: 1900–1934

Early administration of Southern Zaria is described by Brandt as follows:

> When the non-Moslem tribes in Southern Zaria were being re-organised, an attempt was made to reproduce the Hausa model of a territorial unit. To this end hamlets that formed units of the same clans or sub-clans were grouped together territorially wherever possible. In order to provide village heads to control the territorial units so formed, search was made for the traditionally senior family in the unit—the traditional leader of the family was created a village head. (NAK ZARPROF 312 9, 1939)

Brandt stated that the individually appointed village heads received a fixed salary and a position in the local court or governing body. Within Bajju society village heads were still subservient to the ruling elders. Such an individual served as a liaison or intermediary between the elders of the Bajju society and the outside world. The Bajju did not want the ruling elder to hold this position because of the religious sanctions associated with his person. He could not be risked. Brandt recognized this when he wrote:

> The priest was originally the leader of the village. Contact with Hausas however, made it imperative to have some go-between. The priest could not be risked, would not risk himself or could not appear in public as an ordinary man. (ZAN ZARPROF 312 9, 1939)

In appointing chiefs or village heads the British continued a practice the Hausa had begun. The Hausa often installed as chiefs the individuals who paid them the most money. For example, in the early 1900s in the southern Bajju area District Head Liman Kaje of Jema'a Emirate received payment of five pounds from Osuman to be appointed chief of Katssik. Liman had earlier appointed Makoshi, Dakale, and Audu as chiefs of the same village (NAK 2089, 1915). Similarly, he appointed three village heads at Adwan. He justified the appointment of several men to the position of chief because he found it difficult to extract tribute from the population. According to one colonial administrator, the usual fee paid by a Bajju individual to the Hausa for appointment to the position of chief was from three to five pounds and a horse (NAK 2089, 1915).

The British divided the Northern Region into twelve provinces. The Bajju and other minority ethnic groups were placed in Zaria Province. After that all of these ethnic groups lost their independence and fell under Zazzau Emirate, something they had fought so hard to avoid in the precolonial era. Zaria Province was divided into two districts, the Northern Districts and the Southern Districts, with the Southern Districts referred to as Southern Zaria. The Ham (Jaba), A̱gorok (Kagoro), and A̱sholio (Moroa) eventually gained their independence. They had their own rulers rather than the emir at Zaria. The Hausa maintained walled settlements, which they had set up when trading and slave raiding in this area. These became flash points of conflict with the indigenous population.

The Bajju under Jema'a Emirate

While Jema'a Emirate had been a vassal state to Zaria in the precolonial era, in September 1902 the British removed the emir of Jema'a from Zaria to punish Zaria for supporting those who killed Captain Malone, commander of the British detachment at Keffi. The man who ordered his killing, the Magajin Keffi, fled north through Zaria and on to Kano (Smith 1960:202). Jema'a Emirate was thus placed under Nassarawa Province.

The British maintained a presence at Jema'a by posting an assistant resident and twenty-five men in the WAFF from 1904 onwards (Ames 1934:36). Soon this post was upgraded to include a political officer together with the WAFF detachment and a police unit. The political officer functioned to assert British control through collecting taxes, pacifying "pagans," settling boundary and other disputes, administrating law and order, and promoting economic activities that would benefit the administration.

The British imposed taxes as a sign that the population acknowledged Britain's suzerainty (Tremearne 1912:115). The amount of taxes in the early 1900s in Southern Zaria was one shilling and three pence per person per annum (Tremearne 1912:117), though the expense of collecting taxes exceeded the amount of taxes collected. Further, the British often engaged in skirmishes with the villagers in the collection process. It is not difficult to imagine that from the perspective of the indigenous people the early British presence represented a continuation of the practices of the precolonial Hausa-Fulani emirates.

Jema'a became a stopping place on the route from Loko to the plateau during the early colonial period. This route led from Loko through Keffi and Jema'a, and on to the plateau at Assob (Ames 1934:38).

Temple wrote that in 1912 the Bajju were induced to acknowledge the practical suzerainty of the Sarkin Jema'a and to accept as district head Liman Umoru, a Fulani from Jema'a (Temple 1922:194). Two years later the colonial administration removed Liman for malpractices (NAK 2089, 1915). Some of his malpractices led to the attack on the emir and his followers in 1915.

The Bajju and Kanikom attack on the emir of Jema'a

The British encouraged the new emir of Jema'a to tour his area. The acting resident of Nassarawa stated that there were three purposes for this tour. First, the emir was to inquire into the malpractices of the previous district head. Second, he was to collect tax arrears from some villages in the southern Bajju area. Third, he was to tour "the pagan districts in order to make himself known and to obtain recognition of his ascension as usual" (NAK 2089, 1915). In 1915, Abdullahi, the new emir of Jema'a, toured this area. He undertook this tour together with 120 followers including some of his wives and other women who were to cook for them. On June 15, 1915, he went from Unguwar Rimi (Togwoi; Tagwai, J.) to Katssik (Kachim) to inquire about unpaid taxes. At Katssik the Bajju and Kanikom attacked. In the fray five women, including some of the emir's wives, and two youths in the emir's party died; the emir escaped through Madakiya. As the emir's party retreated through Afana (Byena, J.) and Bakin Kogi (*Atacap*, J.), people from those villages joined in the fight. In the first report by the emir's party there were no Bajju or Kanikom casualities. Further investigation revealed that among the Bajju and Kanikom eight persons died and several others were wounded, including a young man with a bullet wound in his thigh. The Bajju seized seventeen goats and took other articles from members of the emir's party during the fray, articles and animals that they later returned.

Following the attack, Bajju and Kanikom messengers came to Jema'a with the offer of chickens to establish peace. The British refused these offerings and demanded that the chief, his elders, and others who had taken part in the skirmish present themselves. Bajju leaders subsequently offered two goats and a sheep as a peace offering, but the British again rejected their offer. They demanded that the Bajju produce those who had killed individuals within the emir's party.

As a result of that attack, the WAFF conducted a punitive expedition. In that expedition they killed four Bajju men at Madakiya, though the people at Madakiya had not taken part in the attack. After this skirmish, they continued their march towards Unguwar Rimi, Katssik, and the other villages involved in the initial attack. The WAFF killed one Bajju at Afana. They then burned the villages of Katssik, Afana, Bakin Kogi, and Abidoko (a Kanikom village) before returning to Jema'a. At Katssik the WAFF utterly destroyed the *abvoi* shrine as they felt that the activities of the instigators of the attack on the emir originated there. (See map 4.1 for the route of the WAFF punitive expedition.)

Discussions in the colonial archives concerning this attack on the emir show a complete lack of understanding of Bajju grievances. They stated that none of the Bajju or Kanikom had any charges against the emir. What they failed to realize was that the emir had no mutually recognized authority over these people. In discussing this incident, some Bajju pointed out that their forefathers realized that the British intended to place them formally under the emirate, something they found unacceptable. When they realized this, some of the villages in the southern Bajju area refused to pay taxes. A second reason that the colonial material records as contributing to this attack was a rumor concerning the coming withdrawal of the British administration, a rumor that they felt originated among people living along the Benue River (NAK 2089, 1915).

Headquarters of Jema'a Emirate

The headquarters of Jema'a Emirate was in the village of Jema'a (also called Gidan Waya, 'the house of the wire', namely the telegraph); however, due to the prevalence of sleeping sickness there, the British moved it to Madakiya in about 1926. Concerning this move, the acting secretary of the Northern Provinces wrote, "the new Headquarters of the Jemaa Division which it is proposed to establish at Madakia will certainly be a Moslem neighbourhood" (NAK K 4046 SNP 17/8 1121). This was seen as in contrast to Jema'a where the Hausa rulers lived as an enclave among the non-Muslim population. However, the British failed to recognize that Madakiya was not a Muslim village but rather a Bajju one; the Hausa continued as a small enclave among the indigenous people.

In 1933 the emirate headquarters was moved again, this time to Katssik, the part that was adjacent to Kafanchan where it continues. At the time of the move the population of Kafanchan was not predominately Muslim; however, Kafanchan may have been more acceptable to the emir because it was larger and its population included multiple ethnic groups, particularly Yoruba who came to this area to work on the railroad and as traders. However, the emir in Kafanchan had influence only over the minority of Hausa who lived there. The local population did not recognize his authority.

Bajju-Agorok boundary dispute

In 1921 the Agorok (Kagoro, H.) wanted to expand the land they farmed in the direction of the Bajju. The land in question was on the border between the Agorok and Bajju near Madakiya. Although there was some uncultivated land to the east, the Agorok did not want it, perhaps because of a smallpox epidemic nearby.

When this dispute reached the colonial administrators, they felt that the land belonged to the Agorok and claimed that the chief of the Agorok did a good job in keeping his people under control. The administration proposed dividing the disputed area equally, but the Bajju objected strongly. When the British referred the issue to the emir of Jema'a, he postponed a decision. One colonial administrator wrote, "There is absolutely no doubt that the Kaje have been the belligerent

party in this affair whilst the Kagorans have, to date, been well disciplined" (NAK 2083, 1921). The British finally awarded a portion on the
northern boundary of the disputed land to the Agorok.

However, this boundary dispute continued to smolder and was not
finally resolved until 1948. At that time the Bajju objected so strongly that
they arrived armed with spears, bows and arrows, and swords. The colonial administration finally sent a man to investigate the issue carefully. He
returned with the report that the land, with the exception of land in the
north ceded to the Agorok in 1921, definitely belonged to the Bajju rather
than the Agorok.

Map 4.1. Map of the WAFF 1915 attack on the Bajju (from NAK SNP 2089)

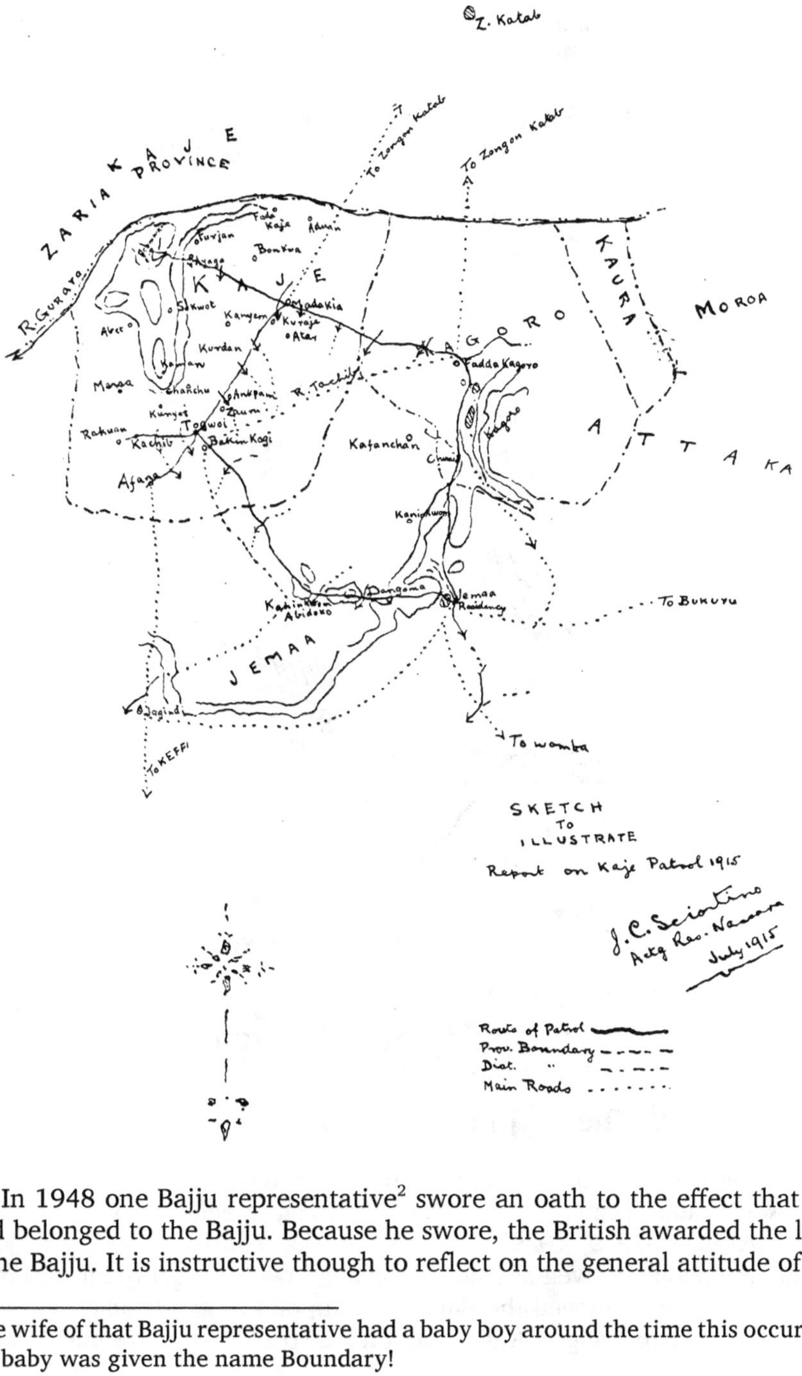

In 1948 one Bajju representative[2] swore an oath to the effect that the land belonged to the Bajju. Because he swore, the British awarded the land to the Bajju. It is instructive though to reflect on the general attitude of the

---

[2] The wife of that Bajju representative had a baby boy around the time this occurred. The baby was given the name Boundary!

British colonial officials towards the Bajju prior to this investigation. They had termed the Bajju as the "rebellious Kaje," and the "belligerent party" (NAK 2083, 1921). Colonial administrators viewed the A̱gorok in Southern Zaria in a more favorable light than they did the Bajju! See map 4.2.

Map 4.2. Map of boundary dispute between the Bajju (Kaje) and the A̱gorok (Kagoro) (from NAK 2083, 1921)

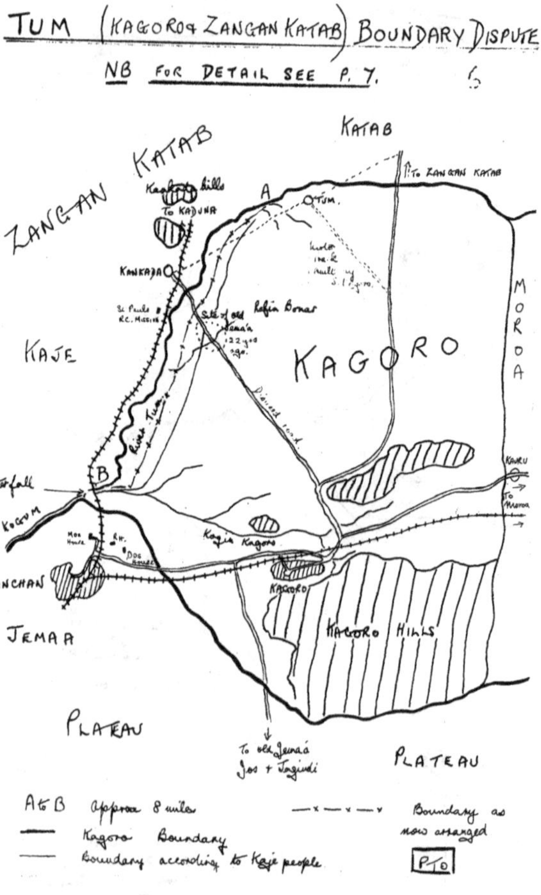

The Bajju under Zaria Emirate

The northern Bajju people in Zaria Province were first placed in Kachia District. Kachia had formerly been a center for Hausa penetration of this area (NAK ZARPOF 312 9, 1939). That penetration consisted largely of slave raiding the people as well as trade along a caravan route through this area. In 1924 the British moved the Bajju, Ba̱kulu, and Angan (Kamantan) from Kachia District to Zangon Katab, another district within Zazzau Emirate.

They did so because they felt that the district head at Kachia lacked the ability to control these people. The British colonial administration did not consult the Bajju concerning what administrative district to place them in. Those who formerly slave raided them were now formally placed over the Bajju and other minority ethnic groups in the area, this time with the backing of the West African Frontier Force.

In 1912 Katuka became the first district head resident at Zangon Katab. After the transfer of these ethnic groups from Kachia District to that of Zangon Katab, the Bajju fell under the jurisdiction of Katuka. The word *katuk ka* is an old Hausa word, derived from *sarauta*, which meant 'the ruler' or 'one who has authority over' (Abraham 1962:783). It was an official Hausa position equivalent to that of 'chief' (*sarki*, H.). However, this word is homophonous with the Jju expression *katuk ka*, meaning 'the night' or 'the evil one'.

In 1924 when Katuka was first given responsibility over these three additional ethnic groups, one colonial administrator wrote, "this meant the addition under Katuka of another very difficult tribe the Kaje" (NAK ZARPROF 607, 1932). He further wrote, "The Kaje have always been recognized as one of the most difficult tribes in Zaria. Fadan Kaje has probably harboured more bandits than any other town in the Southern Districts" (NAK ZARPROF 607, 1932). Their reputation reflected their desire to remain independent, especially from being formally placed under the Hausa who had slave raided them during the precolonial era. At the same time it is true that they raided caravans that traversed through this area.

In reading national archival documents, it is clear that Katuka was taking his orders from Zaria and from the colonial administration. The welfare of the local minority ethnic groups was not his focus. After Katuka served as district head at Zangon Katab for twenty-five years, he received appointment as emir of Zazzau Emirate in 1937. There he was known as Mallam Ja'afaru. He served as emir of Zazzau until his death in 1959 (Yahaya 1980:9).

Considerations of possible administrative changes in Southern Zaria

Some administrators recognized that the administrative problems of Southern Zaria came at least in part from the general discontent of the local ethnic groups. For example, in 1933 G. S. Browne became the lieutenant governor of the Northern Provinces of Nigeria. He reassessed the governance in the non-Muslim areas. He acknowledged that the emirate system with district heads functioned to some extent, particularly in areas where he felt that the organization of ethnic groups was ineffective. However, he stated, "I do not contend for a moment that it [the use of district heads] has not in many places been so used as to break down tribal organisation particularly perhaps in the Southern Districts of Zaria" (NAK ZARPROF 1558, 1933).

Lieutenant Governor Browne requested that these areas be reorganized along tribal lines. The resident responded, "Had these Districts been arranged otherwise from the start, tribal consciousness and tribal machinery might have been preserved to an extent which would have made it possible to utilize them as an effective part of the administration organization" (NAK ZARPROF 1558, 1933). The resident further pointed out that the emir would not agree to such a radical rearrangement since it would have taken control of the non-Muslim areas away from him. Browne responded that the traditional authority of the emirs over the non-Muslim minority groups "consisted in many instances of the right to slave raid them and nothing else," and asserted that these districts "are a part of the Emirate of Zaria by Government's consent only, and this consent can be revoked" (NAK ZARPROF 1558, 1933). He further asserted,

> This was partly on the basis of economy of staff for Government to decide and not the Emir. If Government considers that certain tribes would be better administered by Councils in direct contact with the Emir then the Emir will be directed to remove his direct representative, though why a Council cannot be the direct representative is not evident. This is further evidence of the fallacy that there can be no efficient administration without a District Head and a District, whereas the converse is being proved conclusively elsewhere. (NAK 1558, 1554, 1761; 1934)

The proposal of the secretary to the Northern Provinces was that independent tribal districts be formed for the Gwari, Adara, Kurama, Bakulu, Atyap, Jali, Pitti, Angan (Kamantan), Kuturumi, Chawai, Bajju, and Guri-Sruba Hills. The Hausa settlements at Kajuru, Zangon Katab, Kauru, and Kachia would be treated as enclaves. The village heads would then report directly to the emir. Though this proposal would definitely have been an improvement, it is unclear why the village heads should have reported to the emir rather than to the British district officer or resident.

In this instance a significant change of administration, which would have been far more acceptable to the indigenous people of Southern Zaria, could have been made. In the end the status quo prevailed. The Bajju continued in a subordinate position with respect both to the emirates and the colonial administration.

Under Zaria Emirate: 1934–1960

Spurway, the acting resident in Zaria in a report on Zangon Katab, recommended that no ethnic group be divided between two emirates (NAK ZARPROF 607, 1932). He felt that any division that separated an ethnic group from their ethnic brothers was artificial and unsatisfactory. Ethnic groups that were so divided included the Gwari, Adara, Ham, Bajju,

Rukuba, and Kurama (NAK 1558, 1554, 1761). Following his recommendation in 1934, the administration transferred the southern portion of the Bajju, which was formerly under Jema'a Emirate, to Zazzau Emirate. Similarly, on November 1, 1934, the Ham (Jaba, H.), the Agorok (Kagoro, H.), and the Asholio (Moroa) were transferred from Plateau Province to Zaria Province.

The colonial administration imposed a hierarchical governmental structure, which consisted of village heads (*agwam*, sing.; *bagwam*, pl.), area chiefs (*dagatai*, H.),[3] the district head (*hakimi*, H.) who resided at Zangon Katab, and the emir at Zaria. Although the Bajju traditional political structure consisted of five sections, each under its ruling elder, the administration established eleven area chiefs. Village heads and area chiefs were Bajju, while both the district head and emir were not.[4] Zazzau Emirate contained fifteen districts; the Bajju resided within Zangon Katab District, one of the southern districts.[5] As stated previously, the southern districts were ethnically distinct from the Hausa-Fulani of the emirate.

Bajju efforts to change the political structure

Throughout the colonial era, the Bajju made various efforts to change the administrative structure imposed upon them. They desired independent status, such as that enjoyed by the Agorok, Asholio, and Ham, and a Bajju chieftaincy position. All their efforts towards these two goals proved fruitless throughout the colonial era.

In the early 1930s, when southern Bajju were under Jema'a Emirate, Musa Marsa sought to be chief of the entire ethnic group. Musa Marsa together with his followers went to Madakiya to request the chieftaincy from the emir. Allahmagani, a respected elder at Madakiya, supported his request. However, before he arrived, the emir heard that he was coming. When he arrived, the emir ordered his arrest. Musa Marsa died shortly after his release from prison.

---

[3] Yahaya translated *dagaci* as 'village head' rather than 'area chief' (Yahaya 1980:5). In Southern Zaria the *dagaci* occupied a hierarchical position higher than the village head (Kato 1974:96). Locally both are termed *agwam*. The 'area' in the term 'area chiefs' must be distinguished from an 'administrative area,' which is at the next level above the district. The progression is village head or chief (*agwam*, J.; *sarki*, H.), area chief (*agwam*, J.; *sarki*, H.), area chief (*agwam*, J.; *dagaci*, H.), district head (*hakimi*, H.), secretary to the administrative area, and emir.

[4] According to Yahaya (1980:119) almost all district heads were non-indigenes of the districts to which they were appointed.

[5] The fifteen districts were Ikara, Makarfi, Soba, Kubau, Giwa, Sabon Gari, Zaria da Kewaye, Igabi, Lere, Kauru, Chikum, Kajuru, Kachia, Kagarko, and Zangon Katab. Of these districts the last five were considered the southern districts. The first eight listed comprised the northern districts, while Lere and Kauru occupied an intermediate position between the southern and northern districts (Yahaya 1980:14–15).

In 1939 a local Roman Catholic leader requested that the Bajju and A̱tyap, as well as some other ethnic groups in the area, be formed into a separate administrative unit. The district officer replied that that was "obviously impossible" (NAK ZARPROF 2944).

Usman Akangnet Sakwak (1900–1953),[6] an interpreter at the hospital in Kafanchan, took Musa Marsa as his role model (NAK ZARPROF 3456). In the early 1940s Usman worked towards the establishment of a chieftaincy among the Bajju. He claimed that his father was the *magaji* at Sakwak, his relatives were descendants of Baranzan at Dibyyi, and that therefore either he or one of his older brothers should be appointed to this position. Usman sent a number of petitions to the colonial administration requesting the establishment of this position. He engaged an attorney to write his petitions. In one of his numerous petitions, Usman mentioned the possibility of his being appointed as chief and the *gado* at Dibyyi being appointed as the district head. His basis for this request came from the founding charter of the Bajju. Baranzan, the Bajju founding father, resided at Dibyyi, and A̱nkwak, the founder of Sa̱kwak, was the eldest son of Baranzan. The *gado* at Dibyyi had long been recognized as the most important elder (*gado*) among the Bajju.

Usman attended the church founded by Sudan Interior Mission (SIM). Missionaries took a dim view of his activities. SIM's position was that Christian evangelists should refrain from involvement in politics. Issues such as a change in the status of the Bajju should be left to the government (SIM Zonkwa, Resume for the Third Quarter, n.d., SIM Archives). Though this particular policy applied to evangelists, SIM applied the same principle to the work of Usman. For example, Kirk, an SIM missionary, called him to Jos and asked him to desist from seeking the chieftaincy (NAK ZARPROF C.8/1946). Usman refused to do so and continued to hold meetings with Bajju leaders and other supporters concerning the chieftaincy issue. Though Usman enjoyed widespread support among the Bajju, both with the illiterate and educated, and among Christians and traditional religionists, some objected to his activities. According to one letter to the resident, one elder objected as follows: "Why does he say he is interested in us? He has left the tribe, became a Christian and now professes to be mindful of our welfare. Why should he speak for us and our customs which, as a convert, he scorns?" (NAK 3456).

The colonial administration repeatedly told Usman that any change of administrative structure such as he was requesting had to receive the consent of the emir. So together with some of his followers, Usman traveled by train to Zaria to request the position of chief for the Bajju from the emir. Usman had a limited knowledge of Hausa, so he found himself at a disadvantage when the emir questioned him about what exactly he was requesting. In the midst of a number of questions that Usman was able to answer affirmatively,

---

[6] In the archival records his name is alternately spelled Osuman Sokop and Usuman of Sokop Kaje (NAK ZARPROF 6/1942). My spelling conforms to Bajju pronunciation.

the emir asked him if he was requesting a *lardi* (H.), a 'province'. Usman did not know the word, however in the total context of questions, all of which Usman could answer in the affirmative, he responded "yes" to that question too. That response was clearly unacceptable under the colonial administration and he was promptly arrested. When Usman and his followers found out the meaning of that word, they felt that they had been tricked.

Usman continued his efforts to have the chieftaincy position established. He was again arrested in September 1942. Either during the arrest or shortly afterwards, he was beaten. The colonial medical doctor confirmed that he had been beaten; however, the administration chose to take no action. They said that if he chose to pursue the issue, they would take action. They charged him with refusal to obey a lawful order from the Native Authority in whose area he resided and with conduct liable to cause a breach of the peace. They convicted him on the first charge and acquitted him on the second.[7] He spent two months in jail for that conviction.

In 1946 Usman Sakwak and twelve others were arrested on the charge of causing a riot.[8] This time he and his associates received sentences of twelve months with hard labor. The administration considered permanently exiling him from the Bajju area in order to remove him from his base of popular support. However, the attorney general in Lagos advised against such action because Usman had engaged a lawyer and sought change through peaceful lawful means (NAK ZARPROF 6/1942). He was clearly a thorn in the side of the local administrators.

Among the Bajju he was a respected leader. Chidawa Kaburuk wrote concerning him as follows:

> Mallam Usman was among the first Christians and the literate people in Sakwak and Kajju. He was brave and full of wisdom, foresight and compassion. So he was very concerned about the inhuman treatment that Emirate rule was meting to Bajju. The inhuman treatment spurred him to embark on a struggle to free Bajju from the oppressive Emirate rule. All Bajju supported his move and accepted him as a leader.

---

[7] Yahaya points out that the courts often became tools for suppressing critics of the Native Authority (Yahaya 1980:11). In the case of Usman Sakwak he was not criticizing the Native Authority as much as he was requesting the position of chief, such as other ethnic groups had. Nevertheless his request was a threat to the status quo; the British as well as the Native Authority felt that his movement had to be suppressed.

[8] Those arrested with him were Kwasu Sanke, Abobo Aruwan, Kantiyok Shinkut, Bawwom Bidam, Jatau Bidam, Usman Bvayan, Tanko Kato, Kahuwei Sheyin, Nkut Didam, Laya Sana, and Kwasu Niyrin. Mamman Swam was not arrested with them, but when he heard of the arrest and imprisonment of his colleagues, he trekked to Zaria to join them in prison. All were respected leaders among the Bajju who opposed emirate rule (see Kaburuk 2014).

> Only few Village Heads were reluctant and became
> agents of the Emirate rulers. So in 1946 Usman and some of
> his strong supporters were falsely accused of insurrection.
> They were arrested and imprisoned in Zaria in that year
> without proper trial. Usman died in 1953 but the struggle
> did not die. (Kaburuk 2014:6)

In 1947 the A̲tyap similarly agitated for control of their own affairs.
They did so by having the elders of each of their villages present their
request to the British resident for recognition of their leading *gado* as their
legitimate representative. The A̲tyap specifically requested to meet with
the British resident without an emirate representative present. Though the
resident met with them, each evening he reported what had transpired
to emirate representatives. The A̲tyap request resulted in the arrest of
the *A̲tyap gado*, a man described by the British administrator as ancient,
together with the other elders. They received sentences of twelve months
of hard labor in jail (NAK ZARPROF C8/1946). In the A̲tyap efforts for
recognition of their *gado*, the administration and emir felt that both the
chief of Kagoro and mission adherents had influenced them; however,
investigation did not confirm this. These were in fact the legitimate representatives of the A̲tyap who desired recognition. This can be verified by
examining the names listed in the archival record. Each name listed was
preceded by the title *gado*, 'elder'.

Pitcairn, the resident of Zaria Province, wrote concerning administrative problems in Southern Zaria: "It is really striking to find in Zongon [*sic*]
Katab District (55,000 pagans out of 60,000 total) that the Administrative
control is wholly exercised at H.Q. without a single pagan in the salaried
staff and with no member of the staff having a knowledge of any pagan
language" (NAK ZARPROF C.8/1946).

A recurring theme in the archival material is that if a British resident,
district officer, or assistant district officer devoted more time to Southern
Zaria, the continuing problems, such as the unrest that surrounded Usman
Akangnet Sakwak's efforts to have the chieftaincy position established,
would disappear. One colonial officer's response to this perception was that
he had spent 309 days that year in Southern Zaria. Clearly, the problems
in Southern Zaria were deeper than could be remedied by a colonial officer
residing in the area; the problems related to structural inequality. Until
this changed, there was little possibility of smooth administration. Yahaya
wrote about these problems,

> The Provincial Administration upheld and supported the
> Emir's authority, particularly in crisis situations. Thus the
> Provincial Administration consistently supported the N.A.
> during a wave of political crises in the southern districts of
> the Emirate in the 1940s. The official explanation for these

crises was to attribute them partly to inadequate supervision, or inadequate touring by administrative officers, and partly to the laxity of control of the N.A., but never to the genuine demands by the people for improved social and political conditions. (Yahaya 1980:8)

Local efforts continued for both representation and improvement in services, infrastructure, and facilities in Southern Zaria. In October 1948, a group composed of one Bajju representative each from the Roman Catholic Church, the SIM-founded church, and the Anglican Church presented three requests to the resident at Zaria. They chose to bypass the district head at Zangon Katab, feeling that their requests would not be transmitted further up the administrative hierarchical structure. Their requests were for (1) an all-season road through the area, one that went from Kaduna through Kachia, to Zonkwa, to Kafanchan, and to Unguwar Rimi,[9] (2) permission for schools to go beyond the primary four level, and (3) a chief. The resident replied that their requests had merit. He sent their requests to the emir for considerations. Though the emir listened to them and said that they would hear from him, they received no response.

Government efforts for reform

In 1955 the government instituted reform in its administration by establishing village group councils and by appointing a representative, *wakili* (H.), for each ethnic group. In theory these representatives enjoyed a status equal to the district head. The district head was to serve only as a liaison between them and the emir. In practice these representatives continued to be under the authority of the district head. The office of *wakili* of the Bajju was ineffective, and therefore it was abolished in 1970.

From 1946 until 1960 both colonial administrators and Nigerian leaders sought a viable governmental structure in preparation for independence. The Richards Constitution of 1946 established three regions: the Northern Region, the Western Region, and the Eastern Region. Southern Zarians, as well as other non-Muslim minority ethnic groups who were placed within the Northern Region sought a voice in the Northern Region governmental structure. When they experienced difficulty in obtaining representation, they felt the need for a separate governmental structure. This led to demands for a Middle Belt Region, a region that was never formed.

The political agitation for self-government, elimination of discrimination, and a voice in their own administration continued into the 1950s. In 1953 some of the political leaders of the Bajju and A̲tyap wrote to the newly formed Ministry of Local Government in Kaduna outlining their complaints against the rule of the emirate district heads. These included forced labor

---

[9] At this time the road through this area was passable during the dry season only.

for road construction and other jobs without adequate payment; problems in the market, particularly the demand for eight measures of grain to be given to tax collectors; evil practices of district overseers (*jekadu*, H.); corrupt scribes who included children and elderly persons as tax payers and demanded bribes to remove such individuals from the tax rolls; contemptuous treatment of *arna*, H., 'pagans'; lack of justice for non-Muslims in court; mistreatment of non-Muslim women on market days; the practice of segregation such that a non-Muslim could not build a house near that of a Hausa; discrimination and neglect of education for non-Muslims; problems that occurred when the district head toured non-Muslim areas and showed his contempt for the population and their customs; and lack of peace for the peoples of Southern Zaria (Turaki 1982:230–231). In response to this letter Sir Ahmadu Bello, the Minister of Local Government and Community Development and the Sardauna of Sokoto, toured the area. He heard the same complaints of misrule. He sent his report to C. V. Williams, the resident of Zaria, who responded,

> His honour fully agrees with the Ministry that the problem of unrest in Southern Zaria over Local Government affairs is of great importance in view of the present political situation and danger that agitation for a Fourth Region (Middle Belt) may destroy the unanimity of the region. (NAK ZARPROF C7/1953)

The Ministry recommended that a senior administrative office be set up for Southern Zaria and that a Native Authority subtreasury be established for the area. Sir Ahmadu Bello further brought the matter to the attention of the Executive Council of Northern Nigeria. The Council drew up a list of recommendations for local government of Southern Zaria. Their recommendations included prohibiting discrimination against non-Muslims, village and district councils taking charge of their own affairs, formation of area and outer councils, posting of subtreasury and other Native Authority officers to Southern Zaria, appropriation of government funds to implement these changes, non-Muslim representation on the Native Authority council, and a press release on the political situation in Southern Zaria (Turaki 1982:235–236).

These attempts to rectify the deteriorating political situation in Southern Zaria reached a climax in the 1959 election. Political parties that emerged resulted in Southern Zarians favoring the Northern Elements Progressive Union and the Middle Zone League. The latter later developed into the United Middle Belt Congress (UMBC). This party allied itself with the Action Group that was founded by Awolowo, a Yoruba. In the 1959 election the people of Southern Zaria voted overwhelmingly for the UMBC/AG (Yahaya 1980:155). This contrasted with the Hausa and Fulani emirate rulers and populace who favored the Northern Peoples' Congress. In response to this vote Ja'afaru, the emir at Zaria, called a Bajju representative to explain their voting. This representative responded that although they had presented their requests repeatedly to him, nothing had been done for them, therefore they sought support elsewhere. He and the Bajju he represented wanted attention paid to their repeated requests. The emir offered him a position on the Zaria emir's advisory council. Though the Bajju representative was willing to work within the governmental structure for change in Southern Zaria and was therefore willing to serve on the advisory council, he was never called to do so.

It was not until 1968 that an indigene of Southern Zaria, Bala Gora, an Atyap man, was appointed to the position of district head of Zangon Katab (Yahaya 1980:167). Later the Bajju were granted three district head positions and their own chief. More recently the Bajju have appointed eighteen district heads.

Economic development under colonialism

In 1905, after a WAFF expedition against the Agorok, the acting high commissioner for the Northern Provinces wrote concerning the economic potential for this area,

> To the West and North of the KAGORO range of hills extends a vast grassy plain, well studded with magnificent trees, about 2000 feet above the sea level. It is a land both fertile and healthy, and where the European could live for several years, without endangering his health. It is a land with possibilities of many kinds, and, when fully developed, could compete in commercial importance with any part of Nigeria. Cotton, Indigo, Wheat, Millet and other cereals would yield a rich harvest, and as a grazing country for cattle and sheep it could be unrivalled. Horse breeding would be a profitable enterprise. Judging from what one saw, not many parts of the Transvaal could outrival it in climate, or as a land for profitable agriculture or cattle breeding. (NAK SNP 7/2350/1905:5–6)

This report portrayed the potential this area held for economic development under colonialism. The British recognized the Bajju as energetic farmers who offered the potential for profitable economic development projects, a potential that was not developed by the colonialists. Instead, quite the opposite of economic development occurred; Southern Zaria experienced increased poverty under the colonial administration.

In 1927 there was a shortage of both money and food in Southern Zaria. The price for grass mats, one of the primary sources of income, was 1 shilling 6 pence. A horse sold for 25 shillings and a donkey for 11 shillings

(NAK 59, 1921). In 1931 a famine occurred in this area (NAK ZARPROF 607, 1932). In 1932 one administrator noted that Zangon Katab used to be so full of horses and livestock that it was nicknamed the horse market, but that situation had changed so that it had become rare to find horses there by that date (NAK ZARPROF 607, 1932).

The British introduced ginger and rice as cash crops and in 1932 one administrator wrote, "The Kaje are energetic farmers, and have in one or two cases taken up the farming of ginger" (NAK ZARPROF 607, 1932). He further stated, the "Kaje are renowned as experts in bee-keeping and own a considerable number of goats. Furthermore there is a larger proportion of mat makers among them" (NAK ZARPROF 607, 1932). Temple stated, "They are excellent farmers and breeders of live-stock. They manure the ground with dung from goats and fowls, and ashes" (Temple 1922:195). Another administrator noted, "Economically they are progressive and nearly all law-abiding. They farm the new crops of rice and ginger and cotton as vigorously as their other crops" (NAK 1558, 1554, 1761; 1933).

Colorful sleeping mats woven by both men and women continue to be a source of income. Locally woven mats were often marketed through Hausa middlemen. SIM missionaries introduced economically productive trees, especially citrus trees, mango, and pawpaw, and hog rearing in the early 1930s, which eventually became important sources of income.

From 1914 to 1927 the British administration constructed the eastern branch of the railroad through this area. Many Bajju worked on railroad construction as well as building the road to the tin mines on the Jos Plateau (NAK ZARPROF 607, 1932). While working in the mines the Bajju saw the relationship between other ethnic groups and the colonial administration in which they dealt directly with the colonial administrators rather than through Hausa intermediaries. The Bajju could see that these groups were better off than they were, and this led to attempts to change their status. They desired independent status such that they would deal directly with the administration without Hausa intermediaries (NAK ZARPROF 6/1942).

The southern districts within the emirate were economically depressed compared to the northern districts. The relatively prosperous cash economy of the emirates was based on cotton, tobacco, and groundnuts, all of which grew in the northern districts. Although some groundnuts are cultivated in Southern Zaria, it is too wet for cotton cultivation. They readily adopted ginger and rice growing, with ginger becoming a major cash crop, though the world ginger market was erratic.[10] Further, the local practice of splitting ginger that allows it to dry more quickly lowers its value on the world market.

With the introduction of mission schools and churches, and the beginnings of Bajju insertion into the national economy, families shifted their village residence sites from hilltops and wooded areas to the plains. Waters-Bayer commented on this shift,

---

[10] See Waters-Bayer 1982:19 for a discussion of Bajju adoption of ginger cultivation.

> Judging from the approximate time of the major shifts of families to the new village sites, the settlement pattern of the arable farmers on the Abet Plains must have been strongly influenced by the arrival of the Sudan Interior Mission to Abet in the late 1930's, the establishment of mission schools and churches in the area in the 1940's and 1950's, and the construction of the motorable road from Gidan Maga to Ungwan Rimi (site of a major weekly market near the railway town of Kafanchan) in 1950, followed by the growth of marketing points. The most recently established villages and clusters of compounds are all close to motorable roads. The most common reason given by Kaje informants for shift of dwelling was the attraction of so-called 'civilisation', usually specified as roads and schools. Particularly strong attraction appears to have been exerted by the signs of economic and social progress such as shops of traders and craftsmen, motor transport amenities, dispensary, wells, schools, churches and mosques. (Waters-Bayer 1982:8–9)

While the administration did little to develop this region economically, a cash economy did develop that gradually resulted in Bajju integration into the wider economic structure of Nigeria. Cessation of warfare, the introduction by missionaries of economically productive trees and hog rearing, decorative sleeping mats, and marketing of ginger and other locally produced food products, such as palm wine and locust bean cakes, all contributed to the Bajju entering the wider economy. This was a major change in their economy. Prior to British pacification of this area, there were no markets among the Bajju, and it was not safe for people to enter this area because of the local practice of headhunting.

The general economic situation in the southern districts contributed to their political discontent. Yahaya states, "The relative poverty of the area was to create a sense of deprivation, and this together with an awareness of a separate identity, became the strongest motivations for their resistance of the N. A. system" (Yahaya 1980:16). This political oppression was a major factor in the sense of deprivation that the Bajju and other minority ethnic groups felt. Turaki also expounded on the relative underdevelopment of Southern Zaria, together with their lack of equal participation in the political process by stating, "Southern Zaria was also economically underdeveloped both during the colonial and independent Nigeria. There were no good roads, industries and government schools situated in the area" (1982:391–392).

Overview of the colonial period

The Bajju occupied a position of powerlessness under the colonial administration. They, together with other peoples classified as "pagans," formed the
bottom social class of the social structure in Northern Nigeria. Though the
administration forbade slavery, they put their former slave raiders, namely
leaders from the Hausa-Fulani emirates, in positions of authority over the
Bajju and other non-Muslim ethnic groups. Consequently, the collection of
slaves continued covertly in this area into the early colonial period.[11] The
formal imposition of emirate rule upon the Bajju compounded their problems and resulted in their having no voice in the governmental structure
imposed upon them throughout the entire colonial era.

The Bajju suffered from raids and enslavement by Hausa and Fulani
from the emirates in the precolonial period. In the colonial period the British
continued a similar pattern of oppression that these emirates practiced.
Military personnel of the Hausa and Fulani emirates had burned villages,
engaged in skirmishes, and set up rulers who had no real authority within
the Bajju community. As the colonial administration extended its authority over Southern Zaria, it continued some of the practices of the emirates.
For example, after the attack on the emir in 1915, the Bajju sought peace
through traditional means. However, the British demanded that the Bajju
and Kanikom produce the individuals who took part in the skirmish. In
Bajju precolonial society, to produce the individuals involved was unacceptable as it would have violated the solidarity of the group and the secrecy
associated with the *abvoi* society. When they refused to produce the men,
the British burned their villages, destroyed the *abvoi* shrine, and killed Bajju
indiscriminately.

Because the colonial administration undermined the political authority exercised by the *abvoi* society, it also undermined the existing religious
structure.[12] If the *abvoi* society were to survive, it would have had to change
its functions within society. Even without the introduction of missions into
the area, the *abvoi* society could not have continued as before, given the
new ground rules laid down by colonial administrators.

As the colonial period progressed, the Bajju sought representation
and independent status under the colonial administration through various
means; however, each effort was unsuccessful. The British sided with the

---

[11] Some elderly individuals provided me with firsthand accounts of the capture of
slaves. These individuals were not over eighty years old, which they would have
had to have been if the capture of slaves had ceased with the establishment of the
Protectorate of Northern Nigeria. Since the continued acquisition of slaves was
covert, little data on this activity are available. For example, slave markets had
disappeared so that buying and selling of slaves took place between individuals
rather than in a formal context.

[12] I am grateful to Stephen Nkom for pointing this out to me.

emirates, and the emirate leaders maintained their authority to their own advantage. The losers were the Bajju and other minority ethnic groups in Southern Zaria. These people developed a deep sense that they had been wronged and oppressed; however, they did not lose hope. Christianity brought by missionaries provided an alternative. It provided educational opportunities such that individuals could improve their economic status and in time also their political status. Although British administrators were nominally Christians, the government sought to maintain tight controls over mission activities while it left Islam free to expand.

The widespread adoption of Christianity must be viewed from the position of a people who suffered political and economic oppression. Though this oppression was not the sole motive for the adoption of Christianity, it was significant. Their adoption of Christianity was a form of resistance to oppression. Kato saw the Bajju acceptance of Christianity from this perspective:

> The Kaje people with their traditional dislike of their Hausa overlords saw the missionaries as a buffer between them and their oppressive rulers. Their ready acceptance of Christianity appeared to have been a means of registering their protests against the Muslim rulers. They also appeared to have seen the missionaries as a body which would free them from the domination of the Hausa. (Kato 1974:236–237)

Missionaries entered this context soon after the imposition of colonial rule in northern Nigeria. The following chapter examines the missions and church context of Bajju religious change.

5

Missions in Northern Nigeria

Introduction

In this chapter I examine the context of Christian missionary work in Nigeria in general. It includes attitudes of colonial administrators towards Christianity, some of whom promoted it and others who actively opposed it especially in the Hausa heartland. It was seen as contrary to the colonial leaders' assertion that they would not interfere with the practice of Islam. In many cases the colonialists actively opposed Christian missionaries while encouraging Muslim proselytization. This chapter provides the context for Bajju Christian conversion, which the following chapters build upon.

Early missionaries in northern Nigeria

Christian missionary efforts to reach people with the gospel in northern Nigeria began in the precolonial era. During the 1840s the Wesleyan Methodist Missionary Society wanted to enter northern Nigeria, followed closely by the Church Missionary Society (CMS). In 1855 Bowen, an American missionary with the Southern Baptist Mission, sought to enter the Nupe and Hausa areas (Ayandele 1966:98).

Early Christian missionary contact with various northern leaders included that by Bishop Samuel Ajayi Crowther, a former slave of Yoruba descent, who had been freed by the British antislavery squadron

65

and taken to Freetown, Sierra Leone. There he proved to be an apt pupil who first attended the CMS mission school, then Fourah Bay College. In 1841 Crowther was a member of the British Niger Expedition, an expedition supported by Sir Thomas Fowell Buxton and sponsored by the Society for the Extinction of the Slave Trade and for the Civilization of Africa. Following this disastrous expedition in which 130 members suffered from malaria and 55 died of it, Crowther published his *Journal of the 1841 Expedition* (Crowther 1842). The CMS was impressed with this book, so they called him to England where he spent some time at the Parochial School on Liverpool Street, Islington, London. Eventually Crowther became bishop of Western Equatorial Africa beyond the Queen's Dominions where he headed up the work of establishing schools, churches, mission stations, and an experimental farm at Abeokuta. His approach was to reach *communities* with the gospel, rather than focusing on conversion of individuals.

Crowther was interested in giving the people the Bible in their own languages. For example, Crowther was the translator of the Yoruba Bible, his native language. He also worked among the Nupe, and in 1864 he published his *Grammar and Vocabulary of the Nupe Language*. With the help of a Nupe, he prepared a translation of Matthew in Nupe. In 1870 Crowther went to the Nupe area where he met with Masara, the Muslim emir at Bida. He sought to convince Emir Masara of the need for Muslim-Christian cooperation. He also requested permission to establish a missionary rest house there. In 1873 he again journeyed to Bida where he met with Umaru, Masara's successor. Umaru agreed to protect missionaries who came to staff the mission station established there. The Nupe were predominately animistic at that time, though their rulers adhered to Islam.

In 1892 the Hausa Association was formed in England with the goal of continuing Hausa Bible translation work initiated by J. A. Robinson (Crampton 1975:37), who had begun translation of the Christian Scriptures into Hausa. His brother, Canon C. H. Robinson, who studied Hausa in Tripoli, subsequently published the gospel of Matthew. In 1897 he arrived with a small party of CMS missionaries in Lokoja, and from there they traveled to Kano where they spent three months. After returning to England, Canon C. H. Robinson published several portions of the Bible, a grammatical write-up of the Hausa language, and an account of his travels entitled *Hausaland*. From his interaction with the Hausa, he was encouraged that the Hausa Muslims might be open to the gospel.

In 1893 Kent, Gowans, and Bingham went to Lagos with the goal of moving into the "Sudan,"[1] particularly into northern Nigeria. Bingham remained in Lagos where he was to be a liaison with the outside world while the other two set out for the north. They went beyond Bida, but by the end of 1894

---

[1] "Sudan" is an Arabic word meaning 'Land of the blacks'.

both Gowans and Kent had died. Bingham returned to Canada where he shared with other Christians his vision of reaching the Sudan with the gospel. In 1898 in Toronto he formed the Christian Council for the Sudan. In 1900 Bingham with two others returned to Nigeria, but it was a short trip as Bingham became very ill and so returned home to Toronto. His two companions soon sailed home to Toronto.

Bingham's vision for reaching the "Sudan" continued after colonialism was established. In 1900 three missionaries, Antony, Taylor, and Banfield, were sent to Nigeria. They traveled on the same ship with Lord Lugard who was very friendly with them and promised to facilitate their work in any way. He assisted them in getting to Pategi where they set up their mission work. That work was the beginning work of Sudan Interior Mission (SIM).

CMS missionaries worked primarily in Southern Nigeria, but some CMS missionaries had the goal of reaching the north with the gospel. For example, in 1895 Bishop Tugwell made an exploratory journey to Bida and traveled through the Bassa territory. In 1896 he visited Keffi.

In 1897 plans were underway among Anglican Christians in Britain to send missionaries to Hausaland. Dr. Walter Miller, a recently qualified medical doctor, was one of the new CMS recruits (Crampton 1975:39). Dr. Miller and a few others went to Tripoli to study Hausa with Hausa traders who lived in an enclave there. While in Tripoli, Miller assisted Abdul Majid, a thirteen-year-old boy, on his way to Mecca. When Abdul Majid returned from Mecca, he found a letter from Miller inviting him to England. He accepted this invitation, and when he returned from England with Miller, he accompanied him to Zaria. His family became one of the first Christian families among the Hausa-Fulani (Crampton 1975:41).[2]

After completing his study of Hausa in Tripoli, Miller left Lagos in January 1900 with four other CMS missionaries, including Bishop Tugwell and 240 carriers. This caravan arrived in Zaria in April 1900. On their trip north they crossed paths with a British military party that was seeking to colonize the north, but they moved ahead of the colonialists. They received a warm welcome among the common people, and even from the emir of Zaria. They explained the nature of British intentions to the emir, and he welcomed the British colonialists as allies against the emir of Sokoto who he feared was about to depose him.

When the British arrived in northern Nigeria, Lord Lugard promised the Waziri and the headmen of Sokoto: "The English Government never interferes with religion. Taxes, law and order, punishment of crime, these are matters for the Government, but not religion" (Lugard, as quoted in Turaki 1993:129). Lugard later spoke to the Royal Geographical Society and said, "I added that the British had no intention of interfering with their religion, for

---

[2] There is some question as to which mission, the Methodists or the Church Missionary Society, arrived first in Northern Nigeria. Most agree that they probably arrived around the same time.

under the King's flag all were free to worship God as they pleased" (Lugard, as quoted in Turaki 1993:130). Lugard also stated, "Government will in.no way interfere with the Mohammedan religion.... Mosques and prayer-places will be treated with respect by us" (Lugard, as quoted in Boer 1979:69). However, Lugard was not anti-missionary. For example, Dr. Walter Miller was one of Lugard's closest advisors, and Lugard allowed Miller to preach freely in Muslim areas. He also allowed missionaries to operate in Muslim areas, including at Pategi, Bida, Zaria, Wase, Kontagora, and Katsina (Boer 1979:69). The only condition for missionaries operating in Muslim areas was that the emirs of each area agreed with their being there. In fact, few missionaries were allowed in these areas, as Lugard and other British colonial officers feared that Muslims might perceive their presence as a breach of faith on the administration's part not to interfere with their Islamic religious practices.

British colonial policy was to use Indirect Rule in the colonies they governed. Under this policy they applied the emirate model to non-Muslims; hence the British sided with Muslims and thereby shielded their societies from Christian missionaries. Sanneh states, "In the Muslim world Christianity was stumped by Western imperialism more than by any other force, with the accompanying Western-inspired modernization furnishing the Muslim world with tools with which to launch and to maintain an anti-Christian cultural-resistance strategy" (2012:167).

By contrast, Lugard encouraged missionaries to go to areas where the people practiced traditional religions. He stated, "I have...held out every encouragement to establish missions in pagan centres, which appear to me to need the influence of civilization and religion at least as much as the Mohammedans" (as quoted in Boer 1979:70). His only condition was that missionaries uphold the prestige of the Europeans. Lugard felt that the advantages of missionaries was that they would help bring an ethical system to these groups, namely that of Christianity. To Lugard, Christian education would introduce a moral system.

Dr. Kumm, a German missionary, together with some British Christians formed the Sudan Pioneer Mission, which begun work in Northern Nigeria by 1902; two years later they changed their name to Sudan United Mission (SUM) (Crampton 1975:44). In 1904 Kumm went to Tripoli to study Hausa. Temple, the resident of Bauchi Province, which included the Jos Plateau, invited Kumm to work there. The initial work of SUM was at Wase, a work that was unsuccessful and abandoned in 1909.

In fact, the work of CMS, SIM, and SUM all grew out of what was termed the "Burden of the Sudan." This area was seen as the largest mission field in the world that had no missionaries. The missionary "Burden of the Sudan" contrasted with the "Burden of Empire" position of the colonialists.

After Lugard left his position as British high commissioner, those who followed him were much less sympathetic to Christian missions. His successor, Canadian Sir Percy Girouard, bitterly opposed Christian mission-ary "propaganda" in Islamic areas. He stated,

> Personally I should like to see the [CMS] mission retire entirely from the Northern States, for the best missionary for the present will be the high-minded, clean-living British Resident. The opinion of Residents is absolutely unanimous in considering the presence of the Mission as a menace to the peace of the country... It is a very sad fact that the missions, as constituted, are not of the slightest assistance in admin-istering the country: on the contrary a constant source of worry. They say that their religion and common sense bear no relation to each other. (Boer 1979:72)

C. L. Temple, another British colonial officer, also opposed missions, pre-ferring the indigenous religious institutions. He wanted missionaries out of animistic areas as well as Muslim areas. For example, he refused to allow mis-sionaries to respond to a request made by the non-Muslim Maguzawa Hausa that missionaries come live among them. His reason for this refusal was that he felt this would make them less obedient to the emirs. In fact, over time many Maguzawa Hausa have accepted Christianity, a decision that they have made themselves, while other Maguzawa Hausa have converted to Islam, and some continue to follow traditional Habe (Hausa) religious practices.

When Lugard was in authority, he wanted to have an educational meas-ure passed that favored missions, but the Colonial Office overruled this proposal. The opposition to missions in Muslim areas, and even in some animistic areas, came both from some of the colonial administrators and from the Colonial Office in Britain.

Basically, the relationship between the British colonial administration and missions was an ambiguous one, with missionaries obligated to fol-low colonial policies, while at the same time teaching the worth of each individual, whether Christian, Muslim, or animist. The moral teachings of missions tended to undermine the paternalism that was so much a part of colonialism, though some missionaries were also paternalistic. An example of a missionary who undermined British authority, while also cooperating with it, was Dr. Walter Miller. He "was directly responsible for encouraging the founding of a political organization, the Northern People's Congress, to advance African political aims against British authorities" (Sanneh 1989:118). He was seeking to teach Africans how to work within the British system towards their own goals.

Missions and education

Lugard's policy towards education and educational reform had five goals. These were "the strengthening of government control, more government schools, closer liaison with mission schools through grants-in-aid, government schools inspectorate, and emphasis on character training through religious and moral education" (Kirk-Greene 1966:ix).

In 1908, Girouard, who succeeded Lord Lugard as high commissioner, requested that Hanns Vischer, a political officer, organize the educational system. Vischer was a Swiss missionary in Northern Nigeria. He had taken British citizenship in 1903 in order to enter the Colonial Service and work in the Political Department of the Protectorate. Because of Vischer's desire to fulfill Lugard's promise not to interfere with Islam and to implement Indirect Rule, he insisted that the schools he set up each have a mosque, and he personally paid for the services of an imam for each school.

Three men worked in the Department of Education until 1912. By that date there were five government and Native Authority schools with 350 students in them. At the same time missions had four primary schools and twenty-five elementary schools with an enrollment of 604 students (Kirk-Greene 1966:xiii).

In 1926 the government released the report of the Phelps-Stokes Commission (Awóníyì 1978:88-90). This report specifically called on the colonial governments in Africa to have joint ventures and to cooperate with missions in education and medical work. Cooperation in educational ventures was not as evident as was their cooperation in medical work, specifically in the care and treatment of leprosy patients.

The government maintained its monopoly over the education of Muslims and insisted that missions should confine their stations and educational efforts to predominately non-Muslim areas. It was not until around 1930 that the British colonial administration allowed missionaries to enter Muslim areas. This attitude towards Muslims and missionaries on the part of the British colonial administration resulted in the spread of Islam into areas of Northern Nigeria where it had not been before or where people were only nominally Muslim. There were no such restrictions placed on Muslims as were placed on Christian missionaries. They were free to proselytize wherever they chose to.

The initial goal of the British educational system was to educate the sons of emirs and other Muslim leaders to prepare them to assume roles within the administrative structure, initially as clerks and technical assistants. As Tibenderana (1983) pointed out, the emirs were not opposed to this type of education for their sons and many took advantage of it. He wrote concerning education in Northern Nigeria,

> Up to the late 1940s the development of Western education
> in non-Muslim areas in northern Nigeria was the responsibility of Christian missions, since the policy of the colonial administration was to confine native administration
> schools to Muslim areas. The non-Muslim administrations

were too poor to run schools. Hence during the period...
native administration schools in non-Muslim areas were
one-teacher schools. Because of the low education standard
of one-teacher schools, many non-Muslim parents sent their
daughters to mission schools instead of native administration schools. (Tibenderana 1985:93)

As late as 1932 there were no Native Authority schools in Southern
Zaria other than those maintained at Kachia and Zangon Katab for
Muslims. Those two schools were for the benefit of the children of those
in the Hausa and Fulani enclaves, not for the indigenous population (NAK
907, 1932).

While the colonial administration concentrated its efforts on teaching
Hausa children, it was not until the 1950s that the colonial administration
began to pay attention to education in minority areas. The mission schools
in non-Muslim areas were an important arm of the church; consequently,
education and Christianity arrived together.

Initially missionaries established literacy classes that taught reading,
writing, and notation. Soon afterwards they established more advanced
classes termed Christian Religious Instruction (CRI) classes that taught people to read well enough to read the Bible, writing, arithmetic, and Bible.
These classes were open to anyone, particularly adult converts. One SIM
publication in 1935 stated, "The Educational Work of the SIM is confined
entirely to the Bible instruction, the elements of reading and writing being
taught to those who become interested in the Gospel from an illiterate population" (Beacham 1935:2). In the early days a second goal of these schools
was to train Christian laymen, teachers, pastors, and evangelists. Though
most CRI classes disappeared long ago in the Bajju area, they continue in a
few villages. Today CRI classes have largely been displaced by other schools
that teach illiterate adults to read, such as Day Bible Schools that are held
in a number of villages.

When missionaries first established primary schools throughout
Southern Zaria, they had to campaign to get children to attend the schools.
Later, when interest in attending school increased, some missionaries, for
example those with SIM, required that anyone who attended their schools be
a member of the denomination that had established the school. Therefore,
if a Bajju wanted to be educated, he had to convert to Christianity if he had
not already done so, and occasionally a Christian had to change his denominational affiliation.

Over time the emphasis shifted first to Bible schools, then to primary
schools, teachers' colleges, secondary schools, and finally to seminaries and
advanced teachers' colleges.

In the late 1940s Mgr. Lumley requested government permission to
establish a Catholic men's teacher training college at Kafanchan. The goal
of this college was to train teachers for Catholic primary schools that the

Roman Catholics had set up. After receiving government permission, they established the College of Mary Immaculate as an elementary training college; in 1951 it became a higher training college. In 1955 Roman Catholics, through the missionary Sisters of Our Lady of Apostles, began work at Zonkwa and established a girls' secondary school there.

Some early administrators and missionaries spoke against the evils of "detribalization" (Turaki 1982:150). They feared that if Africans received more education, they would then take jobs with the colonial administration or with other companies and be lost to the work of the church. Later experience with well-educated Nigerians showed that these people were the future leaders of the country. They became government workers who benefited enormously from whatever education they were able to get.

In 1972 the North Central State[3] government took control of all Voluntary Agency schools, including those set up by missions. Since then the level of education offered in these schools has tended to decline, and there has been talk of giving the schools back to the agencies that set them up.

Missions and medical work

While the government focused on the economic sector of the colony, they were glad to leave most of the educational and medical responsibilities to missions. Missions rose to the challenge by establishing schools and a number of hospitals and dispensaries.

Hospitals

Missionaries became involved in medical work early in their ministry. For example, in 1905 Dr. Miller returned to Zaria with permission from the British high commissioner and the emir of Zaria to open a small dispensary. He did so within the walls of old city Zaria, a city where theoretically only Muslims may live.[4] While in Zaria he developed a close relationship with the emir. In 1906 Lugard wrote concerning this,

> This friendly attitude [of the emir of Zaria] and the most remarkable results achieved are probably and almost entirely due to Dr. Miller's exceptional tact and personal influence, together with his absolute mastery of the Hausa language. The Resident...cannot too warmly express his gratitude to Dr. Miller...The Emir himself has apparently formed a close

---

[3] North Central State was later renamed Kaduna State.

[4] I use the word "theoretically" as Dr. Miller, a Christian missionary, was allowed to live there. Our family and a number of our colleagues also lived within the mud walls of old city Zaria. The landlords of the three houses we rented were glad to receive our rent.

friendship with Dr. Miller and invites a frank expression of
his opinions on social abuses which come under his notice. I
believe that a very great deal of good has resulted. (Lugard,
as quoted in Grimley and Robinson 1966:51–52)

In 1929 the colonial administration ejected Miller from Zaria because
they saw the presence of a Christian missionary within the old city as a
threat to their promise of noninterference with the practice of Islam. The
CMS work moved two miles away to Wusasa, which is located outside the
walls of the old city. The buildings there are built in the Hausa style, with
patterns sculpted into the mud walls on the front of the houses. Miller's
intent was to live as much like the Hausa as possible. St. Bartholomew's
Church, the earliest church in Northern Nigeria, was built there and is still
in use. Missionaries also established a large mission hospital at Wusasa.

At Kano Sudan Interior Mission (SIM) established Kano Eye Hospital,
which has both inpatient and outpatient facilities. In 1946 SIM established
Bingham Memorial Nursing Home in Jos to meet the medical needs of missionaries. In 1969 it merged with the African Hospital, which was renamed
SIM Evangel Hospital. In the 1970s Plateau State government took over
Evangel Hospital and a second hospital at Kaltungo. In 1981 the government returned Evangel Hospital to ECWA so that high quality medical services would be maintained for the indigenous population.

Figure 5.1. Saint Bartholomew Anglican Church built in 1929, the
oldest church in northern Nigeria (Norris McKinney).

SUM established a hospital at Vom. The Roman Catholics, through the Sisters of Our Lady of Apostles, established St. Louis Catholic Hospital at Zonkwa. Both hospitals continue to provide excellent care to the local population. These are only two of the medical facilities established by missions in Northern Nigeria. While the government established a hospital at Kafanchan, the local population often bypassed that hospital to go to the dispensary at Kagoro or St. Louis Hospital at Zonkwa because the quality of treatment was better there. The quality of care at Kafanchan General Hospital has also improved.

Mission dispensaries

In traditional culture, health and disease are part of the religion system. Missionaries were concerned with both the people's physical and spiritual wellbeing. To that end Sudan Interior Mission's goal was to have a dispensary connected with each mission station they established. Missionaries initially ran these dispensaries. For example, the Archibalds established a dispensary at Kagoro in 1927 that followed early mission practice summarized as follows:

> In each of the pagan stations we [SIM] start a Medical Dispensary. This work is often used to bring the natives into friendly relations towards us as well as alleviating a great deal of suffering. Each dispensary is fitted with a supply of suitable medicines and these are from time to time replenished and inspected by our field doctor. In case of our last station [in the Rukuba tribe] over 1300 cases were treated in less than two months. (*The West African Yearbook* 1915)

In 1959 SIM set up the SIM Medical Auxiliary Training School (SIMMATS) to train dispensers and medical attendants in a two-year program. The dispensers they trained were to work in the over 110 dispensaries and treatment centers that SIM had established. Nigerian dispensers now run all dispensaries in the area under the sponsorship of The Evangelical Church Winning All (ECWA), the denomination that grew out of the work of SIM. The reputation of these dispensaries is such that people prefer to receive treatment at a church-sponsored dispensary if at all possible rather than at a government dispensary or hospital.

Missions and economic development

As mentioned in the previous chapter, the colonial administration introduced ginger and rice as cash crops into this area. Missions introduced economically productive trees, hog rearing, use of mud blocks in house construction, schools with literacy initially in Hausa and later in English,

Northern Nigerian-style clothing, carpentry, high-grade cheap salt, and Western medicine.

At one point SIM required their missionaries to sign a statement that they had planted a certain number of economically productive trees each year (Gerald Swank, SIM missionary, pers. comm.).[5] Today at the compounds of early Christians, there are large mango and citrus trees, especially grapefruit. The produce from these trees has helped the local population economically and nutritionally.

The educational work of missions has been extremely beneficial to the local population. When independence came, there were educated individuals from various minority groups. They were able to take over as schoolteachers, administrators, carpenters, craftsmen, and so on. Although the government had ignored their home areas, missionaries did not.

Rev. James Mitchell-Innes, an Anglican missionary, had the vision of setting up agricultural stores in this area. While he and his family had to return to the UK due to health reasons, his vision lived on. CMS eventually set up three agricultural stores in the area that sell medicine for animals, animal feed, Christian literature, and other products relevant for a horticultural people. These stores have been quite successful. After CMS set up their stores, ECWA set up a similar store.

Discussion

This chapter has discussed the beginning of missionary activities in Northern Nigeria, including the colonial government's perspectives on missions. Many colonial administrators sought to restrict missionaries from working in Muslim areas, particularly prior to 1930. Hence missionaries were shunted off to work in minority language areas where people practiced traditional religions. The result has been that these areas have produced many very well-educated individuals. Since Christian missionaries taught about the worth of each individual before God and man, their teaching undermined the paternalistic colonial administrative structure. It also meant that many ethnic groups in the Middle Belt of Nigeria are today predominately Christian.

Missionaries set up dispensaries and hospitals that met the physical needs of the local population. In addition, they contributed more towards economic development in minority areas than the colonial administration through planting economically productive trees, introducing hog rearing, education, high-grade cheap salt, and crafts such as carpentry. Missions helped develop southern Kaduna State, though they chafed under the restrictions placed upon them by the colonial administration.

---

[5] When I tried to verify that they had to sign in the SIM archives in North Carolina, I was unable to do so.

The next chapter discusses specific missions and the denominations they established in the Bajju area. It expands upon this brief introduction to mission activities.

6

Mission Societies and Denominations in Southern Kaduna State

Introduction

Christian mission work under the colonial administration

The colonial government sought to maintain some control over missionary activities by requiring them to obtain government permission to establish mission stations, mission schools, and churches. Lugard subscribed to the concept of spheres of influence for different missions so that their work would not overlap and compete against one another (Lugard 1926:596). He stated that this arrangement was in accord with the *Foreign Office Handbook*. This policy occasionally led to problems in the Bajju area, particularly between SIM and Roman Catholic missionaries.

Christianity and education

Christianity and education came together in the non-Hausa areas in Northern Nigeria. Initially missionaries established Christian Religious Instruction (CRI) classes. Later when primary schools were established, the colonial administration allowed them to go through primary 4 only.

After completing primary 4, applicants could apply to the Elementary Training School, established in 1937 at Kagoro. Two years later this school was upgraded to Kagoro Teacher Training College. The goal for graduates from this school was to fill positions in the expanding number of Sudan primary schools. Instruction was initially in Hausa, though in 1949 English became the language of instruction rather than Hausa. English gradually gained importance because it was the language of government and increasingly of education. Graduates received the rank of Grade III teachers. In 1958 Grade III teachers could return for a two-year course to upgrade their certification to that of Grade II. In 1960 Kagoro Teachers' College was upgraded to a Grade II teachers' college with a five-year curriculum.

The colonial administration criticized SIM for providing substandard education. It felt that SIM's only goal was proselytization. They viewed those who graduated from mission schools as having too little education to qualify for jobs, yet enough to make them misfits within the local community. In general, the colonial administrators feared that Western-style education would disrupt African societies, and some spoke against the evils of "detribalization" (Turaki 1982:150).

The situation in which missions provided a lower standard of education than that of the government changed in the 1950s when SIM placed increasing importance on education. This shift in emphasis coincided with the availability of government grants for education to missions. At this point the quality of mission education surpassed that of government Native Authority schools. Evangelization increasingly became the responsibility of Nigerian pastors and evangelists rather than of missionaries.

In some ways the schools undermined colonial control of the area by producing an educated population who became aware of what was occurring in their country. Further, missions taught that all people are equal; hence the governmental structure in Northern Nigeria with the British administration at the top, then Muslims, and finally "pagans" at the bottom of the social hierarchy was not tenable. The colonial government's Mohammedan policies and pagan policies are an example of the class stratified society introduced by the administration.

Bajju response to Christianity

Prior to the coming of Christianity, the Bajju believed in one God as well as an afterlife and punishment for sin after death. Each of these concepts is compatible with Christianity. People found the Christian gospel attractive because it allowed them to know God. Thus Christianity expanded their knowledge of God, the God they already believed in. One person asserted that although they knew God existed, they did not know Him. Another said that though they knew there was an afterlife, they did not know God would be there.

The Bajju reached out and brought Christianity home to their area. While there were missionaries in the area, all sought to serve all of the ethnic groups in the southern Kaduna area, not solely the Bajju. There have been SIM missionaries at Kagoro since 1927, with the first Bajju conversions occurring in 1929. SIM missionaries have been posted to Kagoro, Kafanchan, Unguwar Rimi, and Zonkwa. Roman Catholic missionaries soon followed with missionaries posted to Kagoro, Zonkwa, Mabushi, Kafanchan, and Fadan Kaje. Baptist missionaries have a mission station near Kafanchan, and CMS has maintained a mission station at Kafanchan.

Missions and language

Few missionaries at the various mission stations learned Jju, the language of the Bajju. This lack clearly hindered their ability to communicate the Christian message to monolingual speakers of Jju. It also hindered communication with the vast majority of Bajju who spoke Hausa at the market level or less. Further, it did not allow missionaries to understand the traditional religion or the questions the traditional religious system addressed. Had they understood traditional religion, they could have provided Christian responses to questions raised by traditional religion.

This use of Hausa was also part of the missionization of speakers of the other ethnic groups in southern Kaduna State, including the Atyap, Agorok, Bakulu, Asholio, Angan, Gwong, Ninzam, and Ham, and other smaller ethnic groups. Missionaries considered this a Hausa-speaking area since Hausa is the language of wider communication that is used in the markets where interaction occurs between ethnic groups, at hospitals, and by government officials. Local pastors receive their training in the "vernacular" language, namely in Hausa. Hausa continues to be the primary language of the churches in the area since this is what the pastors have been trained to use. In fact, missionaries and now Christian pastors have been a primary means whereby the use of Hausa has spread to this area. Turaki asserts that "the Hausa language quickly became the common language of the region and a powerful tool for assimilation and communication which the Caliphate used effectively" (2010:71).

In my research sample in 1984, I found 4.5% of the interviewees, out of a sample of 266 individuals, were monolingual in Jju. Most of these monolingual speakers lived in rural areas, were forty years of age or older, and the vast majority were women (McKinney 1990:282, 285). Further, these women attended church daily but did not understand what was being taught. They did not have a response problem, but rather a language problem; they could not understand the message. They formed a linguistically neglected segment within Christian churches.

In 1984 over 90% of the Bajju interviewed indicated that they spoke Hausa at the market level or less. This use of Hausa in the churches has definitely hindered communication of the Christian message to Bajju speakers. A good example of this was one elderly man who attended church regularly but who did not understand Hausa. When asked what he got out of church, he stated that he enjoyed the music. He also said that as a Bajju elder he had to be there. It was his responsibility as an elder in the community. (For further discussion of language use, see McKinney 1990.)

Denominational teachings on morality

Teachings on morality are extremely important topics when discussing the various denominations in southern Kaduna State. From the perspective of the local population the differences between churches are not based on evangelical versus liberal, or on doctrinal differences. Rather, differences in teachings on morality are a primary factor for why a person would attend one denomination rather than another.

SIM, formerly Sudan Interior Mission

Sudan Interior Mission (SIM) established its first mission station at Kwoi in the Ham (Jaba, H.) area in 1910 and a second at Kurmin Musa in about 1921, also in the Ham area. Missionaries trekked out into villages from these stations to evangelize. The earliest SIM missionary visit to a Bajju village that individual Bajju remember was to Zitrung by a missionary who was on his way to Kurmin Musa in 1922 (Asake 1982:96). SIM applied to the colonial administration to open a mission station among the Bajju in 1926; however, none was opened at that time (NAK ZARPROF 264).

SIM missionaries resident at Kwoi and Kurmin Musa studied Hyam,[1] the language of the Ham people. This language is not mutually intelligible with Jju, the language of the Bajju people. Because of this lack of mutual intelligibility, it is unlikely that those missionaries were able to communicate with the Bajju. It was not until they began work at Kagoro and used Hausa that the Bajju began to hear the gospel.

SIM requested permission from the colonial government to establish mission stations among both the Bajju and Agorok. In 1912 the resident at Jema'a na Daroro approved this request. He suggested Fadan Kagoro as the site where they might build among the Agorok and Gidan Atta or Madakiya among the Bajju.[2] Rev. Archibald began construction of a mission house at Madakiya; however, the chief of the village drove him away. The old foundation of that structure was recently located in the soccer field of the school.

---

[1] W. Watson translated Scripture into Hyam with the gospel of Mark completed in 1921 and the gospel of John in 1923 (Report of the United Conference of Protestant Missionary Societies held at Port Harcourt, 1928).

[2] Letter from H. D. Larrimore, The Resident, to Sudan Interior Mission, 2 November 1912, SIM Archives.

The first SIM missionary to visit Kagoro was C. Hummel, an SIM missionary from the Chawai and Rukuba groups north of Kagoro who contacted the Agorok while staying at the government Rest House in 1923. He sought a site to establish a SIM station; however, the district officer ordered him out of the area for fear he would be killed (*The Sudan Witness*, July–August 1934:10). By 1925 SIM had selected the site of the Kagoro mission station; in 1926 they applied for permission to establish it; and in 1927 they received the necessary Certificate of Occupancy (C. of O.).

In April 1927 Tom and Grace Archibald, Scottish missionaries from Edinburgh, arrived at Kagoro together with their one-year-old daughter Gracie and Toro,[3] a Ham evangelist and his family. Hence, a third SIM station in Southern Zaria was established at Kagoro. They began morning and evening prayers as well as regular visitation and evangelism in individual households. Itinerant preaching was perhaps the most significant method Tom Archibald used.

> Within the first six months they had begun classes in Christian Religious Instruction[4] (CRI) which had as their primary goal education of Christians sufficient to read and understand the Bible. In CRI classes they taught reading, writing, arithmetic, and Bible stories. In addition, they opened a dispensary that attracted a steady stream of patients. (Swank (1970:3)

From this beginning at the Kagoro mission station SIM began evangelizing the Bajju.

The early days of the Archibalds' residence at Kagoro were not easy; the local residents did not readily accept their presence. They shot poisoned arrows at them through their windows, windows that they tightly closed with shutters at night. However, in time the Archibalds won the confidence of the local residents. Rev. Archibald preached, provided medical and dental services, and taught literacy classes with the Hausa New Testament as the main textbook. After the entire Hausa Bible was printed in 1932, he used it. Rev. Archibald, although required by the colonial administration to maintain residence standards similar to those of government administrators, lived close to the people. He spent weeks at a time traveling from village to village and encouraged other missionaries to do likewise (Minutes 1935).

---

[3] While we were in Nigeria, Toro died. As he was dying he kept telling those in his room with its kerosene lantern lit, that they should turn down the light. Though they turned it down, he kept telling them that it was too bright and that it was getting brighter, then he died. Some of those present at his death said, "It was as though he was glimpsing heaven!"

[4] Initially these classes were known as Religious Instruction (RI) classes, and subsequently as Christian Religious Instruction (CRI) classes. I refer to them as CRI classes.

Some of the people of southern Zaria said that they knew that the Archibalds loved them because of the way they talked to them and treated them. Rev. Archibald was known as Dachip, 'One who plays', and his wife Grace received the name Dariya, 'Laughter'. Some Christians spoke of them as "our beloved parents" (*Africa Now*, March–April 1972:15). One elderly man recalled Rev. Archibald's presence as follows:

> He always had time to sit by our fires and talk to us. He never refused anything we offered him. He walked from village to village, sitting with us, eating the food we ate, sleeping where we slept, and always telling us of Jesus Christ. (*Africa Now*, March–April 1972:15)

Besides bringing the gospel of Jesus Christ, Rev. Archibald brought light by introducing a type of kerosene lamp known as "Archibalbal." It consisted of a small tin can or pot to hold kerosene together with a rag for a wick. He introduced this lamp because he desired people to study their Bibles in the evenings.

Though Rev. Archibald became popular with the indigenous population, he ran into conflict with at least one of the colonial administrators. In 1951 one administrator wrote, "Mr. Archibald's VALUE TO THE COUNTRY IS IN DOUBT" (NAK ZARPROF C.8/1946, capitals in the original). This assessment of Archibald's work occurred following the period of the 1940s in which the Bajju, Atyap, and other ethnic groups in Southern Zaria sought some measure of self-government. This administrator contended that Rev. Archibald felt that Muslim administrators, including Katuka, the district head at Zangon Katab, pursued anti-Christian policies. This administrator proposed five alternatives:

1. Replace Katuka.
2. Replace Mr. Archibald.
3. Effect a rapprochement between the two.
4. Replace both.
5. Replace Mr. Archibald and give closer administrative advice and supervision to Katuka.

(NAK ZARPROF C.8/1946)

He felt that the first was inadvisable because if Katuka was replaced, the Christians would claim victory and would press for further reforms, which he felt they were not ready for. He also rejected the second because he felt that Rev. Archibald would then be seen as a martyr, resulting in local disturbances. He recommended that the administration follow the fifth alternative. Rev. Archibald would be given one year to remain in the country but during that time he would be restricted to Kagoro District; he would then be expelled from Nigeria. He concluded his letter as follows:

In conclusion I should like to place on record that at our interview, which lasted close on 2 hours, Mr. Archibald spoke with eloquence, with obvious sincerity, and with disarming friendliness. Further, when considering this most difficult problem, due recognition must be given to the magnificent work he has done in this country in particular in Kagoro District. (NAK ZARPROF C.8/1946)

These recommendations were never implemented and the Archibalds continued their missionary work in Nigeria. Their contributions to Nigeria did not remain unnoticed. In 1972 General Yakubu Gowon, head of the Federal Military Government, publicly thanked the Archibalds for their service to Nigeria (*Africa Now*, March/April 1972:15).

Early "Sudan" churches and converts

In January, 1929, Carl Tanis and his wife joined the Archibalds at Kagoro. That year they opened Kagoro Bible School,[5] the first SIM Bible School in Northern Nigeria.[6] The language of instruction was Hausa. It began as a dry-season school only. Tanis also worked with local churches and counseled early Bajju Christians, especially when they were being persecuted.

Figure 6.1. First Sudan church at Kagoro (Carol McKinney).

---

[5] Kagoro Bible School has now been upgraded to Kagoro Theological Seminary.
[6] SIM did not open another Bible school until 1938, when they established Biliri Bible School (Crampton 1975:155).

The Bajju people responded early to mission teaching, as mentioned in the first chapter. Other early Christians, besides those mentioned in chapter 1, included Usman Vayan from Madakiya who in 1930 went to Kafanchan to sell mats. There he heard Rev. Archibald preaching in the market, and he, too, converted to Christianity. Soon after that other Bajju from villages such as Zonkwa, A̱bet, Kamrum, Sa̱kwak, Ka̱tssik, Madakiya, and Unguwar Rimi accepted Christianity. Early Bajju converts walked up to fifteen miles each Sunday to worship with other Christians at Kagoro.

In its early days SIM missionaries devoted most of their energy in Southern Zaria to itinerant evangelizing, planting churches, establishing mission stations and outstations, and teaching the Bible. In 1932 SIM founded churches at Kafanchan and Unguwar Rimi and opened a bookstore in Kafanchan. In 1943 they established a mission station at Kafanchan, and in 1946 they built another at Zonkwa (Swank 1970:11).[7] By 1944 SIM had built fourteen churches, eight of which were in Kajju, and had established eighteen primary schools and 110 CRI classes in Southern Zaria (NAK ZARPROF C9/1939). Churches founded by SIM were initially known as "Sudan" churches (see figure 6.1.).

Eunie Cockerel, an SIM missionary from the United Kingdom, was one of the few SIM missionaries to learn to speak Gorok, the language spoken by the people at Kagoro; she established an orphanage at Kagoro, which in 1942 had eleven orphans (NAK ZARPROF C9/1939). In time the care of orphans passed to Nigerian Christians and the orphanage was discontinued. Members of the Evangelical Church Winning All continue to provide for orphans by gathering money to give to mothers who adopt orphans so that they can purchase powdered milk and formula. Bajju Christians keep pictures of orphans and their adoptive mothers, and on occasion give them public recognition.

Of foremost importance in the goals of the mission was the conversion of individuals to Christianity. According to Smith,

> The Mission on its part taught all converts to respect their elders, kin and affines, to carry out all obligations of kinship, marriage and co-residence not directly contradicting their creed, to maintain exogamy rules, the taboos of Kagoro ritual.... (Smith 1975:13)

The mission also introduced an alternative lifestyle. They introduced schools with literacy in Hausa, Sunday as a day of rest, clothing, carpentry, high-grade cheap salt, building with mud blocks, Western medicine, hog

---

[7] Zonkwa SIM work began as an outstation from Kagoro through the work of Mika, a Yoruba evangelist (Zonkwa, n.d., SIM Archives). In 1935 Kirk and Archibald assisted the Christians at Zonkwa with building their own church. In 1945 Zonkwa was designated a regular station, separate from Kagoro.

rearing, and various fruit trees. They taught that converts should not drink beer, use tobacco, or practice polygamy. Other rules in the early days of SIM mission work prohibited chewing kola nuts, speaking English, women wearing leaves in church, men wearing skins[8] in church, practicing polygyny, and using native tunes for Christian hymns. Second and subsequent wives were not to wear the uniform of the women's fellowship, attend the women's fellowship, singing practices, or hold elected positions within the fellowship. SIM missionaries required polygynists to send away all wives except their first one. Converts were to refrain from participating in the *abvoi* society's activities and dances (Swank 1970:7). Converts were not to cry at funerals in order to avoid displays of excessive emotion.

Figure 6.2. Bajju men wearing skins (Tremearne 1912:178).

---

[8] Men were forbidden from wearing skins in church. They were required to wear skins into the *abvoi* shrine but were forbidden from wearing hats into the *abvoi*.

Figure 6.3. Bajju women wearing leaves (Tremearne 1912:252).

Converts were not to become horn blowers, an inherited position. The mission's reasoning for prohibiting converts from being horn blowers was that they felt horn blowing was associated with their traditional religious practices, and they wanted converts to make a complete break from such practices. The main problem with the prohibition against horn blowing was that missionaries failed to investigate the role of horn blowing within the traditional culture. While it was true that horn blowing occurred at the *ǫbvoi* society celebrations, horns were also blown at occasions to call people to work, to celebrate the fulfilled lives of elderly persons at their funerals, to call people to begin farming at the start of the rainy season, and to call people to war when attacked by others. Horn blowing continues in Bajju culture even though SIM missionaries sought to forbid it. Some Bajju Christian leaders assert that missionaries did not prohibit all horn blowing, but only in those contexts in which it was associated with their traditional religion.

According to Bajju understanding of mission teaching concerning conversion, they were to make a complete break from their past culture and religion. This complete break is summarized in the frequently used confession, "I repent; I leave the old things of darkness; I will follow Jesus" (*N tuba, n wwon nkyang duhu nyyai, n ni tssup Yesu*). The word conversion indicates a change, in this case a change from following "the old things of darkness" to "following God." The missionaries expected a clean break by the Bajju who converted from their traditional religious beliefs and practices. This proved difficult because missionaries failed to study the traditional beliefs and activities. Consequently they did not target their teachings to the areas traditional religion dealt with. As will become obvious later, this resulted in a Christian overlay on their traditional beliefs, with traditional beliefs answering one set of questions and Christianity answering another set.

Individual Bajju occasionally refer to the "rules of following" that SIM introduced. In my interviews on reasons for conversion, one woman responded that she accepted the "rules of following," thereby indicating that she was willing to follow the various rules and regulations that missionaries in SIM-founded churches specified.

Sudan churches practiced discipline for transgression of those rules. If a person admitted a transgression, he was rebuked. It was then announced in church, and he was denied the privileges of membership for a specified period, usually six months to one year; those privileges included participating in communion, saying prayers in church, holding a church office, and doing any church work. During that period church elders watched the behavior of the disciplined individual to see that he had indeed changed. However, if an individual refused to confess to the transgression he was suspected of, he was not rebuked. An example of this form of discipline is recorded in a 1954 quarterly mission report about one individual as follows:

> [X] gave us some trouble. He would not confess to seeking a second wife although evidences were against him. After taking his case to court in Kaduna because we had hindered his work, he confessed that he had sinned. Upon confession the mission dismissed him. Now he is to be disciplined by the church. This will be done Aug. 1st in our next elder's meeting. (*Quarterly Report, Zonkwa,* July 1954, SIM Archives)

The trend among the Bajju is monogamous marriages rather than polygamous ones. Which church a person belongs to is often determined by what that church's position is with regard to polygamy. In most churches polygamously married men cannot hold any office in the church because the Bible teaches that an elder should be the husband of one wife (I Timothy 3:2). In discussing various denominations below, most denominations' position with regard to polygamy is given.

Mission teaching on marriage condemned polygamy, a practice that was prevalent among the Bajju when missionaries first began working among them. Missionaries required that Christian converts send away all but one wife. In 1942 SIM mission policy was that, "It is our solemn duty to show African Christians that polygamy is sin in God's sight, that a polygamist is guilty of theft and adultery" (Sudan Interior Mission, 1942:17–18). Some missionaries did baptize polygamists. However, polygamously married men cannot hold any office in most churches. Breaking up a polygamous marriage often resulted in bitterness within families, splitting up families, depriving children of their mothers, leaving a woman without a husband and her children, and multiple other problems.

Some Bajju elders, such as Dogo, Mutum, and Bakut, dealt with the prohibition taught by SIM, that a man who converts to Christianity send away all but one wife, by allowing any of their wives to continue to live with them in their compounds, but not as wives. This kept their children together with their mothers. In a patrilineal society, the children belong to their fathers, so if a wife is sent away, she must leave her children with their father. Other men who were married polygamously at the time of their conversions decided to keep all the wives they had, but not to marry any more women.

The Bajju traditionally practiced widow inheritance. A brother or other close male relative may inherit a deceased man's wife. The woman does have a choice whether or not she chooses to be inherited by a specific man. When a woman is inherited, this results in keeping the family together. Today many widows decide not to be inherited. Her children stay with the man's brother and his family who are responsible for caring for them.

Polygamy is often very hard on women, who must share a husband with one or more other women. It often leads to jealousy and conflict within the family. In fact, the Jju word *ahwwuk* translates as 'co-wife' and 'jealousy'. Polygamy can also be hard on the husband and children, as this jealousy can permeate throughout all relationships within the extended family.

Growth of SIM work

Christianity expanded rapidly among the Bajju, as reflected by church attendance. In 1939 the average attendance at the SIM-founded church in Zonkwa was eighty-one, while at Unguwar Rimi it was 136 (Swank 1970:9). In addition, there were thirteen CRI classes among the Bajju.

The SIM-founded church denomination is made up of people from multiple ethnic groups. Unfortunately, divisive ethnicity has often plagued this denomination as it has also in other denominations (Maigadi 2006). Local representatives from churches founded by SIM met monthly at Kagoro with Christians from Sudan churches in all of Southern Zaria. They brought offerings from their churches, divided those offerings, and from them they paid each church leader his salary. In 1943 Bajju church leaders decided to form a Local Church Council separate from the Local Church Council at Kagoro.

Evangelical Church Winning All,
formerly the Evangelical Church of West Africa

The Evangelical Church of West Africa (ECWA) was incorporated in 1954 and recognized by the government in 1956. ECWA as a denomination grew out of the work of SIM. More recently the meaning of the initials ECWA has been changed to Evangelical Church Winning All.

Discipline continues today under ECWA leadership, though it tends to be less arbitrary and harsh, basically because the Bajju ECWA pastors understand their own culture and have sought to contextualize Christianity. Among the Bajju, parishioners who desire to have multiple wives, drink alcoholic beverages, or engage in other disapproved activities go to churches of other denominations that allow those behaviors. Some Bajju ECWA pastors have said that if a man comes for communion and they know he is a Christian and he has more than one wife, they would not deny that person communion. However, he would still be prohibited from the position of elder in the church.

During the time we lived in Unguwar Rimi, discipline of Christians did not seem to be a central focus of the church. I only recall one instance where discipline was taken and that was for adultery, an offense that is contrary to both Christianity and Bajju traditional culture.

While missionaries initially helped evangelize this area, evangelism increasingly became the responsibility of Nigerian pastors and evangelists. Missionaries then devoted themselves largely to educational work.

In terms of the indigenous leadership of ECWA, several men from southern Kaduna State have held national leadership positions, including Dr. Byang H. Kato (1967–1970), a Ham man; Rev. Chidawa B. Kaburuk (1984–1987), a Bajju man; Dr. Yusufu Turaki (1987–1993), a Kagoma man; Dr. Musa Asake (2000–2006), a Bajju man; and Dr. Samuel Waje Kunhiyop (2011–2017), a Bajju man.

Roman Catholic missionary work

There were three foci of Catholic work in Northern Nigeria: Catholic priests stationed at Shendam, the site of the first Catholic mission station in Northern Nigeria, which was established in 1907 (Makozi and Ojo 1982:58); Catholic priests in Kaduna; and Catholic priests from the Parish at Udei in the south who came north. These priests served under the Society for African Missions, which was founded in Lyons, France, in 1856 as the Société des Missions Africaines. Although the first priests sent to Nigeria were French, from the early 1930s onward most Society for African Missions clergy assigned to Africa came from Ireland.

The Catholic priests who first contacted the people of Southern Zaria were from Shendam, who trekked through this area on foot. They did

not establish churches or mission stations. Rev. Eugène Sirlinger, one of
the early priests, was later stationed at Kagoro. Rev. Sirlinger is perhaps
best remembered for his gift in learning languages and his desire that
the indigenous people in Northern Nigeria have literacy materials in
their own languages. In 1949 while stationed at Kagoro he translated
the catechism into Gorok (Kagoro) (*Katekism b'umi Oeliem n Gworok*,
1952).

Roman Catholic priests established outstations as they made their
rounds along the railway line while resident at Udei, a practice known
among them as "doing the line." The railroad extends from Makurdi, Udei,
Lafia, Gudi, Kafanchan, and Zonkwa to Kaduna. As Catholics from ethnic
groups in the south moved into Kafanchan, Catholic priests followed in
order to minister to them. The Station Book at Kafanchan records that
the first Catholic marriage occurred there in 1931, and the first baptism
in 1932. By 1933 Rev. Peter Bennett spent part of each year living at
Kafanchan; however, this proved unsatisfactory. In 1935 Mgr. William
Lumley, the prefecture apostolic of Jos, decided that this area needed a
full-time priest. He asked Rev. Tony O'Dwyer to build a mission house
at Kafanchan, which was completed by 1936, and Rev. Michael O'Flynn
was the first resident priest at Kafanchan (Walsh 1983:171–172). In the
early days the main ministry of the Catholic church in Kafanchan was
to Southern Nigerians. For example, by 1940 there were no recorded
baptisms of Bajju people performed at the Kafanchan Catholic Church
(*Kafanchan Station Book,* n.d.).[9] However, the goal of this work was not
only to minister to the southerners who dominated the church at this time,
but also to reach out to the indigenous population.

Prior to this Catholic work, SIM was the sole mission in Southern Zaria.
The Catholics and SIM ran into conflict almost immediately. Archibald at
Kagoro was strongly anti-Catholic. In 1936 Catholic traders resident at
Kagoro requested the Catholic mission to build a church at Kagoro. Although
the chief at Kagoro at first granted permission to build the church, he sub-
sequently withdrew it under pressure from SIM and SIM-related Christians.
He ordered the walls of the church under construction torn down. However,
Catholics readily attracted a congregation from the indigenous population
who found some of the rules of behavior established by SIM difficult to follow. For example, some men did not want to send away all except their first
wives. According to Walsh, "The total prohibition of alcoholic drink by the
S.I.M. was one of the major factors for the success of the Catholic Church in
this area" (1983:177). By 1938, thirty A̲gorok Catholic Christians trekked
to Kafanchan each Sunday to worship. In 1941, two hundred others, who

---

[9] In 1935 the Catholic priest at Kafanchan baptized Moses Moma from Kagoro
and James Gani from Zango. These were the first recorded Catholic baptisms
at Kafanchan of people indigenous to Southern Zaria (Kafanchan Station Book,
n.d.).

broke off from the SIM-founded church, joined them. With this large group desiring to worship in a Catholic church, they decided to go ahead with construction of a church building at Kagoro.

Because they were unable to get permission from the chief to do so, they built a small mud church in the compound of Paul Balarabe. Catholics finally appealed to the authorities in Zaria for permission to build a larger structure at Kagoro; thus they bypassed local Protestant opposition. On January 4, 1945, they applied for the necessary C. of O., and it was granted on February 14, 1947 (Walsh 1983:176). By this time the church had grown to four hundred members. Frs. Sirlinger and Harrison took on the task of building the church, the mission house, and other staff quarters. These were completed in November 1948.

The work at Kagoro increased to the point that in 1948 Mgr. Lumley decided that Kagoro should be designated as a parish separate from Kafanchan. After the Parish of Kagoro separated from that of Kafanchan, the Parish of Kafanchan continued to evangelize and minister to all of the Kagoma, 16,000 Ham, 5,000 Mada, all the Ninzam, 8,000 Nunkas (Nungu?),[10] Numana, 2,500 Agorok in the Jagindi area, the Kanikom, the Kafanchan, and the Bajju (*Kafanchan Roman Catholic Station Book*, n.d.). They also continued to serve southerners resident in the area. Catholics established a primary school at Kafanchan that mainly served the children of the southerners who lived there, as was true also of the CMS school (Walsh 1983:177).

In 1936 Allahmagani, a Bajju elder at Kankada, invited Rev. Gately to establish a school there.[11] At first the resident at Zaria verbally granted permission to build this school, so the Roman Catholic mission proceeded with construction in 1937. Rev. Gately submitted a formal request for a C. of O. on February 15, 1937. However, that resident was replaced before granting the necessary written permission, and the next resident refused to grant it. His reasons were that the area was already served by SIM, and the colonial administration feared friction between Catholic and SIM followers such as had occurred at Kagoro. So the school and the fledgling Catholic mission station at Kankada had to be dismantled. Catholic priests withdrew because they could not obtain a C. of O. However, according to oral tradition the local people believed that the Catholic priests left because of a smallpox epidemic (Interview with A. S., Adwan, November 2, 1983). In the archival records it is clear that the local population was not informed as to what had transpired. It states,

> Local adherents said the priest had not told them that permission had been refused. They imagined the school (which

[10] According to Nitecki (1972:74), the Nungu reside to the north of the Ninzam and the Mada reside on their southwest.

[11] Rev. Gately had previously worked at St. Patrick Roman Catholic Church in Sabon Gari, Zaria (NAK ZARPROF C9/1939).

had not yet been started) had been disallowed by a sud-
den whim of the Emir or of the District Head, with whom
their relations are very strained. (NAK ZARPROF 2944,
1938–1944)

In a confidential letter the administration forbade construction of
any Catholic mission station within a thirty-six mile radius of Kandada
(Allahmagani, D. K. 1984, pers. comm.). Catholic missionaries then moved
to Kurmin Mazuga in 1943 where they opened a primary school as well as
a church. Allahmagani sent his son D.K. Allahmagani there for school and
he subsequently served as headmaster of that primary school for seventeen
years (Interview with D.K. Allahmagani, Kachia Local Authority, Zonkwa,
February 18, 1984).

Other Catholic stations among the Bajju and other Southern Zaria ethnic
groups were established as follows: Mabushi (1952), Zonkwa (1953), Fadan
Kaje (1960), and Gidan Bako (1967) (Rev. John M. Murphy, personal letter, January 25, 1972). Most of these stations, with the exception of that at
Kurmin Mazuga, have been staffed by expatriate Irish priests. Bajju Catholic
churches are divided between two prefectures. Churches in the northern portion of Kajju are under Kaduna Prefecture, while those in southern Kajju are
under Jos Prefecture. Locally Catholic churches are referred to as "Roman"
churches.

According to a history of the Roman Catholic Church in Nigeria,
"Southern Zaria holds the greatest population of Catholics north of the
Niger today" (Makozi and Ojo 1982:62). The Most Reverend Peter Jatau,[12]
the retired archbishop of Kaduna Diocese, is from the Bajju village of Marsa.
In addition, there are eight other ordained Bajju Catholic priests. Not only
are the Bajju active in the ecclesiastic structure of the Catholic Church,
Bajju laymen and women serve at the local level in thirty-eight Catholic
churches in the Bajju area.

The Catholic Church holds ten-week dry-season training courses for
catechists. Those who desire to serve as catechists must complete four
courses, one each year. Only Catholic clergy may celebrate mass, administer communion, and perform marriages. Confirmation is reserved for
the bishop, with local leaders conducting funerals. Because of the small
number of Catholic priests resident in southern Kaduna State, the priests
usually visit each church once every two to three months. Priests usually visit two to three churches each Sunday. They receive all of their
salary from local congregations because they are seconded to the local
diocese.

---

[12] The Most Reverend Peter Jatau was the first indigenous northerner to be ordained
a Roman Catholic priest (Crampton 1975:156).

First African Church Mission Inc.,
formerly the United Native African Church

The United Native African Church (UNA) was brought by Yorubas in the early 1930s to the Bajju area. By 1934 there were eighty members of the UNA Church in Kafanchan (NAK JEMAA 500 265, 1931–1940). In 1942 this denomination spread to Zonkwa. All of the early UNA leaders at Zonkwa were Bajju, with the exception of their pastor who was Fantswam (Kafanchan). Beginning with the church at Kafanchan and the primary school at Zonkwa, UNA work expanded until in 1983 there were twenty-two UNA churches among the Bajju (Interview with Z., Zonkwa, September 27, 1983).

The UNA shares some characteristics with the Cherubim and Seraphim (C&S) in the Bajju area. However, it contrasts with it in that UNA does not practice trances and visions. They do believe in dreams, the content of which may be shared in church when appropriate. UNA members do not leave their shoes at the door as C&S members do, and they do not dance in church through every hymn; however, they do use clay pot drums (*bakinkyim*) to accompany their hymns, as do most Bajju churches.

The leadership hierarchy within this church, beginning with the most senior position and proceeding to the local leader, is shown in figure 6.1. If the local leader performs his duties well, he may be promoted to the office of deacon and later reverend. Unlike in the Roman Catholic and CMS churches, the local leader may administer the Christian sacrament of baptism for righteous persons through sprinkling. Those in the UNA leadership receive training through short courses or from other denominational Bible schools. However, many in leadership positions within the UNA receive little formal training. In addition to those in formal leadership positions in the local church, the elders exercise strong authority. To qualify as elders Bajju men must be married, have children, and be experienced. Age is also important, but because the Bajju tend not to keep track of age, it is difficult to give an exact age when a man may be considered an elder.

Bishop

Arch-Deacon

Full Priest (addressed as Reverend, a permanent position)

Reverend (temporary position)

Deacon

Leader (*Shugaba*)

Figure 6.4. United Native African Church leadership hierarchy.

UNA clergy wear white robes and black sashes with a yellow cross at each end. These robes drape over the shoulders and extend to the hips, rather than to the floor as do those of the C&S. Members may wear white robes to church if they choose to; however, they are not required to do so.

If a member of another denomination desires to change his affiliation to UNA, he is accepted if he left his former church as a member in good standing. However, if there is a problem or question, UNA leadership watch to see how he "walks." They desire that a man not steal or seek the wife or wives of others. The UNA also desire that their members learn to read the Bible.

Members of UNA churches frequently pray for healing for persons who are ill. The leader and the prayer committee pray either at church or at the home of the patient. The bishop may use a stick in praying for an ill individual. If the patient is present, he or she kneels and the leaders and members of the prayer committee place their hands on the patient and pray for healing. They do not use oil or water for anointing the patient, as is practiced by those within the C&S church. UNA churches hold prayer meetings and Bible studies on Wednesdays. UNA members fast and pray if there are problems such that this is necessary.

Annual Meeting

The UNA gather yearly for a central meeting of their churches. This meeting includes UNA churches from other ethnic groups besides the Bajju, including the two UNA churches at Kachia. In addition, leaders of UNA churches meet together every third month in order to discuss problems and needs within their churches. For example, if they know of parishioners who are without food, they provide it.

UNA teaching on morality

One aspect of the UNA movement that attracted the Bajju was its attitude towards polygamy. Polygamists are welcome and may hold leadership positions within this church. Many of the pastors and leaders have more than one wife. For example, the pastor I interviewed had six wives. Because of this, UNA attracts members from other denominations in the area. However, the church does not encourage multiple marriages. One leader stated that a man should have only one wife, but that if a convert has two or more at the time of conversion, he should provide for those he has rather than divorce all but the first, as some churches require.

UNA attitude towards drinking alcoholic beverages also attracts the Bajju. They teach that drinking is not wrong, though drunkenness is. If a member drinks to excess and causes trouble, the church elders will warn him and may request that he stop drinking entirely. This position parallels that of Bajju traditional society.

Church Mission Society and the Anglican Church

In 1934 Anglican Christians established a church in Kafanchan (NAK JEMAA 500 265, 1931–1940) and by the early 1940s they had also established a school there. This denomination arrived in the area through Igbo traders. Initially the pastor at Kafanchan was an Igbo from the southeastern part of the country, and he shared his faith with those around him. Early Bajju Christians included Toro Yashim, Sule Sarki, and two or three others.

In 1956 Ron Freeman, a British Church Mission Society (CMS) missionary who formerly worked at Wusasa, built the CMS mission house located near the hospital in Kafanchan. After he left, the house remained vacant until the 1970s when CMS stationed Elisabeth Newton and Jacqueline Henry there. The James Mitchell-Innes family joined them in 1972. One of their goals was to initiate an agricultural ministry to meet the needs of the local horticultural population. However, due to health problems with their son, the Mitchell-Innes family returned to England. The next CMS missionary to reside at Kafanchan was John Horton, who arrived in 1976. He was soon joined by Sue Davies, who took charge of the Theological Education by Extension (TEE) program. Davies formerly worked on the Nupe Bible translation project at Bida.

Horton continued the agricultural ministry initiated by James Mitchell-Innes. In May 1977, the first CMS agricultural store opened at Kafanchan. A second agricultural store opened at Zonkwa in March 1982, and a third at Gidan Waya in May 1983. These stores have proved quite successful because they meet felt needs of the indigenous horticultural population. The stores stock animal feed, veterinary medicine, and literature (Christian, agricultural, and animal husbandry), and on occasion sell day-old chicks. Store attendants receive training both in agriculture and Bible.

The CMS church experienced rapid growth in southern Kaduna State. According to Horton, the Anglican Church in Nigeria is growing the fastest in this area (Interview with John Horton, January 25, 1984). The diocese formerly included all of the former Northern Region of Nigeria. In 1979 the ecclesiastical hierarchy of the Anglican Church in northern Nigeria divided the diocese into three dioceses that follow state boundaries, each with a bishop who presides over it. These dioceses are as follows:

Diocese of Jos	Plateau, Gongola, and Benue States
Diocese of Kano	Kano, Borno, and Bauchi States
Diocese of Kaduna	Kaduna, Sokoto, Niger States, Kafanchan, and the Federal Capital Area

The Bajju are in the Kafanchan District in the Diocese of Kaduna. Within this diocese there are three church districts, each with a number of churches, as follows:

Zonkwa	43+ churches
Gidan Waya	29 churches
Kafanchan	30+ churches

The Anglicans inaugurated the Dioceses of Kafanchan on September 5, 1990. This important step indicates this denomination has a significant and expanding work in this area.

Among the Bajju there are thirty-nine Anglican churches or "Cemed" churches as they are called locally.[13] A district chairman, an ordained pastor usually with seminary training, presides over each district. Under the chairman are ordained pastors, evangelists, and catechists. CMS conducts training for catechists at their catechist training course at Wusasa. In addition, CMS sends a few students to Emmanuel College in Ibadan each year.

Anglicans, like Roman Catholics, reserve serving communion and performing baptisms and marriages for priests. Within the Zonkwa District there are three ordained men, therefore each man has thirteen or fourteen churches for which he must provide these services. Hastings argues that this results in communion occurring too infrequently in rural churches. He feels that catechists should be taught to serve communion. Although what he wrote was specific to the Roman Catholic Church, he would probably also apply the same to the Anglican Church as it follows a similar pattern (Hastings 1976).

The laity receive training through TEE classes. These train them to conduct services, prepare people for baptism, and perform burials. TEE classes are short classes given during each dry season for five years. Many of the men who become local leaders (*shugabanni*, H.), catechists, and women who become leaders of the women's work receive their initial training in TEE classes.

In addition to churches, agricultural stores, and TEE classes, CMS ministers to the physical needs of parishioners. For example, at Kamaru Station they maintain the Good Samaritan CMS Dispensary.

According to Anglican policy an Anglican priest is not to baptize a polygamously married man. The first wife of a polygamous marriage may be baptized, presumably because it is not her fault that her husband took another wife. However, his second and subsequent wives cannot be baptized if they were Christians prior to marrying this man. Presumably they knew better than to marry a man who already had a wife. However, if women became Christians after their polygamous marriage, then they can be baptized. Anglican priests deny communion to men who practice polygamy whether or not they have been confirmed and baptized. Polygamously married men cannot be elders within the church.

---

[13] Jju has no fricatives in syllable-final position, so the "s" of CMS becomes a stop, a "d," with a short "e" transition vowel preceding it.

Funds for pastors' salaries are centrally set and controlled. Offerings are sent to the central office as the assessment of each church. Pastors receive their salaries from these assessments.

Baptists

Yoruba Baptist traders and others initiated the Baptist work in this area while seeking employment in the north largely with the railroad and the government. They left Ogbomosho and other southern areas where there was a strong Baptist influence, bringing with them their familiar Baptist form of worship.

According to Nigerian archival records there has been a Baptist church at Kafanchan since 1935 (NAK JEMAA 500 265, 1931–1940). According to Baptist archival records at Kafanchan, the Kafanchan Yoruba Baptist Church was established in 1941. A Yoruba named Moses Isola, a tailor, worked with two men, Mallam Soje and Bangoji Bido. They preached the Christian message in various local villages where others also came to Christ. Together they established several Baptist churches in the area with Kafanchan as the center from which Baptist work radiated out into this area. Baptists named this work the Kafanchan Hausa Baptist Association. The term Hausa in this title refers to the fact that the Baptists use Hausa as the language of worship, not because converts were Hausa or that Hausa was the mother tongue of people in this area.

Baptist workers posted to Southern Zaria were initially under the Baptist Home Mission. The Nigerian Baptist Mission (Baptist Home and Foreign Mission Board) took over the work in 1960.

Baptist Home Mission

Baptist home missionaries were largely Yoruba who held supervisory positions over the indigenous Baptist teachers, pastors, and evangelists. The Baptist home missionaries reported to the Nigerian Baptist Convention. Missionaries occasionally visited this area, though until 1963 there was no resident expatriate missionary. Both the Nigerian Baptist Mission and Nigerian Baptist Home Mission have responsibility for Kafanchan District.

Leadership of the Baptist work in Southern Zaria was initially by Moses Isola and Ayo Bello, a teacher. In 1943 Ayo Bello left to attend seminary at Ogbomosho and Pastor J. Ade Keku replaced him as the designated Baptist home missionary. This fledgling Baptist work was organized in 1944 as the Native Baptist Churches Association.

The first Baptist Bajju to join them was Bulus Soje. He had converted to Christianity in the Sudan church in 1942, but then began attending the Baptist church. The next Bajju Baptists were Bangoji, who converted in the Baptist church, and Bature Tonak. Bature had wanted to make a profession of faith in the Sudan church, but his father refused to allow him to. Bature's father was an elder in the men's secret society, and people danced for the *abvoi* at his father's house in Unguwar Rimi. Because his parents wanted him to be active in *abvoi*, he did not tell others of his conversion to Christianity until after his father's death. His motives for conversion were that he liked Christian singing and was impressed with the lives of the Christians (Interview with Rev. Bangoji, Kawo, February 28, 1984).

In 1944 the Baptist church appointed Bangoji Bido and Bature Abet to the position of evangelist; both men received financial support from the American Baptist Mission. In 1948 Rev. Bangoji moved to Kawo, a suburb in the north of Kaduna, near the Baptist Pastors' School. He continued to be active within the Baptist church and traveled widely to evangelize and encourage Baptist Christians. Atuk Nan was another Baptist Christian in Southern Zaria. He originally converted within the Sudan church, then attended the UNA, and finally joined the Baptist church. He too became a Baptist pastor.

Bajju Baptists initially worshipped together with Yoruba Christians. However, to meet the need for a service in a language understandable to them, in 1941 the Kafanchan Baptist Church instituted a service in Hausa; this was in addition to the Yoruba service. In 1945 indigenous Christians built a church separate from that of the Yoruba congregation.

Nigerian Baptist Mission

The Baptist work in Southern Zaria expanded rapidly. Consequently, in 1960 the Nigerian Baptist Convention requested that this work be placed under the Nigerian Baptist Mission (Baptist Home and Foreign Mission Board), and that the Baptist Home missionaries be transferred elsewhere. Until this transfer of administration occurred, the Baptist missionary resident at Keffi, who was in charge of the Benue Association, administered this area. Off and on from August 1963 there has been a Baptist missionary couple resident at Bakin Kogi, a small village about three miles from Kafanchan on the Kafanchan-Kwoi road. Over time various missionary couples have lived there, all working through the Hausa language. Baptist mission reports consistently refer to this area as Hausa speaking, though the 1965 report mentions Baptist work in twelve different ethnic groups (Donald Smith 1965:1, unpublished Baptist files, at Bakin Kogi).

Baptist missionaries have commented on the responsiveness of this area to Christianity. In 1962 one Baptist missionary wrote, "The response to the Gospel in proportion to our outlay has been phenomenal" (Report of the Acting Northern Secretary on the Kafanchan District, 1962, Baptist files, Bakin Kogi). In 1965 a Baptist missionary wrote, "One of the remarkable things about the area is that new groups of worshipping people will spring up and call themselves Baptists even before the missionary hears of them" (Donald Smith 1965:2, Bakin Kogi, Baptist Files).

While statistics are incomplete for Baptist churches, as they are for all churches in southern Kaduna State, the number of preaching stations and churches presented in table 6.1 gives some idea of the growth of this denomination. Not all of these are in the Bajju area, but a substantial number are. Preaching stations represent embryonic churches. In 1944 the first Baptist churches in the Bajju area were at Kanfanchan, Zitrung, and Abet. From Zitrung the work spread to Zonkwa.

Table 6.1 Number of Baptist churches and preaching stations
in Southern Zaria by year

Year	1941	1942	1944	1945	1946	1947	1953	1954, 1955	1962	1965
Number of churches and preaching stations[a]	2	3	6	7	10	16	26	36	65	66

[a] Data are from mission reports on file at the Baptist Mission Station, Bakin Kogi.

In 1947 northern Baptist Christians attended the Nigerian Baptist Convention at Ogbomosho. This was the first year Northern Christians attended.

Baptist educational work

Because of the need for a trained clergy and laity, the Baptists established the Baptist Pastors' School at Kawo, Kaduna. This school consisted of three sections: an English section, a Hausa section, and a women's department. These sections were not mutually exclusive, with women admitted into both the English and the Hausa sections. Those students who take the English course receive a higher starting salary than those in the other two sections even if they fail the course. Clearly it is advantageous to take the English course.

Baptists taught classes in Christian Religious Instruction (CRI). By 1965 there were twelve CRI classes in their churches in southern Kaduna State. These classes taught reading, writing, Bible, simple arithmetic, and occasionally other subjects. They also established primary schools in this area, particularly at Zonkwa and Zitrung.

The indigenous Baptist churches were very much involved in the establishment of schools. For example, in 1957 they requested that the mission establish junior primary schools in the central towns of each of the ten ethnic groups with which the Baptist church worked. The people volunteered their labor together with some of the necessary building materials such as stones, sand, and planks. The Baptist Mission declined as the demand for schools was greater than the mission could readily fill. In 1963 the people at Zirtung requested that primary 5 be added to the school there. The Baptist Mission did fulfill this request. By 1965 there were three Baptist schools in the area.

Organizational structure

Within the Baptist church organizational structure each church is independent. The Baptist churches relate to one another through a loose organizational structure, termed an association, and to a larger organizational unit that comprises several associations, termed a conference. The Baptist churches in Southern Zaria, together with the Baptist churches in Kaduna, Niger, Sokoto, and Kano States belong to the Bethel Conference and the Bishara Baptist Association.

Each local church is expected to be self-supporting. Pastors may "bank" their funds with the missionary advisor who "pays" pastors from their own funds. However, they do not pool their funds and pay each pastor the same salary. They do maintain a salary scale for pastors based on their educational qualifications. Churches try to meet the set salary for their pastors; however, most pastors supplement their income by farming.

Baptists distinguish between unorganized churches or preaching stations and organized churches. Unorganized churches are technically under an organized church. Some churches remain with the status of unorganized churches for years, even though they have a pastor, church building, and meet regularly. An example is the church at Kamrum that constructed its church building in 1966 and was technically still an unorganized church in 1984.

Each Baptist church maintains the same basic number of meetings, which includes Sunday school, followed by Sunday morning worship service, and an evening worship service.

Baptist teachings on morality

The Baptist church teaches that God's ideal is monogamous marriage. Church leaders must practice monogamy. Although polygynously married men are baptized, they are excluded from leadership roles as well as from communion. In practice, a large number of men in Baptist churches are married polygynously. This fact has made it difficult for some churches to find elders for their churches and the elders they do have tend to be young men who have not yet taken a second wife. More recently monogamous marriages appear to be more common than polygynous ones. Baptists feel that with love, patience, and concern, those who commit immoral acts can be won back into a right relationship with the church and with the Lord.

Cherubim and Seraphim Church

The Cherubim and Seraphim (C&S) denomination entered the Bajju area in 1946 through Paul Repair, a Yoruba who worked at Kafanchan. The first C&S church among the Bajju was at Katssik near Kafanchan. Many of the early C&S leaders converted in other churches such as the Sudan before attending the C&S. One senior C&S apostle stated that nearly all of their early members came from other denominations. It is a growing church among the Bajju. For example, in 1984 there were thirty-six Bajju C&S churches.

Cherubim and Seraphim distinctives

Omoyajowo, who wrote on the history of the C&S among the Yoruba, argues that C&S teaching is essentially orthodox in its theology (1982:105–108). However, some of its emphases concerning their doctrines and their forms of worship are distinctive. Omoyajowo asserts that many of their beliefs and practices are Pentecostal in form. He states,

> The C&S believes that this gift [of the Holy Spirit] has been bestowed on the organization as on the day of Pentecost. With the Holy Spirit came various spiritual gifts: prophecy, visions, dreams, speaking in tongues. In this sense, the C&S is essentially a pentecostal movement. (1982:98)

The C&S originated as a movement of revival or renewal within the Anglican Church. This spiritual renewal eventually resulted in the C&S separating from the Anglican Church. C&S churches retain various aspects of Anglicanism. For example, the physical layout of C&S churches resembles Anglican churches. The platform where the pastor and elders sit is often separated from the congregation with an altar, and the two halves of the choir sit facing each other.

Distinctive C&S features include wearing white gowns to services. The gowns signify the great multitude who will wear white clothing before the throne of God as mentioned in Revelation 7:9. Most also wear hats. Some women's hats have *aladura*, 'one who prays', embroidered across the front of them. The C&S white gowns are set off with sashes, usually red, although some are yellow and blue. As in the Anglican Church, those ordained as reverends wear purple sashes to indicate their status. When C&S members travel, they frequently wear their white gowns. When attending a church service, C&S members take off their shoes before entering the sanctuary because the inside is considered holy ground. For the same reason menstruating women must remain outside. Dancing and drumming accompany each hymn sung in church.

From Ash Wednesday until Easter C&S congregants do not beat drums in worship, and they wear red sashes, symbolizing Christ's death. On Easter leaders change to yellow sashes, symbolizing Christ's resurrection, and they beat the drums again, symbolizing their joy because of the resurrection.

Because Christ was in the grave for three days between his death and resurrection the C&S Church claims that when a person dies, that person's spirit remains with the body for three days before going to be with God. There are no special rites to mark this transition other than their daily prayers. They bury a deceased member dressed in a white gown, holding his or her baptismal certificate in his or her hand. A white cloth is placed over the corpse. Some are attracted to the C&S church because of the good burials that people receive there.

The leader uses a rod similar to that used by Moses. One senior apostle also compared this to the walking stick of Elisha, which he gave to his servant Gehazi to lay across the Shunamite woman's dead son in order to restore him to life (2 Kings 4:29, 31). A C&S leader may place this stick on someone in prayer and assert that he or she will receive an answer to the prayer uttered. For example, if a woman wants to conceive a child, the pastor may lay his staff on her and assert that she will conceive; or if a young man wants a job, then he will find employment.

Another distinctive feature of the C&S is their belief in visions. They distinguish between dreams and visions. It is the latter that are important to them. Visions often occur during altered states of consciousness that take place in services, usually during rapid singing and drumming. The individual begins to shake violently, then gradually falls to the floor where women prayer leaders quiet him or her. The individual receives a vision from the Spirit or an angel during the shaking. Someone is appointed in each church to write down the contents of these visions. Later they check to see which visions have been fulfilled. They state that visions come to persons who are sober, not drunk, as a person who is drunk might hear the Spirit but not know what the Spirit is saying. Men, women, and children are all susceptible to visions, although women seem to receive them most frequently.

Typical visions concern such things as information that a certain child is special to the Lord and therefore they should not cut his or her hair for a set period of years as prescribed by the vision. This parallels the account of Samson in the Old Testament (Judges 13:2–5). At the end of the set number of years, the church leader cuts the child's hair and a large feast is held. This feast may include slaughter of a cow to serve the guests. They believe that if the child's hair is cut prior to completion of the number of years prescribed in the vision, the child will die. This belief parallels Bajju beliefs concerning the consequences of swearing an oath falsely. Another common vision tells that a specific woman will bear a child next year at the same time of the year.

If a woman prays for a child, conceives, or if she has difficulty in childbirth, yet the child is born safely, then members of the church give a special thank offering. If the child is male, the thank offering occurs thirty-three days following birth, and if female, forty-six days.

If a person is ill, C&S leaders gather around that person to pray. A person with the Spirit (*Ruhu*, H.) prophesies whether or not the patient will recover. Prayer is also indicated for *wabi* (H.), an affliction a woman may have whose young infants continue to die one after the other. It is as though the spirits are calling the spirit of the same infant back, who is subsequently reborn, then dies again.

The C&S practice fasting. Sometime a person may undertake a lengthy fast for personal reasons. During fasting a man or woman may remain inside the church. A fast may last for twenty days, during which time that person neither eats nor drinks, but devotes him- or herself to prayers. On the twenty-first day the individual may take a small amount of grain. The church members watch that individual, to see if he or she is growing too weak. If that is the case, they take that person to the hospital, for some have died while fasting. One leader stated that not all people have the gift to complete a twenty-day fast.

C&S members meet for prayers twice daily at 5 a.m. and 6 p.m. The church publishes daily Bible readings for these services. C&S members meet twice on Sunday for worship. There may also be special meetings called. For example, the C&S worship on high places during the time of fasting (*kąram ązumi*). This is in imitation of Jesus' temptation by Satan on the high place after fasting (Matthew 4:1–11).

Leadership

The C&S have a hierarchical leadership structure, with a number of positions so that many individuals within a local church may hold an office. Offices include special apostle, most senior apostle or prophet, senior apostle, apostle, evangelist, prophetess, senior mother in Israel, mother in Israel, and leader. Ideally C&S leaders take a one-year training course in Kaduna, but many have no formal training. Others receive their training at schools of other denominations. Inadequate training of leaders is a problem. Omoyajowo states,

> The absence of a trained ministry for an effective spiritual and administrative oversight is a weakness which we have examined. But the C&S explanation, based on the Bible and the guidance of the Holy Spirit in reading and interpreting of the Bible, cannot be ignored. It is not systematic education but spiritual enlightenment which is essential to faith. Nevertheless, some of the sections have become aware that in a quickly developing nation like Nigeria, intellectual development must become a necessary prerequisite for the effective proclamation of the Christian message. (1982:195–196)

In 1984 there were two ordained C&S men who performed weddings and baptisms in the Bajju area. One of these had had a year of formal training with the C&S in Kaduna while the other had received no formal training. The church does not conduct infant baptism. Those who wish to be baptized must first repent and express their desire to follow Jesus, and then attend a baptismal class for one year. Local leaders conduct funerals.

Morality

C&S allow their leaders as well as the man in the pew to have more than one wife. One senior apostle stated that only one wife is recognized, but that people may have more than one. He himself had four. Generally polygamous marriages are accepted.

The C&S teach that when an individual is mature, he or she may drink beer (*nkwwa*). I observed that one C&S leader built a drinking house next door to the house of prayer he had constructed. C&S teaching on drinking alcoholic beverages parallels Bajju traditional society in which a mature individual may drink. However, if one has problems with alcoholism, he or she is warned; problem drinking is not acceptable.

Assemblies of God

Assembly of God churches began in the Bajju village of Afana through the work of an expatriate Assembly of God missionary. There is no Assembly of God mission station in southern Kaduna State and Assembly of God missionaries have not worked extensively in this area. In establishing their work among the Bajju Assembly of God missionaries commuted from Jos and stopped at Afana, a village on the Kafanchan-Kwoi road. In 1984 there were three Assembly of God churches in Afana. Assembly of God pastors receive three years of training at the Assembly of God Bible School located at Saminaka.

Methodist Church

The Methodist denomination began among the Bajju when an expatriate missionary visited Afana and established a Methodist church there. In 1984 there were ten Methodist churches in Kajju. However, there has been little Methodist missionary work in southern Kaduna State. Many members of Methodist churches attended churches in other denominations before attending the Methodist church. Methodist leaders may receive training at Emmanuel College located in the Yoruba region of Nigeria.

Other denominations

By 1984 there were over 185 Christian churches in the Bajju area. All of these were established within fifty-five years (1929–1984). This indicates that substantial religious change has occurred among the Bajju. By 2010 there were at least 198 churches. The new denominations that have come into the area since 1984 are the Apostolic Church, Celestial Church, Church of Christ in Nigeria, now called the Church of Christ in Nations (COCIN), Christian Reformed Church, Deeper Life, Grace of God Church, Jehovah's Witnesses, and Living Faith Church. See Appendix A for villages with specific churches in them.

Interdenominational Christian organizations

Several Christian organizations have conducted work in southern Kaduna State; these organizations are best classified as interdenominational, as they do not have a goal of establishing a separate denomination. Rather they have either targeted a specific segment of the population, such as the youth, or have a specific focus, such as evangelism or Bible translation.

Boys' Brigade and Girls' Brigade

Rev. Archibald introduced Boys' Brigade into Nigeria, when early in his ministry he began a Boys' Brigade group at Kagoro. Boys' Brigade was important in Scotland, Archibald's home country. He brought his own uniform and participated actively in Boys' Brigade. Boys' Brigade has two goals: (1) the importance of spiritual life and discipline, and (2) physical training including games, crafts, and drills.

Boys' Brigade and Girls' Brigade have been active throughout southern Kaduna State, and these organizations attracted many to Christianity. Many of the first Christians in the area were youths, which included some who converted to Christianity through Boys' Brigade and Girls' Brigade.

Members of the Boys' Brigade drill in various dance formations. These activities reach their climax during the week between Christmas and New Year's Day when groups from different villages compete against each other. While the current emphasis in Boys' Brigade is on drill formations and physical training, Boys' Brigade and Girls' Brigade included a Bible study component when they were first introduced.

New Life for All

In 1964 New Life for All (NLFA) began as an evangelistic organization initiated by Gerald and Dorothy Swank, SIM missionaries. The goal of NLFA was to evangelize and encourage the growth of the church. The Swanks perceived that Christianity was limited to a thirty-five mile radius around

Kagoro. Through NLFA they desired to complete the task of evangelism (Interview with Gerald Swank, Dallas, June 13, 1985).

Rev. Ginn, the ECWA pastor at Kafanchan, insisted that the task was too great for SIM and ECWA to complete on their own and therefore he encouraged the organization to include Christians from other denominations. So NLFA includes Baptists, ECWA, and Anglican churches, which Swank and other NLFA leaders perceived to be evangelical. NLFA formed prayer cells and training sessions in preparation for evangelism. One of the unexpected benefits of NLFA was the unity that it brought between individuals within different denominations.

While NLFA maintains its central office in Jos, members of this organization have conducted evangelistic meetings in southern Kaduna State. It is composed both of Nigerian Christians and expatriate missionaries. It also has radio programs.

Bible translation

In 1966 a Bajju representative wrote a letter to Wycliffe Bible Translators requesting that a team come work to provide the Bajju with a Bible in their own language. In 1968 my husband and I received this assignment through Wycliffe's partner organization, SIL International. We began language learning and language analysis while living in Zaria prior to moving to the Bajju village of Unguwar Rimi on December 26, 1968. The Bajju warmly welcomed us and the task assigned to us. They were thrilled as no expatriate had ever learned their language and culture before. As one Bajju said, "Now people will know who the Bajju are!" Our being there contributed to their ethnic pride. Our first assignment was to learn to speak Jju. Second, we were to work on both phonological and grammatical analyses of Jju. We held discussions with various community leaders on the formation of the orthography. We also produced several booklets in that orthography.

When we turned our attention to translation in 1972, leaders of the Bajju community formed the Kaje Bible Translation Committee led by Rev. Makoshi, a Baptist pastor, and Yabo Bayei as secretary. This committee appointed Simon Yashi Waziri to translate the first draft of the New Testament. Simon had graduated from the SIM-founded seminary at Egbaja and had taken a course on principles of translation in Jos to train him in Bible translation. I worked through the first draft of the New Testament to check it exegetically as well as linguistically and noted places where revision seemed necessary. My husband and Rev. Iliya Ahuwan revised that draft. Elisha Sambo coordinated the task of gathering groups of people together to read the draft of the New Testament to ascertain whether the translation was understandable, flowed smoothly, and accurately translated the New Testament into Jju. Based on feedback from Elisha, we revised the New Testament. Rev. Dawuda Maigari contributed to the glossary that is at the end of the New Testament. Many Bajju people made significant contributions to this project. The Bible Society of Nigeria published it in 1982. After an extended delay due to foreign exchange problems, it was finally "launched" on May 5, 1984. At the launching, Kaduna Television televised it and radio Kafanchan broadcast the launching. That day 1,333 copies of the New Testament were sold. The entire edition quickly sold out. The New Testament was reprinted in 2013.

The New Testament is probably more used in its oral form than in the written one. Faith Comes By Hearing recorded the entire New Testament and it is this version that is more used than the written form. The *Jesus* film was also produced, and showing it resulted in greater understanding of the Christian message and in some conversions to Christ. However, Hausa continues to be the language used in church services.

Rev. Chidawa, Rev. Iliya Ahuwan, Rev. Musa, and others are currently working on translating the Old Testament under the auspices of the Bajju Language and Translation Association and the Seed Company. May 5th is now Bajju Day, also known as the day of the Bible *(nom Kpa Kaza),* that is celebrated every year as a special time for this Middle Belt people because it was on May 5th, 1984, that the Jju New Testament was launched.

Because translation and literacy go together, we produced primers to teach people to read in Jju. There was also a pre-primer (Primer 1) to help people who were unable to read begin to recognize and learn letters. Primer 2 introduced some of the more frequently occurring sounds, and Primer 3 focused on introducing the fortis consonants. These primers are being updated.

This language and translation project met with widespread community support. Each edition of a booklet that was published quickly sold out. We also held three Writers' Workshops to encourage local Bajju people to write stories in Jju. Some of these proved quite popular and were reprinted. At the same time it is fair to say that these efforts have not yet produced a body of literature sufficient for an ongoing literacy program. There is need for a body of literature sufficient for a literacy program, as well as transitional reading material for transitioning into reading Hausa, the language of wider communication, and English, the official language, as both Hausa and English are gaining importance in this area.

The federal government has approved the Jju orthography. They have also granted the right to teach subjects in Jju in primary schools and teachers' colleges. If an individual receives a degree in Jju, this qualifies him or her to teach in primary schools. The late Daniel Hywa worked on producing materials in Jju for use in primary and teachers' training schools.

Discussion

This chapter has briefly discussed the introduction of Christianity to the Bajju in southern Kaduna State through various denominations. It began by focusing on the work of Sudan Interior Mission, now SIM, the first mission in this area. It highlighted the work of Tom and Gracie Archibald, the first missionaries in the area. Other denominations soon followed SIM.

The introduction of Christianity included rules of following God. Unfortunately missionaries did not study the traditional religion nor know the questions that traditional religion addressed. This occurred because they did not learn the local languages and cultures.

The positive side of the rules of following was that Christianity looked like what a religion was supposed to look like. Their traditional religion and Christianity both had a lot of rules. In fact, the rules of following God convinced many that Christianity was a true religion that they should accept. The retention of African traditional religious beliefs by Bajju Christians will be dealt with in chapter 9.

There is a lot of overlap between the history, organization, practices, and moral issues of each denomination in the Bajju area. All use the same Hausa Bible and the same Hausa hymnal. All have experienced incredible church growth. In terms of missiology, what occurred among the Bajju would be described as a people movement to Christ. Large numbers of people became Christians within a relatively short time.

One experience we had soon after moving to the village of Unguwar Rimi illustrates this rapid acceptance of Christianity. Together with Mallam Yabo Yashim, our language assistant, we walked down to the wooden bridge that spanned the Atacap River, an all-season river that flows through the area. We stood on the bridge for approximately two hours watching the scene below. During that time I counted sixty people baptized. When we had to leave to go home, there were more waiting on shore for their turns to be baptized. The group that was baptized that day was from churches in one denomination in the southern Bajju area. Similar baptisms were occurring in multiple churches in the area. Clearly, we were in the midst of rapid expansion of Christianity.

7

Religious Change Interview Schedule

Sample population

In order to ascertain why Bajju individuals converted to Christianity, my research colleague Haruna and I administered an interview schedule on religious change to both rural and urban samples in 1984, and Haruna administered it again in the same locations in 2009. The results of these interviews provide a twenty-five-year longitudinal study of religious change. Data obtained provide an emic perspective[1] on reasons for religious change. Factors investigated in the interview schedule included basic demographic data, and data related to religious conversion and affiliation for the sample population. These data included age, sex, highest educational level attained, occupation, language(s) spoken and domains of language use, literacy, religion, reasons for religious conversion, and a few questions on traditional religious beliefs Bajju Christians may have retained. This chapter discusses construction and testing of the interview schedule, sample selection, and basic demographic information about the sample population. In the next chapter I correlate the basic demographic data with responses to questions on religious change.

Constructing and testing the interview schedule

Since we planned to sample both literate and illiterate individuals, we decided to use an interview schedule rather than a questionnaire. We constructed

---

[1] An emic perspective is the viewpoint of an insider within a culture.

the interview schedule initially in English, and then translated it into Jju. Haruna then tested it by administering it to forty Bajju speakers in Jos. Based on the results obtained, we further refined the questions to make sure they elicited the desired information. The interview schedule subsequently went through several revisions prior to being administered to the sample population. The responses obtained in the testing phase were thrown away and did not form part of the research sample.

Even after the interview schedule went through this testing process, there were still a few questions that could have been better phrased. In particular, the questions on marriage needed further refinement because the results did not adequately reflect the facts on the ground. For example, one man, who was living with two wives at the time of this research, had had eighteen wives over the years, including one of Haruna's aunts. The way the question was phrased did not elicit this level of detail.

In actually administering the interview schedule, I instructed Haruna that under no circumstances should we suggest possible answers to questions. The questions could be repeated but no sample answers given. If sample answers had been suggested, people would likely have selected one of those answers. Some of the questions clearly had discrete answers, while others were open-ended. The latter questions on retention of traditional religious beliefs in particular needed to be answered by the respondent without input from the interviewer.

Though we considered having educated individuals fill out the interview schedule themselves, this proved inadvisable. When we tried, individuals discussed possible answers with each other, seeking to arrive at the "correct" answer for each question. Their seeking a correct answer was in accord with their usual consensus decision making process; however, a group answer was unsatisfactory because we were seeking to find out what individuals actually believed. Since the interview schedule dealt with beliefs as well as factual information, answers might be considered "correct" with respect either to Bajju traditional religion or to Christianity. What we were seeking was the extent to which Bajju Christians retained traditional religious beliefs. It was therefore necessary to gather data without prejudice that might have occurred through discussion.

Possible sample bias

In administering an interview schedule, there is always the possibility that respondents would base answers on what they perceive the interviewers would want to hear and thus distort their true answers. The question might be raised as to whether the Bajju would distort their answers in response to a research team that they perceived to be Christian. A related question addressed the concern that some might have been influenced by my personal involvement in the translation of the Jju New Testament.

Some factors point to a minimum of bias in the answers received. First, most individuals interviewed did not know me. I had been out of the country for seven years before returning in 1983 to conduct this research. Previously I had not worked in either Kamrum or Television, the two primary sites where we administered interview schedules. Second, the Jju New Testament was not available to the Bajju at the time we administered the interview schedule in 1984. Therefore, individuals might not have readily identified me as one who had worked on it, nor would their answers have been influenced by it. Third, my impression was that respondents were genuinely trying to answer the queries posed. All interviews were conducted in Jju. Not only did this ensure that interviewees could readily understand the questions, it also enabled the interviewers to understand comments that might have indicated that incorrect answers were deliberately being given. Because of the widespread adoption of Christianity by the Bajju and the fact that the members of the research team were Christians, people felt free to express their opinions to the interviewers.

A further aspect of the research that reduced possible bias is that this research on religious change did not rest solely on responses to the interview schedule. Data gathered through other research methods supplemented and supported data that emerged from the interviews. However, it was important to obtain individuals' perspectives on why they converted to Christianity, and their perspectives were best obtained through administering an interview schedule.

Sample selection

The rural and urban composition of the sample selected reflects the geographic distribution of the Bajju population in general. Though adequate statistics on rural-urban Bajju population are not available, in 1963, 7.2% of the Bajju were urbanized (Adedeji and Rowland 1973:223). The proportion of urbanized Bajju has risen steadily since then.

The sample consisted of the following rural and urban respondents.

Table 7.1. Number and percentages of urban and
rural respondents—1984 and 2009 samples

Rural—urban samples	Number of respondents per year	
	1984	2009
Rural	192 (72.2%)	31 (49.2%)
Urban	74 (27.8%)	32 (50.7%)
Total	266 (100%)	63 (100%)

Rural sample selection

For the rural sample population, the village where interviews were conducted needed to be representative of rural Bajju. The village selected was based on the following criteria: (1) It needed a population that was not intermixed with other ethnic groups. Thus a village such as Zonkwa, where the population includes Bajju, Atyap, Igbo, Hausa, Fulani, Bakulu, Agorok, and members of other ethnic groups, did not meet this criterion. (2) The village selected needed to be readily accessible by road, though not necessarily a main road, to allow access. This criterion meant that a village such as Ayagan, which is not readily accessible by road, did not qualify. (3) The village needed to be one of the long-established Bajju villages, not a village whose existence in a particular geographic area began comparatively recently. This criterion meant that some of the villages on the northwest side of Fadan Kamantan did not qualify. (4) The chief of the village needed to agree to our administering the interview schedule to the people in the village. (5) Some members of the village needed to have converted to Christianity. As demonstrated in the chapter on Christian denominations, all Bajju villages met this criterion.

The Bajju village of Kamarum (Kamaru Kaje, H.) was selected for the rural sample population. This village is readily accessible by a road that branches off at Unguwar Rimi from the Kafanchan-Kwoi road. This road continues to Bebyet and on to Zonkwa. Kamarum is located approximately eight kilometers from the Unguwar Rimi road junction. The population of Kamarum is composed primarily of Bajju, though in administering the interview schedule in 1984 we encountered one non-Bajju family and one Bakulu woman who married a Bajju man. Consequently, this village met the criterion that the population was primarily Bajju and not intermixed with multiple ethnic groups who might have influenced individuals in some way concerning religious change. Kamarum is also a traditional Bajju village that has been at its current location for a long time. The chief of Kamarum cordially welcomed the researchers. Kamarum also met the fifth criterion since there were four churches in it in 1984.

The rural sample consisted of adult respondents of Kamarum, with the exception of one section of the village. This section was omitted because it was geographically separated from the main part of the village by several kilometers and was not readily accessible. In the sampling procedure followed in 1984, the researchers interviewed all adults fifteen years of age and older who were at home at the time we came to the household. This sampling procedure yielded a convenience sample. Because the sampling technique did not involve sample selection based on a complete census of every adult of the village, a few adult residents in the village may inadvertently have been omitted. A second problem with this sample selection procedure was that the number of individuals resident within households is flexible depending upon the day of the week. For example, postprimary students who are ordinarily away during weekdays tend to be home on weekends and holidays. Even with these sampling procedure problems, most of the adult members of Kamarum were interviewed in 1984. A smaller sample population was interviewed in 2009. Again, every adult in each compound sampled was interviewed.

The 1984 sampling procedure resulted in 130 interviews in Kamarum that came from seventy-six households. This corresponds fairly closely with the number of individuals that one might find within each Bajju compound. For example, Gozuk found that in Bebyet (Abet, H.) the average number of individuals, including children, resident within each compound was nine, though household size ranged from two to twenty-five persons (Gozuk 1981, as quoted in Powell 1981:99). If we assume a similar number of persons resident within Kamarum compounds, the number of adults per compound interviewed was probably fairly close to the actual number of adults who lived there. A smaller sample population of thirty-one adults was interviewed in 2009.

During the interview period in 1984 one elderly man died, and out of respect for his bereaved family, that household was omitted. Interestingly, however, the deceased was included in the sample as he was living and available to be interviewed on the day before his death. His death came as a surprise to us as he seemed healthy on the previous day. Two other individuals were excluded also due to illness, one of whom was close to death with tuberculosis.

In addition to the rural sample population interviewed at Kamarum, we interviewed sixty-two individuals who live in Kajju but who were not selected from Kamarum. These individuals composed the nonrandom rural sample and have been so designated in the data presented. These respondents came from Sakwak, Ayagan (Furgyem, Kukwan), Dihwan, Katssik, and Madakiya. We included them in order to have individuals in the sample who attended churches other than the four churches located at Kamarum. To obtain this nonrandom sample, we stationed ourselves along the road that leads out of Unguwar Rimi towards the interior of the Bajju area on Wednesday, market day, and interviewed people who passed by.

Urban sample selection

Criteria for selecting an urban sample included the following: (1) The population needed to include a sufficient number of Bajju living within one geographic area to allow for randomization. (2) The population needed to reside close enough together so that once households were selected in the randomization process, those households would be readily accessible by walking. (3) The population needed to live in an urban environment. Several suburbs of Kaduna were considered and Television (also known as Unguwar Maichini) was selected because it met the above criteria. This suburb was named after a television transmitting station that was burned in the 1975 coup attempt. Television, though a suburb of Kaduna, is under Kachia Local Government. It is composed of three sections: Unguwar Yelwa, Unguwar Kadara, and Unguwar Bajju. We administered interview schedules in Unguwar Bajju.

The method utilized for sample selection within Television in 1984 involved obtaining a list of all Bajju household heads in Unguwar Bajju from a long-term resident, then randomly selecting households from that list. The list consisted of seventy-seven households headed by Bajju. From that list, fifteen households were randomly selected by tossing a coin approximately ten times per selection.[2] Because of this randomization procedure each Bajju household in Unguwar Bajju in Television had an equal probability of being selected. Haruna and I both interviewed people from each selected household, with the exception of one household where a recent death in the family had occurred. From the fifteen households selected, we interviewed fifty-two individuals, which included all of the adult members of fifteen years and older who were home when we came. One time the coin flips landed on the local drinking establishment, so we all trouped in and interviewed the people there. Needless to say, they generously offered us some of the local brew.

Problems with urban sampling are greater than those associated with rural sampling because urban environments are more diverse in terms of socio-economic and educational statuses. The sample population interviewed at Television was composed largely of those from the lower socio-economic spectrum of urban Bajju. Therefore, in 1984 we supplemented the interviews conducted at Television with an urban nonrandomly selected sample of respondents. The goal of use of this additional urban sample was to include persons who had received more education and represented a higher socio-economic level than the majority of the respondents in Television. Twenty-two secondary school students, university graduates, and others were interviewed. Table 7.2 presents the sample composition of randomly and nonrandomly selected respondents.

---

[2] In this method of successive coin flips, the first flip determined whether the household should come from the upper or lower range of the seventy-seven households. The second flip determined whether the middle number of the thirty-nine should be included with the upper or lower range. The third and subsequent flips narrowed the range of possibilities until one was selected. Each selection took approximately ten coin flips. As we walked from household to household, my husband Norris, who devised this randomization method, spent his time flipping a coin to determine the next household to sample. His actions brought stares and comments such as "What is he doing?" I was not sure how to tell them in Jju that he was selecting a random sample.

Table 7.2. Sample composition—1984 and 2009 samples

	1984		2009
	Randomly selected	Nonrandomly selected	Nonrandomly selected
Rural	130	62	31
Urban	52	22	32
Column total	182	84	63

In 2009 the sample population at Television consisted of interviews with thirty-two individuals all of whom were selected nonrandomly.

Demographic characteristics of the sample

Demographic data collected on the sample population included age, sex, highest level of education attained, occupation, and economic status.

Age

The first question on the interview schedule asked the age of the respondent. In 1984 this question often brought laughter, which turned out to be a delightful way to begin the interview. One person responded, "Whoever knows a thing like that?" While people keep accurate ages today, traditionally this was not a statistic that people kept. This meant that for the 2009 sample population we had accurate information on people's ages while we did not for the 1984 sample.

We asked both how old a person was, and what year they were born. The interviewers made age estimates based on various criteria. For example, names often reflect what was happening around the time of a person's birth, so occasionally it was possible to correlate a name with the year a person was born. Ages of elderly individuals were estimated based on whether or not they remembered the construction of the railway through Kajju. Sometimes age estimates were based on relative ages of individuals with respect to each other. People would often know who was older or younger than themselves. Even with these efforts the ages we recorded were frequently estimates.

Sex

In 1984 males made up 36.5% of the sample, while females made up 63.5%. The number of males and females in the sample is correlated with rural and urban samples (see table 7.3).

Table 7.3. Sex of respondents—1984 sample

Sex of respondent	Rural		Urban		Row total
	Random	Nonrandom	Random	Nonrandom	
Males	35	22	22	18	97
Females	95	40	30	4	169
Column total	130	62	61	22	266

Table 7.4. Sex of respondents—2009 sample

Sex	Rural	Urban	Row total
Males	19	23	42
Females	12	9	21
Column total	31	32	63

Education

The highest educational level of interviewees attained varied from university graduates to individuals with no formal education. Table 7.5 presents the highest level of education attained by individuals within the sample. In 1984 approximately half of the sample (48.1%) had received some formal education, while the other half (51.9%) had received none. In the 2009 sample only seven respondents, or 11.3% of the sample, had received no formal education.

Table 7.5. Highest educational level attained

Highest educational level attained	Frequency	
	1984	2009
None	138 (51.9%)	7 (11.3%)
Primary incompleted	22 (8.3%)	11 (17.7%)
Primary completed	36 (13.5%)	6 (9.7%)
Secondary incompleted	14 (5.3%)	8 (12.9%)
Secondary completed	2 (.8%)	4 (6.5%)
Teachers' college incompleted	16 (6%)	6 (9.7%)
Teachers' college completed	10 (3.8%)	1 (1.6%)
Advanced teachers' college completed	0 (0%)	8 (12.9%)
Bible school incompleted	5 (1.9%)	0 (0%)
Bible school completed	8 (3%)	0 (0%)

Polytechnical school incompleted	0	2 (3.3%)
Polytechnical school completed	2 (.8%)	4 (6.4%)
University incompleted	0	1 (1.6%)
University completed	4 (1.5%)	0 (0%)
Christian Religious Instruction	8 (3%)	0 (0%)
Other: Staff Training Center, Computer school, Military, Firefighter's course (1 each)	1 (.4%)	4 (6.4%)
No response	0	1
Total	266	63

Economic status

Though it is desirable to have information on individual respondents' income, this type of data was not readily obtained because many of the individuals interviewed lived at a subsistence level and grew most of the food they consumed. Therefore, in order to have some measure of the economic status of respondents, we collected in-kind data; however, no effort was made to convert in-kind data to an approximate monetary value.

Gugler and Flanagan state, "For Nigeria, most rural-urban comparisons reveal a substantial and widening income differential, with rural incomes less than half of urban incomes" (1978:58). However, in contrast to their findings, urban dwellers in Television who work in the private sector perceived that they had fewer material possessions, such as radios and bicycles, than their rural counterparts. Further, most urban dwellers in Television had to purchase grain and other food. Though a few were well-to-do, most represented the urban poor. In contrast, the economic status of those in the urban nonrandom sample was higher than in the urban random sample and the rural samples. The exception to this was the student population, who were characterized by a relatively low economic status, though not social status, as is probably typical for the majority of student populations worldwide. They have the potential, based on their educational background, to do better economically in the future than those without their education.

In comparing in-kind data for the random urban and rural samples, the only significant differences were in the number of houses, goats, radios, cows, televisions, pigs, and sewing machines. Only for the last three of these variables did urban dwellers rank higher than rural dwellers. Hog rearing flourished in this suburb of Kaduna and provided a ready source of pork for urban residents. In fact, when our research team first arrived at Television, people's first reaction was that we had come to buy a pig. Then when we took the camera out of the van, their second reaction was that we had come to take pictures. When they realized that we understood what they were saying, they crowded around and we were able to tell them why we had come.

One further measure of economic status was the number of plots of land that a person farmed. Powell found that at Bebyet each plot was approximately ¾ hectare (almost 2 acres), and the average farmer cultivated 1½ to 3¾ hectares (five to ten acres) or two to five plots of land (1981:84).

Only 15% of rural males reported having no plots of land to farm; many of these respondents were young men who attended school. In 1984 within the random rural sample from Kamrum 77.1% of the 35 male respondents farmed two to six plots of land or 1½ to 4½ hectares; this is assuming that each plot is approximately ¾ hectare as measured by Powell in Bebyet. If the random and nonrandom rural male samples are combined, 79.2% farmed two to six plots of land. No rural farmer in the sample cultivated only one plot. Further, the urban farmers cultivated less land than their rural counterparts, with one to two plots (¾ to 1½ hectares) most commonly reported.

Responses from women indicated that the number of plots they cited reflected either the number that their husbands farmed or, for some widows, the number of plots that they farmed with male help. Bajju women do not own land and rarely hoe it, other than for their bean fields (the *kạdak*) adjacent to their compounds. If possible, men prepare their fields for them.

Traditionally, a Bajju farmer measured his economic status in terms of having a house, grain sufficient to feed his family until the next harvest, and animals. In administering the interview schedule, each respondent was asked about his or her father's economic status. Responses to this question were based on individuals' personal perception. Some individuals qualified their response, such as their father was wealthy because he had lots of goats. Results for this question are in table 7.6.

Table 7.6. Father's economic status

Perceived economic status of father	1984	2009
High income	70	9
Middle income	115	40
Low income	76	14
Missing value	5	0
Column total	266	63

In terms of women's work, many reported that they do housework, which includes a broad spectrum of activities. In the rural setting Bajju women collect and chop firewood, pound grain, cook, wash cooking utensils and clothes, plant seeds, carry loads, haul water, care for children, market surplus produce, weave colorful sleeping mats, carry the crops home after harvest, and the list continues. Men prepare the ground for planting, do some planting such as sowing millet in seed beds and transplant it when approximately 30 centimeters (one foot) tall, plant yam tubers, weed the fields, harvest the crop, do house construction and repair during the dry season, work as carpenters, bricklayers, etc. Farming is thus a communal activity shared by men, women, and children. In addition, some men, women, and children do petty trading. Most are actively involved in church and other religious activities.

The language context

The language context of missionary work relates to education, evangelization, church planting, and communication in general. Turaki captures its importance as follows:

> The value of education had been identified quite early in mission work. Education was the most powerful tool and means of evangelization and church planting in the Mission Field. The reason is simple, Christianity is a "literate" religion. The deep truths, values and principles of the Word of God, the Holy Scriptures have to be read, learned and taught, and literacy is a potent vehicle to achieve this. (1993:136)

He further asserts:

> Education was primarily auxiliary to and also a hand-maid of evangelism and church planting. The goal or the end is not education in itself but the attainment of the knowledge of the Gospel of Christ. (1993:136)

The Bajju live in a multilingual context in southern Kaduna State, where Jju, Hausa, and English are spoken by the Bajju. Christianity was presented to them in Hausa and Hausa continues as the language used in Christian contexts. It is important to note what language is used in various contexts (for example, home, church, work, market), and how they evaluate their speaking ability in each language. See tables 7.7 and 7.8.

Table 7.7. Languages spoken in various contexts

	Home (Karyi)		Church (Coc/ Makaranta)		Work (Pfong)		Market (Tunga)	
	1984	2009	1984	2009	1984	2009	1984	2009
Jju (Kaje)	241	51	86	10	182	24	42	3
Hausa (Kpat)	0	7	67	27	16	4	36	18

English (Shong)	0	1	9	15	24	19	0	2
Jju-Hausa	9	2	93	6	8	4	117	10
Jju-Hausa-English	15	0	2	1	21	0	45	17
Hausa-English	0	2	5	4	1	3	20	12
Not applicable	0	0	0	0	0	9	0	1
Missing value	1	0	4	0	14	0	6	0
Column total	266	63	266	63	266	63	266	63

Answers to questions on languages spoken and understood point to how much Christianity is really understood if it was presented in the language of wider communication, namely, Hausa, rather than in their mother tongue, Jju. The next chapter raises the issue of Bajju Christians retaining traditional religious beliefs. Some reasons the Bajju have retained traditional beliefs may relate to the language choice by missionaries, pastors, and elders in using Hausa in church services rather than Jju.

Initially missionaries in this area began learning various local languages that were necessary for communicating the Christian gospel. For example, portions of Scripture were published in the following languages: Iregwe (1926), Jaba (1924), Chawai (1923), and Rukuba (1924) (Turaki 1993:198).

Part of their reason for using Hausa derived from colonial language policy. For example, in 1908 the secretariat of Northern Nigeria wrote a letter to Sudan Interior Mission concerning language use in education:

> Language in education. That Hausa or another well established native language should be the primary medium in education. That in any case Hausa should be taught in all schools. English should not be taught in the primary school and the character of all schools today is considered to be primary. Advanced or intelligent pupils or sons of Chiefs of importance might with advantage be taught English at a later date but here again the teaching of Hausa should be continued and perfected. It is desirable that Hausa should be taught in the Roman character. (Letter from the Secretariat, Northern Nigeria, to SIM, November 16, 1908, SIM Archives)

In 1910 Christian missions that worked in Northern Nigeria met in Lokoja and adopted this language policy. Those missions were the Church Mission Society (CMS), Sudan Interior Mission (SIM), United Mission Society (UMS), Dutch Reformed Mission, and Sudan United Mission (SUM) (Turaki 1993:141).

Lugard felt that promoting English would aid Africans in trade and allow them access to literature (Lugard 1926). At the local level he was in favor of promoting a lingua franca, such as Hausa, which he felt Africans could easily learn. He indicated his attitude towards the use of minority languages, particularly towards mission use, as follows:

> Missions, on the other hand, being concerned with evangelization only, have no desire to promote intercommunication for trade and other purposes, and are generally content to study a local dialect, and translate the Scriptures and textbooks into it. I concur with Lord Kimberley's dictum, that though instruction in English must of necessity at first be given through the medium of the vernacular, Government encouragement should not be exerted to stimulate or preserve these native tongues. (Lugard 1926:454–455)

After approximately 1930, missions decided to use Hausa, the language of wider communication, rather than any of the indigenous languages, in Christian contexts. Turaki asserts, that the SIM perspective was as follows:

> Hausa is becoming more and more the lingua franca of the pagan tribes in the Northern provinces of Nigeria, which is eliminating to a great extent the necessity of laborious translation work in the numerous other languages. In Bauchi province alone one hundred different languages (not dialects) are spoken by its one million inhabitants, but all can now be reached through the Hausa, and that means also the Hausa Bible. (1993:198)

The major impetus for Hausa use in mission work and in churches came from publication of the Hausa Bible in 1932. After its publication, few missionaries made the effort to learn to speak the local languages of Northern Nigeria. The task would have been difficult because most were unwritten and unanalyzed, with language learning materials unavailable for the minority languages spoken in the northern portion of Nigeria.

Gradually some missionaries and colonial administrators came to assume that everyone in Northern Nigeria knew Hausa. As noted under the discussion of the colonial context, in the early 1930s one administrator believed that the Bajju village of Madakiya was a Hausa-speaking village.

Many local Christians today recognize the need for minority language translations of Scripture and development of a literature in those languages, as well as the need for people to learn English, the official language. At the same time Hausa continues to be the language of the church. Missionaries and church leaders have contributed significantly to the spread of Hausa in rural areas in Northern Nigeria. Turaki concurs when he states, "The missionaries themselves contributed immensely in making both English and Hausa the trade languages and lingua franca for northern Nigeria" (1993:188). He further states,

Where Hausa was primary, one must be versed in it before grad-
uating into English. English was a reserve for advanced education. Thus, it was prestigious to be schooled in English. English
bestows prestige, privilege, and higher social status and standing in society. Within the British colonial context, English was a
civilizing tool and a language of advanced education. (1993:190)

When SIM set up Kagoro Bible School in 1929 the language of instruction was Hausa. It was not until 1949 that English became the language
of instruction and the English Bible Institute became part of the Kagoro
Training Centre. Turaki asserted that it was not until 1955 that English
became the language of instruction (Turaki 1993:147).

As a result of these policies SIM set up language schools for their missionaries. Those schools were for teaching Yoruba for missionaries working
in the Western Region and Hausa for missionaries working in the Northern
Region. "This fact made the study of smaller languages and translations a
matter of personal interest for individual missionaries" (Turaki 1993:231).
However, one of the early missionaries who had worked on learning a
minority language asserted that even though she knew the local language,
SIM urged her to use only Hausa (pers. comm.).

Given the language policies that missions and the colonial administration
imposed on the indigenous population, I asked interviewees what languages
they actually spoke in the village and urban areas. In table 7.8 people evaluated
their speaking abilities in Hausa, English, and Jju. The results in 1984 indicate
that the Bajju ranked Jju as the language they spoke and heard best. Hausa
ranked second in speaking ability, followed by English. If "market" speaking
ability in Hausa is combined with the categories of "hear a little" and "none,"
responses indicate that 66.5% of the Bajju population in 1984 had a limited
knowledge of Hausa. As education, urbanization, upward occupational mobil-
ity, migration, and other aspects of Nigerianization continue, this is changing.

Table 7.8. Perceived language-speaking ability for sample population

	Jju		Hausa		English	
	1984	2009	1984	2009	1984	2009
Very well	214	36	30	21	13	10
Well	40	4	57	20	28	19
Well enough for market use	10	13	97	18	40	14
Hear a little	1	9	68	4	26	10
None	0	1	12	0	158	9
Missing value	1	0	2	0	1	0

No response	0	0	0	0	0	1
Column total	266	63	266	63	266	63

The greatest change in language ability in the 2009 sample is with nine younger respondents indicating they "hear a little" Jju rather than it being their most important language. English is the official language, and it is the language of education and government. Other factors include the use of modern media, such as the Internet and cell phones, where knowledge of English is advantageous. There is also the pernicious spread of Hausa, especially as it is the language of the church and market. The result is that Jju is losing out, though it continues as the first language for most Bajju.

When translations of the New Testament and the entire Bibles become available in various local languages, it remains an open question whether or not churches will continue to use Hausa as the church language or switch to using the vernacular. If this is to change, the change needs to start in Bible schools and theological seminaries where new pastors would be taught to use their own languages in church services. Currently congregants must filter the Christian message through a language many do not understand very well. For example, when my husband read passages from Mark in Jju to some church elders and pastors, their response was, "So that's what that passage means"—passages they had read multiple times in Hausa.

Discussion

This chapter summarized the sample population results of basic demographic data for an interview schedule that was administered in both Kamarum Kaje and Unguwar Maichini, a suburb of Kaduna, also known as Television. Various characteristics of this sample population in 1984 were that males composed 36.5% of the sample, while females comprised 63.5%. There was a diversity of occupations represented as well as a wide range of educational levels. Plots of land farmed in the rural area ranged from two to six or 1½ to 4½ hectares. In the interview schedule we asked people to evaluate their speaking ability in Hausa, English, and Jju. If the categories of "hear a little" and "none," are combined, responses indicate that 66.5% of the Bajju population in 1984 had a limited knowledge of Hausa. In the 2009 sample this had dropped to 34.9% of the population. In the next chapter these sample characteristics are correlated with other aspects of the culture, particularly with various traditional religious beliefs.

8

Religious Change Statistics

Following questions that elicited basic demographic information, the next questions focused on religious change. They included questions on religious preference, reason(s) for conversion, reason(s) for rejection of Islam, denominational affiliation, who influenced a person to convert, and which traditional beliefs have been retained by Bajju Christians. Traditional religious belief questions included prayer to God through the ancestors, ancestors speaking to individuals through dreams, *nkut* beliefs, afterlife beliefs, and reincarnation.[1]

The question of whether the respondent's father or mother was a Christian provided evidence of religious change. Responses to this question are in tables 8.1 and 8.2.

Table 8.1. Parents' religious preference—1984 sample

	Yes	No	Missing value	Row total
Father a Christian?	144 (54.1%)	120 (45.2%)	2 (.8%)	266
Mother a Christian?	165 (62%)	98 (36.8%)	3 (1.1%)	266
Column total	309	218	5	

---

[1]For further information about Bajju conversions see McKinney 1994 and for information on retention of Bajju religious beliefs see McKinney 1986.

Table 8.2. Parents' religious preference—2009 sample

	Yes	No	Don't know	Row total
Father a Christian?	49 (77.7%)	13 (20.6%)	1	63
Mother a Christian?	57 (90.4%)	6 (.09%)	0	63
Column total	106	19	1	

In the results to the 2009 sample question there were fewer respondents whose parents were not Christians than in the 1984 sample. This indicates that the Bajju have continued to convert to Christianity. Data concerning respondents' religious preference are below.

Religious preference

Three questions concerned religious preference for those in the sample, with respondents answering affirmatively to one of the three. The questions are as follows:

1. Are you a Christian?
2. Are you a Muslim?
3. Are you a traditional religionist? (Literally, the question translated as "Do you follow praying to God as did your fathers?")

In the 1984 sample all but two respondents responded that they were Christians. Forty-three individuals (16%), who were mostly in their teens and twenties, stated that they had been Christians since birth. The remaining 221 or 83% stated that they had converted to Christianity. These statistics revealed that this sample met a necessary criterion in which to study religious change, namely that they have experienced such a change. In the 2009 sample 100% of the sample responded that they were Christians. Within this sample twelve respondents (20%) stated that they had been Christians since birth and were raised in Christian families.

None of the respondents indicated that they were Muslims. The term for Muslim in Jju is "One who bows [in prayer]" (*antyok tswa katassi*). Included within the 1984 sample were two elderly men who were formerly Muslims but who were now Christians. If we had encountered any Bajju Muslims in the households where we administered the interview schedule, we would have interviewed them. The lack of Muslim Bajju in either the rural or urban contexts reflects the religious preference of the Bajju generally. Though a few are Muslim, most are now Christians.

Earlier I stated that almost one hundred percent of the Bajju are Christians. This figure is based on my extrapolation to the entire population of the results of this question on religious preference in the 1984 and 2009 samples.

Reasons for religious preference

Three follow-up questions dealt with reasons for individuals' religious preference:

1. Why did you become a Christian?
2. Why are you not a Christian?
3. Why did you become a Christian rather than a Muslim?

If an individual stated that his or her religious preference was Christianity, we asked questions one and three. However, if the individual responded that his or her religious preference was Islam or Bajju traditional religion, then we asked question two.

Responses to the first open-ended question fall into religious, sociological, and miscellaneous categories, with a couple respondents who gave no response. None of the respondents phrased their answers in terms of political or economic reasons. However, historically both political and economic factors were involved since the political context was characterized by oppression during the precolonial and colonial eras. Responses to this open-ended question are summarized below:

Religious reasons for accepting Christianity

1. To follow God
2. To find God after death
3. Because Jesus died for us; Christ suffered for us
4. For salvation; to receive life; to receive eternal life
5. To be in God's light
6. To flee from those causing death through *nkut* during an epidemic
7. To pray to God
8. Because of factors in traditional religion—for example, an incident in the *ǫbvoi* shrine; to leave the wicked deeds of *ǫbvoi*
9. To be a child of God
10. To escape God's fire (hell); to avoid God's judgment
11. Convinced by sermons
12. To find peace of mind
13. To free myself from a demon
14. African traditional religion died out so I became a Christian
15. Wanted to know God's Word and read
16. I accepted Christ as my Lord and Savior

Sociological reasons for accepting Christianity

1. Others were converting, so he or she followed them
2. Attracted by the behavior of Christians; for example, Christians were not beating their children
3. To learn to sing
4. Attracted through Boys' Brigade
5. Not being a Christian made one feel inferior
6. People were rejecting the old ways, so he or she followed them
7. A relative (husband, brother, mother, etc.) was a Christian so he or she also converted
8. Born into a Christian home so he or she followed the form of worship of others in the family
9. Because of problems with alcohol
10. "Civilization"
11. Admired Christianity, preaching, and mode of dress
12. Their life was not good, so they decided to become a Christian

Miscellaneous reasons for accepting Christianity

1. To run from troubles
2. To learn to read and write
3. It is the truth
4. To receive a good burial
5. Own thoughts, own decision

Personal reasons for accepting Christianity

1. No reason
2. Do not know

Responses to this question of why people became Christians are presented in table 8.3 for the 1984 sample and in table 8.4 for the 2009 sample. Though a few individuals gave more than one answer to this question, the statistics come from the first answer received. Because some respondents interpreted this question as "Why are you a Christian?" their responses include both reasons for change and reasons for Christian preference.

Table 8.3. Reasons for respondents' Christian preference—1984 sample

	Urban		Rural		Row total	Percent
	Random	Nonrandom	Random	Nonrandom		
Religious	32	19	65	45	161	59.6%
Sociological	18	3	47	11	79	29.3%
Miscellaneous	1	0	7	8	16	5.9%
Don't know	1	0	9	4	14	5.2%
Column total	52	22	128	68	270	100%

Table 8.4. Reasons for respondents' Christian preference—2009 sample

	Urban	Rural	Row total	Percent
Religious	20	16	36	57.1%
Sociological	12	9	21	33.3%
Miscellaneous	0	2	2	3.2%
Don't know	0	4	4	6.3%
Column total	32	31	63	99.4%

In response to the question of why an individual was not a Christian, in 1984 one man stated that he had been a Christian but now was "resting" from Christianity. A second elderly man stated that he was following the beliefs and practices of the Bajju fathers.

Note that in both the 1984 and 2009 samples religious reasons predominated, with sociological reasons coming in next. This was a movement of religious change for the Bajju.

Responses to the third open-ended question concerning why individuals converted to Christianity rather than to Islam, produced answers that fell into sociological, religious, political, and personal categories.

Sociological reasons for rejecting Islam

1. Relatives (such as parents, sons, and daughters) were not Muslims
2. Other Bajju were not Muslims
3. Followed the religious practices of other Bajju
4. Instructed by father not to become a Muslim

Religious reasons for rejecting Islam

1. Wanted to follow God
2. Want to go to heaven to find Jesus
3. Islam does not have the right teaching
4. There is no life in Islam; it does not lead to life
5. Muhammad did not die for us, but Christ did
6. Because of Jesus; he washes us and wants to receive us; Jesus is the truth
7. Islam does not lead to heaven following death
8. Islam is no better than traditional religion

Political reasons for rejecting Islam

1. Not a Hausa
2. Christianity came first

Personal reasons for rejecting Islam

1. Wanted a Christian funeral
2. No reason; do not know
3. Islam is not true
4. Does not like Islam
5. Because of the trouble the individual was experiencing

While respondents most often gave religious reasons for conversion to Christianity, they more frequently cited sociological reasons for rejecting Islam. Religious reasons ranked second to sociological reasons in their reasons for not becoming a Muslim.

Table 8.5. Reasons for rejection of Islam—1984 sample

	Rural		Urban		Row total	Percent
	Random	Nonrandom	Random	Nonrandom		
Sociological	44	18	11	7	80	30.1%
Religious	53	42	24	13	132	49.6%
Political	8	1	0	0	9	3.4%
Personal	15	14	1	1	31	11.7%
No response	8	3	3	0	14	5.3%
Column total	128	78	39	21	266	

Table 8.6. Reasons for rejection of Islam—2009 sample

	Rural	Urban	Row total	Percent
Sociological	15	16	31	49.2%
Religious	10	12	22	34.9%
Political	0	0	0	0.0%
Personal	3	4	7	11.1%
Don't know	3	0	3	4.7%
Column total	31	32	63	

Economic factors in conversion

It is significant that respondents did not mention economic factors either as a motive for conversion to Christianity or as a reason for rejection of Islam. Prior to administering the questionnaire, I formulated two hypotheses that related to economic factors in conversion.

1. Most shopkeepers, chiefs of markets, and entrepreneurs are Christians.
2. Conversion to Christianity occurred first among members of the higher economic bracket because of perceived economic advantage Christianity offered converts.

Because 99.2% of the sample was Christian in 1984 and 100% in 2009, I was unable to prove the first hypothesis. In order to have tested that hypothesis, the sample would have needed to include a significant number of respondents who were not Christian for comparison. Problems with testing the second hypothesis were (1) inadequate data to delineate who composed the higher economic bracket of the population at the time of their conversion, and (2) difficulty in identifying a means of measuring perceived economic advantage. Thus, I was unable to prove or disprove either hypothesis. Impressionistically it appeared that those who converted to Christianity have benefited economically. This benefit often took the form of access to education provided by mission schools; and education opens opportunities for economic advancement.

Influence of individuals in conversion

Various individuals, usually within a person's family, influenced people to convert to Christianity. The question "Who led you to become a Christian?" sought to obtain information about the influence of specific individuals. Tables 8.7 and 8.8 summarize the results obtained from this question.

Table 8.7. Individual who influenced the respondent to
convert to Christianity—1984 sample

Individual		Percent	Percent
Evangelist, pastor, church leader			16.7%
Church, Boys' Brigade			2.0%
Family:	Father	24.4%	
	Mother	3.6%	
	Child	4.0%	
	Brother, sister	11.0%	
	Extended family	6.5%	
	Spouse	1.2%	
Total family			50.7%
Friend			5.3%
Missionary			2.0%
Self			8.5%
God			5.7%
Other			8.5%
Total			99.4%

Of the respondents, 50.7% reported that they converted through the influence of their families, including their mother, father, child, brother, sister, extended family, or spouse. The father had the greatest influence within the family; his influence accounted for 24.4% of individuals' reasons for converting to Christianity. This is expected given that the Bajju are a patrilineal society. Within the family one's spouse had the least influence, accounting for only 1.2%.

Table 8.8. Individual who influenced the respondent to
convert to Christianity—2009 sample

Individual		Number	Percent	Percent
Evangelist, pastor, church leader		16		31%
Church, Boys' Brigade		0	0	
Family:	Father	7	13%	
	Mother	5	10%	
	Father and mother	12	23%	
	Child	0	0%	

	Brother, sister	3	6%	
	Extended family	5	10%	
	Spouse	0	0%	
Total family		20		39%
Friend		3		6%
Missionary		8		15%
Self		2		3%
God		0		0%
Other		3		4%
Total				100%

The picture is not as clear-cut for the 2009 data as for the 1984 sample in terms of who led someone to become a Christian. The mother and father together have increased in importance, though the father continues to be the most important in influencing an individual to become a Christian. The total family accounted for 39% of those who influenced people to become Christians. The next most important people who influenced people to convert are pastors and missionaries.

Christian conversion and knowledge of Jesus

To elicit information concerning knowledge of Christian beliefs, we asked "Who is Jesus Christ?" Many Christians would assert that in order to be a Christian one must acknowledge Jesus as the one who died for their sins and was resurrected. In asking this question some individuals asserted that they were Christians, yet they lacked knowledge of who Jesus is. These individuals may be placed in a folk Christian category.

Responses to this question are as follows:

1. Son of God
2. Spirit
3. Lord
4. Creator
5. Savior
6. Messiah
7. The one God made
8. God's Father
9. The greatest prophet
10. The one who is everywhere
11. Do not know, no response

In 1984 responses that identified Jesus as God's Father or the one God made are not representative of biblical Christianity per se; however, they do indicate that the individual associated Jesus with God in some way. In response to this question 20.8% of those who gave Christianity as their religious preference responded that they did not know. This lack of knowledge of basic Christian teaching cuts across denominations, though in general, individuals affiliated with ECWA had knowledge of Jesus more frequently than those respondents in other denominations. Figure 8.1 presents a chart of the frequency of responses to "Who is Jesus Christ?" for the 2009 sample.

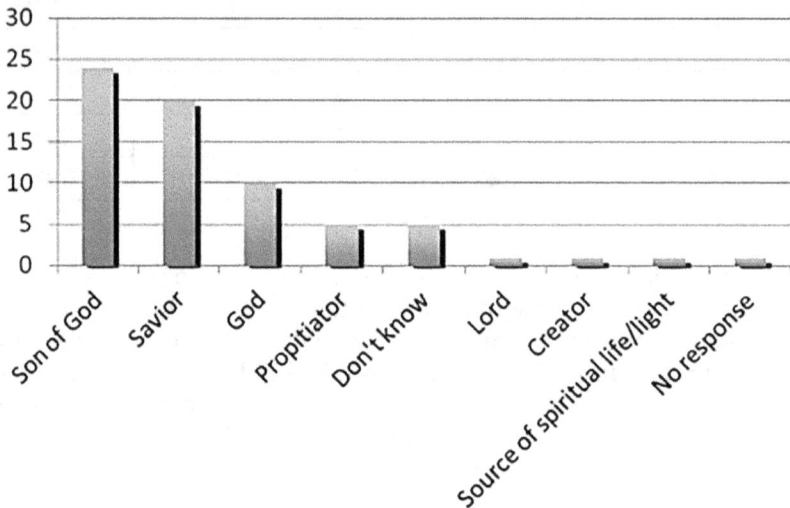

Figure 8.1. Responses to "Who is Jesus?" in 2009.

Table 8.9 correlates lack of knowledge of Jesus with denominational affiliation.

Table 8.9. Lack of knowledge of Jesus correlated
with denominational affiliation—1984 sample

Denomination	Number in sample	Frequency of lack of knowledge of Jesus	Percent of respondents per denomination
Anglican (CMS)	40	8	20.0%
Baptist	26	8	30.7%
Catholic	66	24	36.3%
Cherubim and Seraphim	31	9	29.0%
ECWA	85	5	5.8%
Methodist	5	0	0.0%*

United Native African	12	1	8.3[a]
Column total	265	55	

[a] Not statistically significant, as the total number of respondents for these denominations was too small or not represented in this sample.

I further correlated lack of knowledge of Jesus in the 1984 sample with the highest level of education the respondent had achieved. These results are presented in table 8.10. Lack of knowledge of Jesus correlated positively with lack of formal education. However, it is significant that there were a few in the total sample who received formal education and who did not have knowledge of Jesus. Students in Nigerian schools are required to study Religious Knowledge (RK); they may select either Christianity or Islam. If they selected Christianity for RK in school, as the vast majority of Bajju students do, most students should have been exposed to basic Christian knowledge about Jesus.

Table 8.10. Lack of knowledge of Jesus correlated with highest educational level achieved—1984 sample

Highest educational level achieved	Lacked knowledge of Jesus				Row total
	Rural		Urban		
	Nonrandom	Random	Nonrandom	Random	
None	9	35	0	5	49
Primary incomplete	0	0	0	1	1
Primary completed	0	3	0	0	3
Secondary incomplete	0	0	0	1	1
Secondary completed	0	0	0	0	0
Teacher's College incomplete	0	0	0	0	0
Teacher's College completed	0	0	0	0	0
Bible school incomplete	0	0	0	0	0

Bible school completed	0	0	0	0	0
Technical School Completed	0	0	0	0	0
Christian Religious Instruction	0	0	0	0	0
Other	0	0	0	0	0
Column total	9	38	0	7	54

I further correlated lack of knowledge of Jesus with age and sex of respondents. The results are presented in tables 8.11 and 8.12, respectively.

Table 8.11. Lack of knowledge of Jesus correlated with age of respondent—1984 sample

Age	Lacked knowledge of Jesus				Row total
	Rural		Urban		
	Nonrandom	Random	Nonrandom	Random	
15–19	0	0	0	3	3
20–24	0	3	0	0	3
25–29	0	0	0	0	0
30–34	0	0	0	0	0
35–39	0	1	0	1	2
40–44	1	2	0	1	4
45–49	1	3	0	0	4
50–54	0	6	0	1	7
55–59	2	6	0	0	8
60–64	1	5	0	0	6
65–69	2	2	0	0	4
70–74	1	4	0	0	5
75 +	1	6	0	1	8
Column total	9	38	0	7	54

Table 8.12. Lack of knowledge of Jesus correlated with sex of
respondent—1984 sample

Sex	Lacked knowledge of Jesus				Row total
	Rural		Urban		
	Nonrandom	Random	Nonrandom	Random	
Male	4	4	0	2	10
Female	5	34	0	6	45
Column total	9	38	0	8	55

If we combine information from tables 8.10–8.12, those who lacked knowledge of Jesus lacked formal education, and in the rural sample were forty years of age or older. Further, within the rural random sample, lack of knowledge of Jesus correlated positively with the sex of the respondent. Female rural respondents who were forty years or older were more apt to lack this knowledge. We may characterize this segment of the sample population as folk Christians; they identified with Christianity but lack knowledge of Jesus. This group usually attended church daily, but they lacked this basic Christian knowledge. This was due to Hausa being used in church. This segment of the population was much less likely to know the language of wider communication than men or younger women. They fall into a linguistically neglected group within the Christian church.

In the 2009 sample all respondents knew who Jesus was, so there are no tables to identify who lacked this knowledge.

Influence of dreams in conversion

We asked individuals about the influence of dreams in their conversion to Christianity. Specifically we asked, "Did you have a dream that influenced you to become a Christian?" Table 8.13 presents responses received to this question.

Table 8.13. Influence of dreams in conversion

Did a dream influence you to become a Christian?	1984 Frequency	2009 Frequency
Yes	122 (46.2%)	29 (46%)
No	133 (50.4%)	33 (52%)
Don't know	8 (3.0%)	0 (0%)
Missing value	1 (.4%)	1 (2%)
Column total	264 (100%)	63 (100%)

In 1984 since 46.2% asserted that dreams influenced them to convert to Christianity, these data add confirmation to Fisher's assertion that dreams may be an avenue for the acceptance of new ideas, including religious conversion (1979:217). In the 2009 sample dreams continue to have a significant influence on almost half of the population sampled in their conversion to Christianity.

Christianity and retention of traditional religious beliefs

In religious change, people often add new beliefs to previously held ones rather than replace them. Areas of traditional Bajju beliefs included on the interview schedule were ancestors speaking to individuals through dreams, prayer to God through the ancestors, death caused by *nkut*, belief in reincarnation (McKinney 2017), and the place of the afterlife.

In compiling data on these topics, place of residence, whether rural or urban, did not correlate significantly with the belief in focus, except where otherwise indicated. There was also no significant difference between responses from the random and nonrandom samples. Therefore, tables in this section omit the distinctions between rural and urban, and between random and nonrandom sample populations except where relevant.

Do the ancestors communicate through dreams?

The Bajju pay close attention to those dreams in which the ancestors speak to them, but not all dreams are significant to the Bajju. Therefore, we asked whether the ancestors occasionally speak to them through dreams. Results are summarized in table 8.14.

Table 8.14. Belief that ancestors communicate through dreams

Do ancestors occasionally speak to you through dreams?	Frequency and Percent	Frequency and Percent
Year of sample	1984	2009
Yes, unqualified	137 (51.9%)	29 (46%)
Yes, Christian ancestors	2 (.75%)	33 (52%)
No	122 (46.2%)	0
Don't know	2 (.75%)	0
Missing value	1 (.4%)	1 (2%)
Column total	264 (100%)	63 (100%)

Affirmative responses fall into two categories. The first was an unqualified "yes," and the second "yes" was qualified by being Christian ancestors who did so. If these two responses are combined, in the 1984 sample 52.6% of the sample population responded that ancestors occasionally speak to them through dreams. Almost all respondents in the 2009 sample affirmed the importance of ancestors speaking to them through dreams. These data indicate that dreams continue to be important for Christians.

In interviews with missionaries and church leaders, I asked what they taught their congregations about dreams. One C&S leader responded that visions rather than dreams are important. A UNA leader stated that significant dreams that their members have are shared in church services. Some SIM missionaries have taught that ancestors do not speak to individuals through dreams; however, some ECWA Bajju pastors teach that ancestors may speak to individuals through dreams.

The question may justifiably be raised as to whether or not this traditional Bajju belief is compatible with Christian teaching. Evidence for asserting that Christians may have significant dreams comes from Acts 2:17, which quotes from Joel 2:28 as follows:

"This is what I will do in the last days, God says:
I will pour out my Spirit on everyone.
Your young men will see visions,
and your old men will have dreams" (*Good News Bible* 1966:159)

Since theologians disagree on the role of dreams in conveying God's messages to Christians, the question of whether or not this factor should be viewed as a retention of Bajju traditional religious beliefs or as a manifestation of the Holy Spirit is ambiguous.

Responses by two individuals who said traditional religion was their religious preference indicated that the ancestors occasionally speak to them through dreams. One elderly man gave an ambiguous answer when he stated that the ancestors do not speak, but he hears them!

Prayer to God through ancestors

Traditionally people would go to the gravesites of their ancestors to pray to them, as the ancestors are viewed as being closer to God than those who are still living. For example, if a woman is barren it may be because she offended a deceased parent. Therefore, she would go to the gravesite of that person to pray for forgiveness and to ask that she may be able to conceive a child. For this reason, we asked whether people continue to pray to God through their ancestors. Table 8.15 presents the results of responses to this question.

Table 8.15. Christians praying to God through ancestors

Do you pray to God through your ancestors?	1984 Frequency and percent	2009 Frequency and percent
No	193 (73.1%)	41 (65%)
Yes	67 (25.4%)	21 (33%)
Yes, Christian ancestors	3 (1.1%)	0
Don't know	1 (.4%)	0
Missing value	0	1 (2%)
Column total	264 (100%)	63 (100%)

In the 1984 sample 73.1% of the respondents no longer pray to God through their ancestors, whereas 25.4% continue to do so. This practice has been modified by three individuals who stated that they pray to God through the Christian ancestors. This follows the same pattern of Christian Bajju who claimed that it is Christian ancestors who occasionally speak to them through dreams. Table 8.15 indicates that for the 2009 sample the role of the ancestors continues to be important for Bajju Christians.

Belief in *nkut*

We asked Bajju Christians about their continued belief in *nkut*, the pervasive explanatory system that deals with the ultimate causes of misfortune, illness, evil, and death. We asked, "Can people die from *nkut*?" Table 8.16 summarizes the responses to this question.

Table 8.16. Belief in *nkut*

Can people die from *nkut*?	1984 Frequency and percent	2009 Frequency and percent
No	161 (60.9%)	29 (46%)
Yes	54 (20.5%)	32 (50.8%)
Don't know	47 (17.8%)	1 (1.6%)
Missing value	2 (.8%)	1 (1.6%)
Column total	264 (100%)	63 (100%)

In the light of changing beliefs and the advent of Western medical disease etiology, some respondents do not know what to believe. However, the majority of respondents replied that people do not die from *nkut*. Christian missionaries generally (1) were unaware of this widespread belief system, (2) taught that the power of Jesus was stronger, or (3) taught that such beliefs were superstition. The third position was that taken by some Roman Catholic missionaries. Therefore, some individuals who accepted Christianity when it was first introduced no longer believe in *nkut,* while younger individuals continue to subscribe to it. One individual explained this by stating that it was natural for young men to believe in *nkut* because they were the ones against whom it was most frequently practiced. Individuals who believe in *nkut* point to the evidence that young men are those more frequently killed in road accidents. For the 1984 sample further research indicated that in rural contexts it was females ages 50 to 60 years of age who most often believed in *nkut.* In urban contexts it was male respondents who believed in *nkut.*

Interestingly, both traditional religionists responded negatively to this question. One specifically said that individuals die because of God, not because of *nkut.*

Data for the 2009 sample on belief in *nkut* indicate that it continues to be strongly held by Bajju Christians with almost one half of the population sampled believing in it.

Belief in reincarnation

Traditionally the Bajju believed that those who die as infants, as well as youths, females, and those who have not fulfilled their functions of being married and having children are reincarnated (McKinney 2018). The elderly, particularly elderly men, were believed to enter the underground world of *ayabyen.* They become ancestors who watch over the living. The belief in reincarnation is rather loose. A person can be reborn as a bird, animal, or other human. Reincarnation is not based on merit as it is in Hinduism.

Names may indicate that people believe a child is a reincarnated person. For example, the name Abrak means 'he has returned'.

In seeking to find out whether or not people continue to believe in reincarnation, we asked about reincarnation of an old person, a youth, and a baby. Traditionally people believed that the latter two categories were reincarnated as well as women and single individuals. Table 8.17 presents the results from this question from the 1984 sample.

Table 8.17. Belief in reincarnation—1984 sample

	May an individual be reborn after death?			
	Yes	No	Don't know	Missing value
Old person	64 (24.2%)	157 (59.5%)	41 (15.5%)	2 (.8%)
Youth	62 (23.5%)	157 (59.5%)	42 (15.9%)	3 (1.1%)
Baby	68 (25.7%)	152 (57.6%)	42 (15.9%)	2 (.8%)

For persons in each age category, over 23% of the sample responded affirmatively concerning reincarnation beliefs. Though beliefs in reincarnation have changed, as is evidenced by negative responses by 57.6% of the sample for an infant, there remains a question in the minds of over 15% of the population.

One young man explained that he did not believe in reincarnation until he spoke with one of the elders of his village who assured him that people could be reincarnated. Another young man was unclear on the difference between belief in reincarnation and Jesus' teaching concerning being "born again" (John 3:3). A third individual responded affirmatively and added that he believed it but had no proof.

Table 8.18. Belief in reincarnation—2009 sample

May an individual be reborn after death?

	Yes	No	Don't know	Missing value
Old person	14 (22%)	42 (67%)	6 (10%)	1 (2%)
Youth	10 (16%)	47 (77%)	5 (8%)	1 (2%)
Baby	19 (30%)	38 (60%)	5 (8%)	1 (2%)

Belief in the place of the afterlife

Beliefs in an afterlife exist within the cosmologies of both Bajju traditional religion and Christianity. Therefore, the question did not ask whether one believed in an afterlife. Rather it sought to identify whether the afterlife was associated with the traditional concept of an underground world known as *ayabyen* or with heaven known as *tazwa* or *karyi Kaza. Tazwa* translates as 'sky', 'up', or 'heaven', and *karyi Kaza* as 'God's house'.

This question is perhaps the weakest about retention of traditional religious beliefs because both Christianity and Bajju cosmologies share a belief in an afterlife and because the question was not phrased to distinguish the two. Instead the question asked where the respondents would go after death. This resulted in 8.3% responding that they did not know. In retrospect, the question should have asked the name of the place of the afterlife and about its existence. These data are still included because they do indicate a continued belief in an afterlife. Results are in table 8.19.

Table 8.19. Belief in an afterlife

Where will you go after death?	1984 Frequency and percent	2009 Frequency and percent
Underground world (ayabyen)	9 (3.4%)	0
Heaven, God's house (tazwa/karyi Kaza)	225 (85.2%)	63
Don't know	21 (8%)	0
Missing value	9 (3.4%)	0
Column total	264 (100%)	63 (100%)

One Bajju pastor said, "We knew there was an afterlife; but we did not know that God was there."

In the 2009 sample all respondents said the afterlife is in heaven or God's house. Most Bajju Christians no longer believe in the concept of an underground world.

Discussion

Within a fifty-five-year period the Bajju moved from having no Christians to almost 100% of those sampled claiming to be Christians. Clearly a massive change of religion occurred. During our time living among them, we were in the midst of what missiologists term a people movement to Christ. The church is now a central institution among the Bajju, as indicated by over 60% in the 1984 sample reporting that they attend church daily. While the consensus decision making and communalism that are so much a part of their culture are major factors in this religious change, there are additional factors that must be taken into account.

Ethnohistorical factors, particularly their long-term relations with the Hausa-Fulani emirates and colonialism, provided the context that made religious change possible and perhaps even necessary. For example, by the colonial administration failing to recognize the real leaders among the Bajju, namely the elders, it undermined the traditional religion and political organization. Having no political representation throughout the colonial period led to real frustration among the Bajju. The colonial administration formally imposed two emirates on the Bajju; this put their society under intense pressure. Those who formerly slave raided them were now formally placed over them with the backing of the West African Frontier Force and the colonial administration. Various efforts, as for example by Musa Marsa and Usman Sakwak, to have a chieftaincy position established were frustrated. These efforts might have led to some change in their status with respect to the colonial administration and the Native Authority system; however, these efforts were frustrated.

From a Bajju perspective this clearly was a religious movement. They converted because they believed in God and could now know and follow Him. A number of the early Bajju converted because of their desire to learn to read and write. Many saw that traditional religious practices, such as *abvoi*, did not bring peace, but rather were oppressive. Hence, in conversion they renounced their former religious practices and turned to Christianity. It allowed them to know God, to have a new identity, and to find peace with God and mankind. Christianity also raised the status of women who could now actively participate in Christian churches. Formerly they were excluded from the *abvoi* society.

9

Factors affecting Bajju
Christian Conversion

After briefly describing some of the Bajju traditional culture, including their religious beliefs and practices, their interactions with two Hausa-Fulani emirates in the precolonial era, the colonial era, and their interaction with missionaries, we are in a better position to address the basic question addressed in this study, namely, what were the main factors that contributed to the widespread adoption of Christianity by the Bajju? The results of this study demonstrate that when asked, individual Bajju cite religious reasons as their primary motivation for converting to Christianity. The issue of traditional religious beliefs retained by Bajju Christians was also addressed. In this chapter their traditional religious beliefs are compared with a Christian perspective, with biblical references included.

The Bajju view Christianity as the true religion, one that enables them to know God and to be with Him after death. It gives them hope in the midst of difficult situations. Islam is the other religion in Northern Nigeria that they could have adopted, but they did not do so. They saw Islam as similar to their traditional religion. They assert that Jesus died for their sins. This contrasts with their view of Mohammad, whom they assert did not die for their sins.[1]

---

[1] During the course of my research I encountered one Bajju man who had been a Christian but later became a Muslim, indeed an *alhaji*, a man who had made the pilgrimage to Mecca. In order to understand where he stood on a key Christian theological issue, I asked him, Who is Jesus Christ? His response was "He's the Savior, the Redeemer, the one who rose; everyone knows that!" meaning he still

This study also identified various stresses that influenced the Bajju and played a major role in their Christian conversion. For example, the political oppression they suffered in the precolonial and colonial eras resulted in incredible stress for this ethnic group as well as for other minority groups in southern Kaduna State, and indeed in the entire Middle Belt. During the precolonial Hausa-Fulani era, the Bajju and other minority ethnic groups suffered the loss of their most productive men and women to slave raiders each dry season. Their oppression continued under colonialism when the Bajju had no political representation but found themselves formally placed under two emirates, those of Zazzau and Jema'a. When they sought to resolve conflicts with the emirates and colonialists through traditional means, those means failed. For example, when colonial officials demanded the surrender of those who attacked the emir of Jema'a's group in 1915, the Bajju offered chickens as payment for their fine and the return of the items they had taken from the emir's party. Their offers were rejected; rather, the colonial officials demanded the actual attackers. Because of the communal nature of their society, the Bajju refused to surrender those who had participated in the attack. When their offers did not satisfy the colonial officials, the WFAA attacked and burned some of their villages, including villages that had not been involved in the attack. It is not hard to see that the British colonial administration resembled a continuation of the oppression they suffered under the emirates, though now with superior weaponry.

Further, the elders in the community were not recognized as the political and religious leaders of the community. Instead, first the Hausa-Fulani emirates' representatives and then the colonial administration appointed chiefs through whom they could implement Indirect Rule. This undermined their traditional religio-political system. This was true not only for the Bajju but also for other related minority ethnic groups in this area.

During the colonial era, beginning in 1927 Christian missionaries entered this area and began to have an influence on the traditional religion and culture, particularly on the *abvoi* society. Missionaries condemned anything related to this society. In fact, there were several power confrontations between traditional Bajju religion and Christianity, and in those encounters the *abvoi* society was unable to effectively counter Christianity.

Traditional religious beliefs and Christianity

Some Bajju Christian leaders assert that their acceptance of Christianity benefited from the fact that there was little in their traditional religious beliefs

---

held some of his earlier Christian beliefs. To become a Muslim implies a change in identity. This new identity is seen in that he gave his children long Muslim names. The local people's reaction to his Islamic conversion was that it was not good for him to return to the home area as he had abandoned his cultural roots. There is strong social pressure against conversion to Islam in this area.

that contradicted Christianity. Given this assertion, I charted the similarities and contrasts between their traditional religious beliefs and Christianity. Tables 9.1–9.3 present multiple similarities between their traditional culture, including religious beliefs, and Christianity. Some of the "rules of following [God]" put forth by the early missionaries paralleled their traditional religion, which also had various rules that individuals had to follow. In fact, it was those "rules of following" that convinced many Bajju that Christianity had to be a true religion; it looked like their traditional religion. On the other hand, tables 9.4 and 9.5 show contrasts between Bajju traditional culture, religious beliefs, and Christianity.

Table 9.1. Religious similarities between Bajju traditional religion and Christianity

Domain	Traditional Bajju religious beliefs and practices	Christianity
Religion	Belief in God (*Kaza*)	Belief in one God as the Trinity: Father, Son, and Holy Spirit (God the Father—John 5:18, Ephesians 1:3; God the Son—Mark 8:27–29; God the Holy Spirit—John 14:25–26, Acts 2:17–18)
	Belief in spirits (*aninyet, natenyrang*,[a] *gajimale, baconcong*)	Belief in demons (Luke 8:27–33)
	Blood sacrifice necessary for the forgiveness of sin and for cleansing the community of the consequences of an offense	Blood sacrifice necessary for the forgiveness of sins (Leviticus 17:11)[b]
	Belief in an afterlife located underground where bodies are buried (*ayabyen*)	Belief in an afterlife/heaven (Matthew 5:19, 2 Peter 3:13, Revelation 4 and following)
	Belief in dreams, particularly those from ancestors, and visions	Belief in dreams and visions (Genesis 37:5–7; Acts 2:17–18, 10:9–16)
	Repentance through the drinking ashes ritual (*sswa batwak*) necessary for forgiveness	Repentance necessary for the forgiveness of sins (Luke 24:47)

[a] Some assert that some spirits are not evil while others are; they simply want to live their lives without human interference, for example, stepping on their babies or houses. When this happens, they retaliate by inflicting injury to people's legs, which is as high as they are able to reach. Turaki asserts that evil spirits are equivalent to the fallen angels in the Bible, who are known as unclean spirits, familiar spirits, demons, principalities, and powers (2006:65–66).

[b] Fulfilled by Jesus' sacrifice of himself.

Table 9.2. Similarities between Bajju social issues and Christianity

Domain	Traditional Bajju beliefs and practices	Christianity
Social issues	Kind treatment of visitors and guests (*bgyecen*) in their midst	Kind treatment of visitors, widows, orphans (Leviticus 19:33–34, James 1:27[a])
	Polygyny, polyandrous-polygynous marriage, and monogamy practiced	Many OT patriarchs were polygynists: Abraham (Genesis 11:29, 25:1); Esau (Genesis 26:34); Jacob (Genesis 29:16–30, 35:23–26); Solomon (1 Kings 11:3), etc. Deuteronomy 17:17 states that kings should not have many wives. Monogamous marriages are required of church elders (1 Timothy 3:2)
	Widow inheritance[b]	Levirate (Deuteronomy 25:5–10)
	Homosexuality condemned	Homosexuality condemned (Romans 1:26–27; 1 Corinthians 6:9)
	Adultery within the extended family dealt with harshly	Adultery and fornication condemned (Leviticus 18:6–17; 1 Corinthians 5:1, 5; 1 Corinthians 6:18–20)
	Drinking alcoholic beverages that causes problems condemned, being an alcoholic condemned; persons with an alcohol problem are told to stop drinking	Drinking alcoholic beverages that causes problems condemned; being an alcoholic condemned (Proverbs 20:1; Romans 14:21; 1 Timothy 5:23). Some Christians condemn drinking all alcoholic beverages
	Immorality condemned	Immorality condemned (Galatians 5:19–21, Ephesians 5:3–5)
	Beliefs in the kinship-based ancestors (*bgbvoi*)[c], with some feared and some respected	Belief in the godly ancestors (Hebrews 11)

[a] Today the Bajju chief specifically cares for widows near Christmastime. The church provides for orphans by allowing other women to raise them and giving those women money to purchase formula.

[b] The difference between widow inheritance and the levirate is that with the levirate any children born to the union belong to the deceased husband, while with widow inheritance any children born to the union belong to the biological father.

[c] Some Bajju Christians assert that they pray to God through the Christian ancestors.

Table 9.3. Similarities between Bajju economic and political structure and the biblical context

Domain	Traditional Bajju beliefs and practices	Christianity
Economic structure	Horticulturalists, rural and urban dwellers	Horticulturalists (Genesis 26:12), and pastoralists (Genesis 47:3–4); urban and rural dwellers in NT (Luke 1:39-40; 2:8)
Political structure	Governed by elders (*bagado*), chiefs, district heads, and formerly by emirs	Church governed by God through the apostles, elders, deacons, prophets, teachers, pastors, evangelists, those with gifts of healing, those with gifts of administration, helpers (Matthew 10:41, 1 Corinthians 12:28, Ephesians 4:11–13)
	Murderers are killed	In the OT murderers were killed (Numbers 35:30)
	Homicide dealt with by exile to a neighboring ethnic group for a set period of time	Israelites established cities of refuge for those who committed homicide (Deuteronomy 19:4–7)
	Theft condemned	Theft condemned (Exodus 22:1–4)

Table 9.4. Contrasts of religious beliefs and practices between Bajju
traditional religion and Christianity

Domain	Traditional Bajju religious beliefs and practices	Christianity
Religion	Witchcraft beliefs *nkut*	Witchcraft condemned (Deuteronomy 18:10–12, Galatians 5:19–21)
	Belief in the mother of God *anaa Kazα*[a]	Mary, the mother of Jesus (Luke 2:4–7)
	Belief in physical reincarnation	Belief in being born again spiritually (John 3:5–8)
	Food sacrificed to spirits	In OT food was sacrificed to God by the Levites (Exodus 20:24); in NT food sacrificed to idols is not to be eaten (Acts 15:29). Jesus was the final sacrifice for sin (Hebrews 9:28), therefore other sacrifices are no longer necessary.
	abvoi society maintained the myth that it was all-knowing (omniscient) and everywhere present (omnipresent)	God is omniscient (Psalm 139); and omnipresent[b] (Genesis 28:15; Deuteronomy 31:6; Joshua 1:5; Matthew 28:20)
	Sacrifices made to the ancestors or spirits for sins	Jesus was the final sacrifice for sin (Hebrews 9:11–14)
	Spirit possession *bvori*, divination, sorcery, and magic practiced	Jesus cast out demons that possessed people (Matthew 8:28–34); diviner at Endor called up Samuel (I Samuel 28:7–19); divination, sorcery, and practices of mediums condemned (Leviticus 19:26, 20:26–27), practice of magic condemned (Revelation 21:8)

[a] There is no Christian parallel to the belief in the mother of God. The closest parallel is that Catholics refer to Jesus' mother as "Mary, the mother of God." The concept of a mother of God has largely disappeared among the Bajju.

[b] God is not a territorial god whose residence is specific to one area, but rather he is with people wherever they are.

Table 9.5. Contrasts of religious beliefs and practices
between Bajju social structure and Christianity

Domain	Traditional Bajju religious beliefs and practices	Christianity
Social structure	The seventh day was a work day, like any other day	The seventh day is a day of rest (Exodus 23:12; 31:12–17)[a]
	Polygamy practiced by elders	Monogamy required of church elders (1 Timothy 3:2)
	Women excluded from the men's secret organization *abvoi*	Men, women, and children are included as Jesus' followers and are in the church (Matthew 12:50, 14:21, 19:13–15, 27:55–56; Acts 1:14)
	Women had low status, equivalent to uninitiated boys	Christianity elevated the status of women, for example, some of Jesus' followers were women (Matthew 14:21; 15:22–28, 38; 27:55–56; 28:1–8) and he healed women (Mark 5:22–29).
	Men were known to be very kind at home and very wicked in the bush	Christians are to lead holy and godly lives (2 Timothy 1:9)
	Infanticide and euthanasia justified in some circumstances	Infanticide and euthanasia condemned (Leviticus 18:21, 20:1–5)
	Oathtaking practiced	In the OT oathtaking was common (Numbers 30:2). In the NT a person is not to swear an oath (Matthew 5:33–37).[b]
	Do not talk about evil or sin; to do so will cause sin to occur	Belief in original sin (Psalm 51:5; Romans 3:9–18)

[a] When Christianity first came and instituted a day of rest each week, many Bajju Christian men lost their wives. Their fathers-in-law did not want lazy sons-in-law, ones who did not work on Sunday, so they came and took their daughters home with them.

[b] When in court jurors and witnesses are required to swear to tell the truth, often stated as "I swear to tell the truth, the whole truth, and nothing but the truth, so help me God." It is equivalent to karyong ami, 'It is true', that Bajju Christians often assert.

Religion and social structure contrasts between Christianity and Bajju traditional culture

Tables 9.4 and 9.5 presented notable contrasts of religion and social structure between Christianity and Bajju traditional culture. For example, belief in the mother of God, in witchcraft (*nkut*), and the men's secret society (*abvoi*) contrast with Christian beliefs. Belief in the mother of God has basically disappeared. In this research we found that only very elderly individuals knew this belief.

Belief in witchcraft continues today. Some assert that it is a demon or evil spirit that enters an individual and causes that person's spirit to leave, meet with other spirits in the spiritual realm, and results in others suffering evil, misfortune, illness, or death. Christianity teaches that individuals can become spirit- or demon-possessed. In contrast with traditional belief in *nkut*, when an evil spirit possesses an individual. It does not cause that person's spirit to leave its host's body during sleep to harm others in the spiritual world but rather affects that individual and those who are physically nearby that person. It is this part of the belief that is problematic.

In the past it was diviners *(babvok)* who identified those who used their witchcraft substance to harm others. Today some pastors identify those who practice *nkut*. Women are most often accused of this activity, though men may also be accused. Those accused are beaten. If a woman is accused, she is beaten, and then sent back to her father's compound. Traditionally, if a *gado* found that someone was a witch, he would fine that individual to punish him or her.

Religious factors affecting Christian conversion

The Bajju primarily cited religious reasons for their conversion to Christianity because many of the beliefs taught by Christianity were in agreement with their traditional religious beliefs. For example, the Bajju knew there was a God, and Christianity enabled them to know Him, the same God they already knew existed. The Bajju knew there was an afterlife, but they did not know that God would be there. They knew that actions contrary to the rules of the society needed to be dealt with, which they did through fines, sacrifices, repentance, and prayers to the ancestors. Christianity taught about sin, Jesus Christ's death as the ultimate sacrifice for sin, the need for repentance, and forgiveness of sins.

The early missionaries introduced a rather legalistic form of Christianity. Hence Christianity looked like a true religion because their traditional religion also had such rules and taboos. In this case the "rules of following [God]" affirmed Christianity rather than distracted from its veracity.

Christianity rejected *nkut*, magic, sorcery, and other antisocial beliefs and practices. It also rejected the work of the diviners. Christians felt that diviners simply caused trouble in the community. For example, if a diviner asserted that a child would be born with a deformity, but the infant was normal at birth, the diviner lost credibility within the community. That child might receive the name *Baryat abrak,* meaning 'the words [of the diviner] are lost'. The Bajju realized that the predictions of diviners were often wrong.

Beginning in 1927 Christian missionaries entered this area where they provided an alternate ideology and teachings from Hausa-Fulani emirates, colonialism, and Islam. Missionaries brought education and an ideology of equality between people that contrasted with their inferior status under the emirates and the colonial administration. It also brought a means of knowing God, forgiveness of sins, hope, and belief in heaven.

Christian missionaries established schools. Some Bajju saw schooling as a way to understand and get out from under the oppression that they were experiencing under the emirate system and colonialism. This was certainly Allahmagani's goal in inviting Roman Catholic missionaries to establish a school at Madakiya. However, when that request was rejected by the colonial administration, he sent one son away to be educated. He felt that if they "knew book," they would be able to stop such unfair seizure of his property as had occurred earlier when the district officer took most of his animals to pay the taxes for the entire village.

While Christianity brought a new religious belief system, one with a number of similarities with their traditional religion, it contrasted with traditional religion in that men, women, and children are allowed to worship in Christian churches. Women were no longer excluded from religious practices as they had been under their traditional religion. Thus Christianity raised the status of women in comparison to their status under traditional religion.

Christian missionaries also brought innovations, such as carpentry, building with mud blocks, high-grade cheap salt, productive trees such as citrus, and hog rearing. These innovations helped the Bajju economically. The colonialists brought ginger growing and dry rice cultivation.

The work of Christian missionaries pointed to the hope that things could be different, that there were ways of responding to the oppression that they were under, and that they as a people had worth before God. One Christian said, "Without missionaries where would we be? We'd be the poorest of the poor."

Bajju conversion began among the young men, but gradually the entire society converted. In 1929 the first conversions occurred, and today almost one hundred percent of the Bajju are Christians. This is amazingly rapid religious change. According to missiologists, a people movement to Christ occurred. Churches tend to be full each Sunday and church meetings are common.

Religious factors are also prominent in Kunhiyop's study of Bajju Christian conversion. Among young Christian converts, he found that "Bajju converts would point out a definite time of unbelief or rebellion and change of religion" (2005:131). Second, "their conversion brought about a clear break with the past and marked a new life-style" (2005:132). Third, "all these converts acknowledged that their conversion happened when they placed their faith in Jesus Christ" (2005:132). Fourth, their conversion was the result of the preaching of an evangelist, a pastor, or a Christian relative who witnessed to them. Church service, a revival meeting, or watching a movie were listed as the most important places where these converts heard the gospel. The story of Nicodemus (John 3) and the story of the rich man and Lazarus were some of the themes mostly preached about at these meetings. A popular movie titled *The Burning Hell*, which recounted a similar story as that of the rich man and Lazarus, played a significant role in the conversion of these converts (2005:133).

In exploring who influenced an individual to convert, I found that the father has the greatest influence on an individual's conversion to Christianity, while the mother has less influence. This is understandable, given that this is a patrilineal society. Women marry into extended families but retain membership in their fathers' patrilineages and are never fully incorporated into the lineages of their husbands. However, in the 2009 sample respondents often listed both their mother and father.

There were also some major additions to their religious traditions that Christianity brought to the Bajju that do not have parallels in their traditional religion. These include the following:

1. Belief in Jesus as the Messiah (John 4:25–26)
2. Belief in the Savior and his salvation (Psalm 27:1, John 4:42, 1 Thessalonians 5:9, Hebrews 2:3, and Revelation 19:1)
3. Belief in the Holy Spirit (John 14:15–18, Acts 2:1–12)
4. Belief in Satan, the devil (Revelation 12:7–9; 1 John 3:8)
5. Belief in hell (Matthew 5:22, 29; Luke 12:5)
6. Belief in angels (Psalm 91:11; Numbers 22:23)

Political factors affecting Christian conversion

When beginning this study on Bajju religious change, I hypothesized that Bajju Christian conversion would largely be in reaction to Islam, the religion of the Hausa and Fulani, because of the oppression that they had experienced by representatives of the emirates. However, when asked, political reasons did not play a major role in individuals' Christian conversion as indicated in their responses above. However, if viewed from a macro-political level, their actions were certainly in opposition to their oppressors.

In their local political structure, they had a series of oaths that were used to deal with problems within the community. When Christianity came, the taking oaths changed. They considered the biblical text of Matthew 5:34 in which Jesus told his disciples "Do not swear at all: either by heaven, for it is God's throne; or by the earth, for it is his footstool; or by Jerusalem, for it is the city of the Great King." Bajju Christians take this admonition seriously. After reading this verse, many Christians refuse to take oaths. Hence the assertion 'It is true', *kạryong ạmi*, came into widespread use due to the influence of Christianity.

Christian churches among the Bajju are often used to resolve conflict within the community. This conforms with Bajju tradition in that the *gado* had both religious and political functions within the community. In some ways pastors now have both functions. Following a church service, a pastor may ask his congregation to stay in order to deal with some problem within the community. People recognize the authority of his office and expect him to do so.

Churches began to have political functions when they were first established by missionaries. Churches punished men for taking a second or subsequent wife, for drinking, for chewing kola nuts, for becoming a horn blower when the circumstances involved the traditional religion, for taking part in the *ạbvoi*, etc. They similarly punished women for being second or subsequent wives. They were not allowed to wear the cloth of the women's group within the church. Although some of these breaches can be viewed as moral issues within the community, the punishments the churches meted out included forbidding a man from attending church for a specified period of time, such as six months. Such men were not allowed to hold positions within the church or to receive communion. These punishments stigmatized people and can be viewed as political in nature.

Further, the fact that the other major religion in northern Nigeria, Islam, does not distinguish between religion and politics forces Christians to do likewise. Not to do so would put Christians at a distinct disadvantage. The concept of a separation of church and state is not applicable in the situation the Bajju find themselves in, though some missionaries advocated this separation. This position reflects their home culture more than a local Christian perspective.

Social factors affecting Christian conversion

There is a major contrast between Bajju traditional social organization and Christianity in terms of the status of women. Most Bajju women are very involved in churches today, while all women were excluded from the practices of *ạbvoi*, other than to provide cooked food for the men. Women were not allowed to enter the *ạbvoi* shrine. They were actively discriminated against, while Christianity welcomes them into Christian churches. Women have found that Christianity liberates them from their treatment under Bajju traditional religion.

Language factors affecting Christian conversion

The language used within the men's *ạbvoi* organization was Jju. This contrasts with the language used in Christian contexts, namely Hausa. When missionaries first went into minority areas in northern Nigeria, they began learning local languages and translating the Bible into those languages. Missionary language policy changed in 1934 when the entire Hausa Bible became available, which became the primary resource used in Christian practice in minority language areas in northern Nigeria. Those missionaries who had learned to speak a local language were now required by their missions to use only Hausa. Missionaries set up vernacular (Hausa) Bible schools to train Christian pastors. Because their training has been in Hausa, pastors continue to use Hausa in Christian contexts. It is what they are trained to use even if many in their congregations do not speak it or speak it very poorly.

In 1968 one missionary told my husband and me that the Bajju were without excuse for not understanding and accepting the gospel of Jesus Christ as it had been preached throughout their area in Hausa. The problem with his argument was that at the time he said this, over 4.5% of the Bajju were monolingual in Jju and over 60% said that they spoke Hausa at the market level or less. There clearly was a disconnect between that missionary's perception of the language situation and what was happening within the villages. However, missionaries and some Christian leaders commonly assert that "everyone knows Hausa."

There were various reasons why missionaries chose to use Hausa. First, they felt that it was asking too much for local Christians to learn more than two languages; their own language and Hausa were sufficient. Second, if all Christians knew Hausa, there would be a unity of all believers as Christians. Third, they could move missionaries between different mission stations, and they would be able to minister at each place immediately without having to learn another language. Fourth, they viewed Hausa as the lingua franca in the area and assumed that everyone knew it. Fifth, if there are speakers of several languages present, the use of one language allows all to hear the Christian message. Sixth, the Hausa Bible was available for evangelism.

One legacy of the missionary era is that Hausa continues as the language of the church. Since missionaries learned Hausa, they failed to understand the questions the traditional religious belief systems addressed. Missionaries asked converts to leave the old things of darkness and follow God, but they rarely addressed what those old things of darkness were in the light of a biblical perspective. They knew the answer, namely Christ, but they did not know the questions the local population was dealing with. The result of this oversight is that Bajju traditional religious beliefs coexist with Christianity. The traditional religion answers one set of questions and Christianity addresses a different set. Turaki summarized this issue as follows:

> Anyone introducing a new religion needs to be aware that the traditional religious system will persist if a new religion fails to both address and assuage the same social and psychological needs as the older religion. To introduce a new

religion effectively, it requires knowledge of the theological foundations of the traditional religious system and also knowledge of how to apply the message of the new religion to meet the social and psychological needs of the individuals and communities. This applies in Africa regardless of whether the new beliefs being introduced are those of Christianity, Islam, or modernism. (2006:19)

Since the church language is Hausa and traditional religious beliefs are articulated in local languages, those issues are rarely addressed in church, even in situations where all the people who attend a church speak as their first language a language other than Hausa.

A major factor that motivated some people to convert to Christianity was their desire to learn to read and write. Kunhiyop states, "Nearly all early converts interviewed indicated that the interest to read and write was a major motivation to Christian conversion" (2005:120). Being literate opens opportunities that are not available for those who are illiterate.

Questions to be answered

By and large early missionaries to this area did not study the traditional religion or teach a biblical perspective on those traditional religious beliefs. Kunhiyop observed that:

Many Bajju Christians indicate ignorance on Scriptural truths and how they apply to their lives in different situations. Though the interviews indicate that early converts were enthusiastic about their faith and attempted to apply their faith in every situation, very little was done by early missionaries to interact with Bajju traditional beliefs and practices.... Apart from the superficial condemnations, Christianity really had little to say about African traditional religion in the way of serious judgments of value. Consequently, old beliefs and customs did not die out. Because they were not consciously dealt with, they went underground. So these ways became part of the new "Christians" hidden culture. (2005:148)

If Christianity is to foster people's growth in Christ, it must address the same questions traditional religion asks, questions such as: Why do people suffer evil, misfortune, illness, and death? What causes evil? Is it caused by *nkut*? What does the Bible say about *nkut* or does it even address *nkut*? Can one's spirit leave one's body at night to meet with other spirits in the spiritual realm to cause significant problems for others in the physical realm? Does a demon enter the body of an individual such that that individual practices *nkut*? What is the difference between traditional beliefs in reincarnation and the Christian belief in being born again? Why do babies continue to die? Is the spirit world calling those babies back, who are then reborn? What is the role of the ancestors within Christianity as opposed to their roles within traditional religion? Can the ancestors speak to people through dreams? What are the differences or similarities between their traditional concept of an underground world (*ayabyen*) and heaven?

Some local Christians have addressed some of these issues. For example, Kaburuk wrote on marriage (1976), and Kunhiyop addressed the questions of why people become ill, die, suffer misfortune, and evil from a biblical perspective (1988). Kunhiyop also wrote on the spiritual reasons for Bajju Christian conversion (2005). Asake looked at the biblical perspective of leadership versus the traditional concepts of leadership (1998). While not dealing specifically with Christian conversion in southern Kaduna State, Turaki studied how the colonial administration institutionalized the inferior status of the minority people of this area (1982). His study outlines the context within which Christianity thrived in this area. There are other local scholars as well. Educated Christians are well aware that in order to bring people to Christ it is necessary to understand their traditional religious beliefs, yet pastors continue to minister solely in Hausa and largely do not address these issues.

Local efforts at Bible translation also point out that to reach people with the gospel it is important that they have the Scriptures in their indigenous languages. In 1984 the Jju New Testament was dedicated. The day of its launching, Bajju Day, is celebrated annually on or around May 24. The Bajju Language and Translation Association is continuing the task of translation from its office at Zonkwa. They have the entire Old Testament drafted, with some books consultant-checked, and they are busy revising the New Testament. Their goal is to have the entire Bible in Jju. At the same time, Scripture use and reading in Jju are limited.

The Atyap people have completed the Tyap New Testament. The Gwong (Kagoma) also have a translation project in progress as do the Ham (Jaba) people. Translation work continues in various other minority languages in the area.

Today the Bajju area is largely multilingual with Jju, English, and Hausa spoken. The language of the home continues to be Jju in most cases, though in some areas children have asked their parents to speak to them in English rather than in Jju. In many cases their parents have complied, though some now recognize that by doing so their children are not speaking the local language or speak it very poorly. Jju continues as the primary language of the home. It seems incongruous that Hausa is used at church, even when the entire congregation is composed of Jju speakers, the pastor is Bajju, and people speak Jju at home.

When asked why the young people are not learning Jju, people suggested several answers. First, there is the widespread use of information technology, which largely uses English. Second, English is the language of education as well as the official language. Third, there is the pernicious spread of Hausa.

Today the church has been indigenized with Bajju pastors and leaders in local churches, Christian seminaries, Bible schools, and national Christian leadership positions. Further, the culture in general has changed. Modern conveniences such as cell phones are now ubiquitous, and people rely on cars, taxies, motorcycles, and bicycles. Roadside stands where people sell multiple commodities are found throughout the area.

Education is highly valued. The expectation is that children will attend school and become educated. They pursue education as far as they are able, with many receiving their BA, MA, and PhD degrees both from universities in Nigeria and from universities in various countries throughout the world.

The Bajju have entered the twenty-first century, and the effects of globalization are plainly visible in the area. Their Christian commitment allows them to be part of the worldwide Christian and secular communities.

Appendix A

Villages with Churches
among the Bajju

Representatives of the several denominations active in Kajju have reported the following to be villages in Kajju and neighboring areas with churches of that denomination that have Bajju people as major attendees. While this listing includes most churches in the Bajju home area, new churches continue to be built, so I make no claim that this listing includes all churches in the Bajju home area.

The denominations that have churches in more villages represent those that have been in the Bajju area for a long time. In the following list, denominations are listed in alphabetical order.

Anglican (CMS) Churches

Abet	Katssik Unguwar Sarki
Abodari	Katssik Unguwar Zamani
Afana Daji	Kurdan
Afana Gida	Kurdan Daji
Assako	Kurmin Baba
Ayagan	Kurmin Sara
Aziho	Kwagiri
Boro	Madakiya
Cenccuk	Pan Zakki

Fadan Kaje   Rikawan
Farman Dutse   Sakwak Daji
Farman Gida   Sakwak Gurio (2 churches)
Gumel   Tsohon Gida
Kamaru Station   Tsoryang
Kanem   Unguwar Rimi
Kankada   Zauru
Katssik Bakin Kogi   Zonkwa
Katssik Sabon Gari   Zitrung Pama

Apostolic Church

Zonkwa

Assembly of God Churches

Afana (2 churches)
Katssik
Madakiya
Unguwar Rimi
Zonkwa

Baptist Churches

Azansak (Madauci)   Kankada
Atacap (Bakin Kogi)   Madakiya
Bebyet (Abet) (2 churches)   Marsa
Cenccuk Karyi   Sakwak
Kamaru Station   Unguwar Rimi
Kamrum   Zitrung (2 churches)
Kurdan   Zonkwa (2 churches)

Celestial Church

Zonkwa

Cherubim and Seraphim Churches

Abet   Dihogwei
Abet Daniel   Farman
Abvan Karyi   Furgyem (Ayagan)
Adom (Madakiya)   Jei
Akudan   Jei Karyi

Aribvon
A̱rika̱wan
Atat
Azakwa
Bebyet Azonkwa
Bebyet Jatau
Bagwa Loko
Bvonkpang
Byena

Jei Gida
Kamrum
Kanshwa
Madakiya Station
Madobya (near Tsoryang)
Marsa
Unguwar Rimi
Zatsak
Zitrung

Church of Christ in Nigeria

Zonkwa

Christian Redeemed

Madakiya
Zonkwa

Deeper Life

Dihwan
Madakiya
Zonkwa

Evangelical Church Winning All (formerly, Evangelical Church of West Africa)

A̱dwan
Akudan (Zauru)
A̱rika̱wan
A̱tacap (Bakin Kogi)
Ayagan
Bebyet (Abet)
Byena (Afana)
Cenccuk Karyi
Dihogwei (Fadan Kaje)
Dihwan Jjim (Farman)
Jei (Fadiya Gida)
Jei (Fadiya Tudan Wada)
Kamarum
Kamuru Station
Kanshwa (Tsohon Gida)

Katssik
Kpunyai
Kurmin Baba
Madakiya
Marsa Daji
Marsa Gida
Madauchi
Sakwak
Tsoryang
Unguwar Rimi
Yaribuwan
Zitrung Gida
Zitrung Tudan
Zonkwa (3 churches)

Grace of God Church

Zonkwa
Kafanchan

Jehovah's Witnesses

Zonkwa

Living Faith

A̱dwan
Kafanchan
Zonkwa

Methodist Churches

A̱dwan	Madakiya (2 churches)
Afana	Madobiya
A̱ka̱don	Marsa
Kachia	Zitrung
Kamuru Station	Zonkwa

Redeemed Church

Madakiya
Zonkwa

Roman Catholic Churches

Abet	Katssik Gida
Adwan	Kpunyai
Afana	Kurmin Baba
Bayindusi	Kurmin Mazuga
Cenccuk Kayit	Mafo Fadi
Dibyyi (Kurmin Bi)	Marsa Daji
Dihwan Jjim (Farman)	Marsa Gida
Fadan Kaje	Rufin Juma
Furgyem (Ayagan)	Tsoryang
Jei (Fadiya) (3 churches)	Unguwar Rimi
Kafom	Zagom
Kamaru Station	Zauru (2 churches)

Kamrum

Kanyem Daji

Kanyem Gida

Katssik Daji

Ziti (Ayagan)

Zitrung (2 churches)

Zonkwa (3 churches)

Seventh-day Adventist

Unguwar Rimi

First African Church Mission Inc.
(formerly, the United Native African Churches)

Abet (2 churches)

Adwan (2 churches)

Akudan

Arikawan

Atsotsun (Bankwa, H.; Ayagan)

Byena

Cenccuk

Dihwan Jjim

Gumel

Kamarsa

Kanyem

Katssik

Kurmin Baba

Madakiya

Unguwam Kpaa

Unguwar Rimi

Zagom

Zitrung Karyi

Zitrung Kpang (Zitrung Fama)

Zonkwa (2 churches)

Appendix B

Interview Schedule

Date_____

Place_____

Will you answer some questions about your choice of religion and religious beliefs? Yes _____ No _____

Please fill in only one form per person. Be truthful in your answers.

1. Year of birth (*Anzan dirya ba na byin?*) _____

2. Your approximate age (*Za mang a yet?*) _____

3. Sex: Male (*Antyok*) _____   Female (*Arembyring*) _____

4. Current marital status:

<table>
<tr><th>Man (Antyok)</th><th>Woman (Arembyring)</th></tr>
<tr><td>Married (nyreng)</td><td>Married (nyreng)</td></tr>
<tr><td>Single (kaseyang)</td><td>Single (kaneyang)</td></tr>
<tr><td>Widowed (akpatyok)</td><td>Widowed (antyok u a kan kwu)</td></tr>
<tr><td></td><td>Inherited (assak ambyring)</td></tr>
<tr><td>Divorced (tyet nyreng)</td><td>Divorced (tyet nyreng)</td></tr>
</table>

How many times have you been married? (*A kan bvwa banyreng ba mang?*)	How many times have you been married? (*A kan bvwa banyreng ba mang?*)

5. How many wives do you have? (*A shyi bu banyreng ba mang?*) _____

    How many wives does your husband have?
(*Antyok nwan a shyi bu banyreng ba mang?*) _____

6. What is your home village? (*Kankrang nwan ka?*) _____

7. Your wife or husband's home village?
(*Kankrang ambyring/antyok nwan ka?*) _____

8. How many children do you have? (*Nawon na mang a shyi mi?*) _____

9. How many of your children are still living?
(*Nawon na mang an shyi acet?*) _____

10. Do you have a child born between the following dates?

	1 July 2005–30 June 2006		1 July 2004–30 June 2005		1 July 2003–30 June 2004	
	Living (*ashyi acet*)	Dead (*a kwu*)	Living (*ashyi acet*)	Dead (*a kwu*)	Living (*ashyi acet*)	Dead (*a kwu*)
Boy (*Kaseyang*)						
Girl (*Kaneyang*)						

11. How many of your children are 4 years or younger?
(*Nawon na mang nwan a tat arya apfun ba'?*) _____

12. Occupation (*Pfong*):

Farmer (*Akeyak*)	_____	Trader (*Azzap nkyang*)	_____
Pastor (*Pasto*)	_____	Teacher (*Azzek*)	_____
Blacksmith (*Apfu*)	_____	Student (*Kawon myyam*)	_____
Nurse (*Abrang likita*)	_____	Doctor (*Likita*)	_____
Traditional doctor (*Abvok*)	_____	Traditional priest (*Gado*)	_____
Chief (*Agwam*)		Carpenter (*Kafinta*)	_____
Tailor (*Atywei batro*)		Soldier (*Soja*)	_____
Housework (*Pfong karyi*)	_____		

Other (specify)
(*Bạnyet npfong zan; ạnzan pfong?*)

13. Education (*Bvwo*)

	Completed (*A tyak myyam a*)	Not completed. How many years completed? (*A tyak ba'. Za mang a tyak?*)
Primary		
Teachers College		
Advanced Teachers College		
Secondary		
Bible school		
Seminary		
Technical school		
Agricultural school		
University (What degree?)		
Other (*Ạnzan*)		

14. Did you attend a mission/church school?
(*A yin yya makaranta mission o?*) Yes (*Ee*) _____ No (*Kai*) _____

15. How much education did your father complete?
(*Ạnzan makaranta ạtyyi nwan na tyak?*) _____

16. Did your father attend a mission school?
(*Ạtyyi nwan ạ yin yya makaranta mission o?*)
Yes (*Ee*) _____No (*Kai*) _____

17. How much education did your mother complete?
(*Ạnzan makaranta ạna nwan na tyak?*) _____

18. Did your mother attend a mission school?
(*Ạnaa nwan ạ yin yya makaranta mission o?*)
Yes (*Ee*) _____ No (*Kai*) _____

19. What further education do you plan to take?
(*A cat myyam kyang yaan o?*)

20.   What is your clan? (*Sot nwan ji hwa?*)_____

21.   Economic status (*Zwa nwan ji/Zwa antyok nwan ji?*)

House (*A byyi karyi?*)	_____	Grain (*A byyi, yak ya na na*_____ *maai tyak dirya ni?*)	
Bicycle (*Akeke*)	_____	Cow(s) (*Nyak mang?*)	_____
Motorcycle	_____	Computer	_____
Radio	_____	Car (*Mato*)	_____
Goats (*Bvon mang*)	_____	Refrigerator	_____
Television (TV) ____	_____	Cell phone	_____
Computer	_____	Camera	_____
Digital camera	_____	Video camera	_____

22.   Your father's wealth (*Zwa ji atyyi nwan nu na byyi ni*)

Rich (*A byyi zwa bagangang*) _____
Sufficient but not rich (*A byyi a maai maai*) _____
Poor (*A byyi bacincong*) _____

23.   What language(s) do you speak? (*Anzan nwap ryat?*)

	Jju	*Kpat* (Hausa)	*Shong* (English)
Home (*Karyi*)			
Church (*Coc*)			
Work (*Pfong*)			
Market (*Tunga*)			

24.   How well do you speak? (*Anzan nwap a ryat ansham?*)

	Jju	*Kpat* (Hausa)	*Shong* (English)
Very well (*Batsutswat*)			
Well (*Ansham*)			
Well enough to use in the market (*Bvwo maai maai si sak ju nin dyat a kasuwa ni*)			
Hear a little (*Bacincong*)			
None (*A hok ba'*)			

	Yes (*Ee*)	No (*Kai*)
25. Are you a Christian? (*A yet antyok tssup o?*)	_____	_____
Are you a Muslim? (*A yet antyok tswa katassi?*)	_____	_____

Are you a traditional religionist?
(*A tssup naai Kaza da batyyi nwan ba?*)   _____   _____

26. What year did you become a Christian/Muslim?   _____
    (*Anzan za a nwa tssup a?*)

27. Why did you become a Christian?
    (*Anzan an byyi a yin nwwa tssup a?*)

28. Why are you not a Christian?
    (*Anzan an byyi a yet antyok tssup ba'?*)

29. Why did you become a Christian rather than a Muslim?
    (*Rot anzan an tssup Yesu, amma a rak tswa katassi ka?*)

30. Who is Jesus Christ? (*Anyan a yet Yesu Kristi?*)

31. If you are a Christian, what church do you attend?
    (*Ka a yet antyok tssup, anzan darik a cong?*)

Anglican (*CMS*)	_____	Methodist (*Methodis*)	_____
Apostolic	_____	Baptist	_____
Roman Catholic (*Roman*)	_____	United African (*Africa*)	_____
ECWA	_____	Cherubim & Seraphim (*Sarafu*)	_____
Assembly of God	_____	Other (*Anzan?*)	_____

32. Why did you choose that church? (*Anzan a byyi an tssa darika ayyu?*)

33. Did you attend another denomination before going to that one?
    (*A kan cong darika ayaan o?*) Yes (*Ee*) _____ No (*Kai*) _____

    If yes, which one did you attend, and why did you change?
    (*Ku a kan cong darika ayaan, anzan darika a yin cong?*
    Rot anzan a yin shei?)   _____

34. Is or was your father a Christian?
    (*Atyyi nwan nu a (yin) yet antyok tssup o?*)
    Yes (*Ee*) _____ No (*Kai*) _____

35. Is or was your mother a Christian?
    (*Ana nwan nu a (yin) yet antyok tssup o?*)
    Yes (*Ee*) _____ No (*Kai*) _____

36. Is the pastor of the church you attend Bajju?
    (*Pasto coc u a cong ni a yet antyok Bajju o?*)
    Yes (*Ee*) _____ No (*Kai*) _____

37. Do all the people in your house attend the same church?
(*Sarei banyet kayat karyi nwan ka a cong darika yring o?*)
Yes (*Ee*) _____ No (*Kai*) _____

38. What church do they attend? (*Anzan darika ba cong?*) _____

39. Have you been baptized (*Ba kan na yya baptisma?*)
Yes (*Ee*) _____ No (*Kai*) _____

40. When you first heard about Christianity, was it presented in what language?
(*Karam ka a yin hok baryat tssup ba ni, a yen hok zen ...?*)

   Jju _____   *Kpat* _____   *Shong* _____

41. Who led you to become a Christian? (*Anyan a yin na brang a san Yesu?*)
Pastor (*Pasto*) _____ Missionary (*Bashong*) _____
Mother (*Anaa*) _____ Father (*Atyyi*) _____
Your child (*Kawon nwan*) _____ Another person (Specify)_____
                     (*Anyan?*)

42. How often do you attend church? (*A cong naai Kaza anzan karam o?*)
Daily (*Kozan katuk*) _____ Weekly (*Kozan sati*) _____
Once a month (*Krang _____ Seldom (*A nat tityen o?*) _____
kayring a hywan o?*)
Only on holidays (*Bu _____ Never (*A cong ba'*) _____
karam pfuwi o?*)

43. Do you attend (*A cong...*)

	Yes (*Ee*)	No (*Kai*)
Women's fellowship (*Zumunta banrying*)	_____	_____
Men's fellowship (*Zumunta bantyok*)	_____	_____

44. Is your husband/wife a Christian?
(*Antyok nwan/ambyring nwan a yet antyok tssup o?*)
Yes (*Ee*) _____ No (*Kai*) _____

45. What church does your husband/wife attend?
(*Anzan darika antyok nwan/ambyring nwan na cong?*) _____

46. When you die, where will you go after death?
    (*Kąram ka an kwu ni, ąnzan kąret a ni nat?*)
    Yabyen _____   Tazwa ko Kąryi Kąza _____

47. Did you have a dream that influenced you to become a Christian?
    (*Bązzak tazwa tssup Yesu a yin na brang kąram ka a yin san Yesu nee?*)
    Yes (*Ee*) _____ No (*Kai*) _____

48. Do your ancestors occasionally speak to you through dreams?
    (*Bąnyet nwan ba ą kan kwi ni a na ryat ba nwan I bązzak o?*)
    Yes (*Ee*) _____ No (*Kai*) _____

49. Do you pray to God through your ancestors?
    (*Kąram ka an shyi naai Kąza ni, a na naai kąyat diyrek bątyyi nwan ba
    ą kan kwi nee?*)
    Yes (*Ee*) _____   No (*Kai*) _____

50. Can people die from *nkut*? (*Bąnyet ba kwi rot nkut o?*)
    Yes (*Ee*) _____   No (*Kai*) _____

51. If a person dies, can he be reborn?
    (*Ką ąnyin a kwu, ą bo ni brek ba ku byin brak o?*)

	Yes (*Ee*)	**No (*Kai*)**	**Don't know (*A bvwo ba'*)**
Old person (*Ąkukwo ąyin o?*)	_____	_____	_____
Youth (*Hwwung o?*)	_____	_____	_____
Baby (*Kąbawon o?*)	_____	_____	_____

52. Do you drink wine? (*A sswa nkwa na?*) Yes (*Ee*) _____   No (Kai) _____

53. Were any of your relatives taken into slavery?
    (*Bąnyet nwan a yin shyi kąyat bąnyet ka ba yin pyyem dikwwa ti nee?*)
    Yes (*Ee*) _____ No (*Kai*) _____ Don't know (*A bvwo ba'*) _____

54. Who caught them? (*Bąnzan a yin bą pyyem?*) _____

55. How were they caught? (*Ba yin bą pyyem ni?*) _____

56. Do you know where they were taken or what happened to them?
    (*A bvwo kąbvwa ka ba yin nat ba mba nee, bu kyang a yin ba shya nee?*)

Questions for older women only:
57.   Is your life better now as a Christian than it was before you became a
      Yes (*Ee*) _____   No (*Kai*) _____

58.   If it is better, in what ways is it better?

Appendix C

Jju–English Glossary

Glossary abbreviations

adj.	adjective	NP	noun phrase
adv.	adverb	pl.	plural noun; multiple action verb
H.	Hausa		
J.	Jju	sing.	singular noun; single action verb
L.	Latin		
lit.	literally	v.	verb
n.	noun	VP	verb phrase

Abrak, n. Name meaning 'he has returned'; name given a person who is reincarnated.

abvoi/abvwoi/abwei/bvai, sing.; _babvoi,_ pl., n. (1) Men's secret ancestral organization. It was celebrated at the end of March and early April. This well-organized religious system was led by men, through which they spoke to and governed the community. Young men were initiated into this organization when the older men thought they were ready. The Bajju have officially renounced this traditional men's ancestral organization because they adopted Christianity, and because of some of the negative practices of this society, which became burdensome. (2) An ancestral spirit. (3) _Abvoi_ Name given to an infant boy born when this ancestral organization was celebrating.

abvok, sing.; *babvok,* pl. n. (1) Diviner who was clairvoyant and on occasion could become spirit-possessed in order to ascertain the cause of and solution to some problem within the community. (2) Medical practitioner, both traditional and modern; Bajju doctor; seer; prophet; healer-diviner. Such persons were able both to see the ultimate cause of an illness or problem, and to treat illnesses through herbal medicines. They were also consulted before some activities, such as hunts and war. They used a variety of means, including throwing rocks or cowries to foresee the outcome of an activity. (3) Sorcerer, sorceress.

aconcong, sing.; *baconcong,* pl., n. Water spirit that lives in clear still water, as well as in the bush, in trees, in a forest, or in caves.

agwam, sing.; *bagwam,* pl.; H. *sarki,* n. Chief, king, derived from the English word *govern.*

akinkyim, sing.; *bakinkyim,* pl., n. Clay pot drum that comes in various sizes, some so large that they are set on the floor while played. These are women's instruments usually played in church and other Christian contexts.

akwwa, sing.; *bakwwa,* pl., n. Slave.

aladura, n. One who prays; from *dura,* Arabic, 'to pray'.

alhaji, H., n. Title for a Muslim man who has made a pilgrimage to Mecca, Saudi Arabia.

Anaa Kaza, NP. Mother of God.

aninyet, sing.; *baninyet,* pl., n. Tall spirit.

arne, sing.; *arna,* pl.; H., n. Pagan.

ashong, n. (1) Color red. (2) White person.

ayabyen, n. Underground world where the ancestors reside; residence for those who fulfill their roles in society following death; world of ancestral spirits; the afterlife.

Bakpat, n. Hausa people.

Baryat abrak, NP. Name meaning 'the words are lost'.

bvori, n.; H. *bori,* Spirit-possession cult, which received its name from the village of Bori in northern Benin.

dagaci, H., n. Village head, area chief.

eyecen, ayecen, sing.; *bayecen,* pl., n. Visitor, stranger, guest.

fansa, H., n. Ransom, redemption of someone from slavery. In precolonial days this consisted of a number of cowries paid to redeem a person taken as a slave.

gado, sing.; *bagado,* pl., n. (1) Respected elder, ruling elder, priest; religious, political, and jural leader. (2) Custom.

gajimale, n. Spirit that lives in clear still pools of water, in trees, bushes, caves, or under mountains. It can also reside in one's room. It can appear as a beautiful woman to a man or as a handsome man to a woman. While it can transform itself, it cannot transform its toes, which are like those of horse hooves. The Bajju believe that to see one can cause blindness.

Ham, n. Ethnic group located south of the Bajju, also known as the Jaba. They speak the Hyam language.

hakimi, H., District head.

hong, n. White person.

jekadu, H., n. Overseer.

jihad, H., n. Struggle, a struggle to purify Islam, a holy war in the name of Allah.

jizya, H., n. Payment made for protection by non-Muslims who live in the territory conquered by Muslims.

kadak, n. Garden in the area adjacent to the compound, where women farm broad beans, sponges, various greens, tomatoes, okra, and other plants for sauces.

karam azumi, NP. Time of fasting.

karyi, n. House; household, compound.

karyi Kaza, NP. God's house, heaven.

karyong ami, NP. 'It is true', an oath taken to assert that what one says is the truth.

katanyrang, sing.; *natenyrang,* pl., n. (1) Small white or black spirits that are invisible to everyone but diviners. They do not like loud noises or light. They tend to surround their villages with thorn bushes. After they have abandoned a village, anyone can see their abandoned houses. When white people first came to this area, they were identified as white spirits. Wicked spirits are thought to be short with big heads. Since they are invisible, people may inadvertently step on them or their children. They then retaliate by inflicting paralysis and other problems on one's legs, severe fevers, mental illness, or epilepsy on people. (2) Satan.

Kaza, n. (1) God, Supreme Being. (2) *kaza.* Up, tall, above. (3) North. (4) Name given an infant son as a shortened form of 'God sees them'. It refers to someone practicing *nkut* against a woman, but she conceived and bore a son in spite of *nkut.*

Kuyambana, H., n. Lit., 'The one responsible for worthless people', the military officer in charge of a heavily armed cavalry used to collect slaves.

Kpat, n. (1) Hausa language. (2) Sound of a slap.

lidifi, H., n. (1) Heavily armed cavalry. (2) Quilting for cavalry horses worn for protection.

ma'aji, H., n. (1) Treasurer. (2) Store.

magaji, H., n. Leader, official position.

makaranta, n. (1) School. (2) Church.

nkut, n. (1) Spiritual power used to harm or protect, the power of medicine and witchcraft. Those believed to practice *nkut* may be accused of causing in the spiritual realm physical illness, misfortune, evil, or death of another individual. It is an innate inherited spiritual capacity that an individual has in which his or her spirit leaves the body, meets with other witches in the spiritual realm resulting in problems for other people in the physical realm. Children are told to close their witchcraft eyes so that they do not harm others. The Bajju distinguish two types: *atsatsak nkut,* 'good protective witchcraft', and *abibyyi nkut,* 'evil witchcraft'. (2) Evil person. (3) Name given an infant boy so that an evil spirit's power cannot hurt him. The logic is that if he is already *nkut,* no further *nkut* can harm him.

nkwwa, n.; H. *bukutu,* n. Guinea corn beer.

pfong, n. Work.

riga, H., n. Gown worn by men.

Ruhu, H., n. Spirit.

rumada, rinji, H., n. (1) Slave village, slave camp. (2) Slave living near his master's village.

samame, H., n. Raiding.

shugaba, sing.; *shugabanni,* pl., H., Leader, as a local church leader

sswa batwak, VP. To swear an oath on ashes; lit., 'to drink ashes', 'to repent', 'to lick ashes'; repentance. This was a means of retracting an oath. It is a means of repenting from one's acts or words or from one's ancestor's words or actions.

tazwa, n. Up, heaven.

tunga, n. Market.

wabi, H., n. An affliction a woman may have whose young infants continue to die one after the other.

wakili, H., n. Representative.

yan kasa, H., NP. Sons of the land.

Yesu, n. Jesus.

zango, zangon, H., n. (1) Camping place used by traders along a caravan route. (2) Walled enclave maintained in the territory of another ethnic group. (3) Ward of a village or town.

Appendix D

Archival References from the National Archives of Kaduna (NAK)

Archive abbreviations

ACC	Agency Number
JEMAA	Jemaa Division
JOSPROF	Jos Province
NAK	National Archives Kaduna
SNP.	Secretary to the Northern Provinces
ZARPROF	Zaria Province

1. National Archives material

List	Acc. No	Title	Year
a. Nassarawa Province			
SNP.	7/2148/1903	Military operations in the South-east of Zaria—Report on.	1903
SNP.	7/2350/1905	Opening up and bringing under control of administration, the Dist. S.E. of Nassarawa and S.W. of Bauchi Provinces.	1905
SNP.	K 2985	Kaje tribe anthropological notes on. 1914.	1914

SNP.	2089	Kaje and Kanikwon—Rising against emir of Jema'a—Attack on emir and Kaje patrol. 1915.	1915
SNP.	208/1918	Gazeteer—Plateau Province.	1918
K4046 SNP.17/8	1121	Pagan subjects under Mohammedan rulers.	

b. Zaria Province

ZARPROF	59/1921	Kajuru District—Administrative Affairs of. 1921.	1921
ZARPROF	264	Zaria-Plateau Provinces—Tribal adjustments between.	
ZARPROF	C 6/1942	Osuman Sokop Kaje	1942
ZARPROF	607	Zangon Katab notes on, Report by Mr. M. V. Spurway.	1932
ZARPROF	873 638		1937
ZARPROF	907	Lere District notes on.	1932
ZARPROF	190 C. 4001	Islamic law as applied to Christians. 1938.	1938
ZARPROF	2944	Roman Catholic mission, Certificates of occupancy at Kankada. Zangon Katab District	1938– 1944
ZARPROF	C 9/1939	(1) Missionary activities (2) Itinerant missionaries (3) Missions leper colonies	1939
ZARPROF	312 9 (also 3316)	Notes by P. F. Brandt, On the social and economic organisation of the tribes in Southern Zaria.	1939
ZARPROF	3456	Usuman Sokop Kaje: Petition by (2) Kaje tribe	
ZARPROF	C 7		1953
ZARPROF	C.8/1946	Zangon Katab District—Unrest in (1946).	1946– 1951
ZARPROF	1554	Pagan administration: NA policy with regard to.	
ZARPROF	1558	Pagan administration—Southern Districts Zaria Emirate.	1933– 1934
ZARPROF	1761	Reorganisation of Southern Zaria anthropological.	
ZARPROF	2083	Kagoro: Proposed boundary adjustment. 1921–50	

c. Jemaa Division

JEMAA   500 265   Religious denominations 1931–40.

2. Nigerian Baptist Mission Archives, Bakin Kogi, Nigeria. Smith, Don and Betty Ann. 1965, Kafanchan Baptist Association. (Typewritten manuscript).

3. Roman Catholic Mission Archives. n.d. Kafanchan Roman Catholic Station Book Kafanchan (Handwritten manuscript).

4. Sudan Interior Mission (SIM) Archives, Scarborough, Ontario. *Africa Now.* 1972, March–April, p. 15.
Archibalds and Kagoro. n.d. (Typewritten manuscript).
Kafanchan. n.d. (Typewritten manuscript).
Larrimore, H.D., the Resident. 2nd November 1912. Letter to Sudan Interior Mission.

References

Abraham, R. C. 1962. *Dictionary of the Hausa language.* Second edition. London: University of London Press.

Abubakar, Sa'ad. 1977. *The Lamibe of Fombina: A political history of Adamawa 1809–1901.* Zaria, Nigeria: Ahmadu Bello University Press.

Adamu, Mahdi. 1978. *The Hausa factor in West African history.* Zaria, Nigeria: Ahmadu Bello University Press.

Adamu, Mahdi. 1979. The delivery of slaves from the Central Sudan to the Bight of Benin in the eighteenth and nineteenth centuries. In Jon S. Hogendorn (ed.), *The uncommon market: Essays in the economic history of the Atlantic slave trade,* 163–180. New York: Academic Press.

Adedeji, Adebayo, and L. Rowland, eds. 1973. *Management problems of rapid urbanisation in Nigeria.* Ile-Ife, Nigeria: University of Ife Press.

Ames, C. G. 1934. *Gazetteers of the northern provinces of Nigeria,* vol. IV, *The highland chieftaincies (Plateau Province),* with a prefatory note by A. H. M. Kirk-Green. Jos, Nigeria: Jos Native Administration. Reprint edition. London: Frank Cass.

Annual reports, Northern Nigeria, 1900–1911.

Asake, Musa Nchock. 1982. Tarihi shigowar bishara a kasar Kaje [History of the Good News among the Kaje]. Kafanchan, Nigeria: Evangelical Church of West Africa.

183

Asake, Musa Nchock. 1998. An exposition of I Timothy 3:1–7 and Titus 1:5–9, with application to Bajju ECWA churches in northern Nigeria. PhD dissertation. Dallas Theological Seminary.

Awóníyì, Timothy A. 1978. *Yoruba language in education, 1846-1974: A historical survey.* Ibadan, Nigeria: Oxford University Press.

Ayandele, E. A. 1966. *The missionary impact on Nigeria, 1842–1914.* London: Oxford University Press.

Ballard, J. A. 1972. Pagan administration and political development in Northern Nigeria. *Savanna* 1:1–14.

Barrett, David B., George T. Kurian, Todd M. Johnson, eds. 2001. *World Christian encyclopedia: A comparative survey of churches and religions in the modern world.* New York: Oxford University Press.

Bayei, Yabo. 1983. *Gan Bajju* [Bajju proverbs]. Jos: Nigerian Bible Translation Trust.

Beacham, C. Gordon.1935. Annual field report for Nigeria and French West Africa, 1934. In *The Sudan Witness,* May–June, 6:1–5.

Besmer, Fremont E. 1983. *Horses, musicians, and gods: The Hausa cult of possession-trance.* South Hadley, MA: Bergin and Garvey.

Boer, Jan Harm. 1979. *Missionary messengers of liberation in a colonial context: A case study of the Sudan United Mission.* Amsterdam: Rodopi.

Cohen, Abner. 1969. *Custom and politics in urban Africa: A study of Hausa migrants in Yoruba towns.* Berkeley: University of California Press.

Crampton, E. P. T. 1975. Christianity in Northern Nigeria. In Ogbu Kalu (ed.), *Christianity in West Africa: The Nigerian story,* 1–237. Ibadan, Nigeria: Daystar.

Crowder, Michael, and Guda Abdullahi. 1979. *Nigeria: An introduction to its history.* London: Longman.

Crowther, Samuel Ajayi. 1842. *Journals of the expedition up the Niger in 1841, with appendices and a map.* London: Hatchard.

Evans-Pritchard, E. E. (1937) 1976. *Witchcraft, oracles and magic among the Azande.* Oxford: Clarendon Press.

Fisher, Allan G. B., and Humphery J. Fisher. 1970. *Slavery and Muslim society in Africa.* Garden City, NY: Doubleday.

Fisher, Humphery J. 1979. Dreams and conversion in Black Africa. In Nehemia Levtzion (ed.), *Conversion to Islam,* 217–235. New York: Holmes and Meier.

Good News Bible. 1966. American Bible Society.

Grimley, John B., and Gordon E. Robinson. 1966. *Church growth in central and southern Nigeria.* Grand Rapids, MI: William Eerdmans.

Gugler, Josef, and William G. Flanagan. 1978. *Urbanization and social change in West Africa.* Cambridge: Cambridge University Press.

Gunn, Harold D. 1956. *Pagan peoples of the central area of northern Nigeria.* London: International African Institute.

Hannerz, Ulf. 1978. Town and country in Southern Zaria: A view from Kafanchan. Unpublished ms.

Hastings, Adrian. 1976. *African Christianity.* New York: Seabury.

Horton, Robin. 1971. African conversion. *Africa* XLI:85–108.

Ikime, Obaro. 1977. *The fall of Nigeria: The British conquest.* London: Heineman.

Isichei, Elizabeth, ed. 1982. *Studies in the history of Plateau State, Nigeria.* London: MacMillan.

Johnson, Todd M., David B. Barrett, and Peter F. Crossing. 2012. Christianity 2012: The 200th anniversary of American foreign missions. In *International Bulletin of Missionary Research,* 36(1):28–29.

Kaburuk, Chidawa. 1976. Polygyny in the Old Testament and the church in Africa. S.T.M. thesis. Dallas Theological Seminary.

Kaburuk, Chidawa. 2014. *Prisoners of faith and hope.* Zonkwa, Nigeria: Jju Language and Bible Association.

Katekism b'umi Oeliem n Gworok. 1952.

Kato, Marcus. 1974. A study of traditional social organization among the Kaje with reference to social change during the recent past. MA thesis. Ahmadu Bello University, Zaria, Nigeria.

Kirk-Greene, A. H. M. 1966. Introduction. In Sophia Graham (ed.), *Government and mission education in Northern Nigeria 1900–1919 with special reference to the work of Hanns Vischer.* Ibadan, Nigeria: Ibadan University Press.

Koelle. 1963. *Polyglotta Africana,* reprint. Quoted in Isichei (ed.), 1982:39.

Kunhiyop, Samuel Waje. 1988. Developing the Christian core among the Bajju with special application to the belief in *nkut.* MA thesis. Western Conservative Baptist Seminary, Portland, OR.

Kunhiyop, Samuel Waje. 1993. A theological analysis of Bajju conversion to Christianity. PhD dissertation. Trinity Evangelical Divinity School, Deerfield, IL.

Kunhiyop, Samuel Waje. 2005. *Christian conversion in Africa: The Bajju experience.* Jos, Nigeria: ECWA Productions.

Lovejoy, Paul E. 1983. *Transformations in slavery: A history of slavery in Africa.* Cambridge: Cambridge University Press.

Lovejoy, Paul E., and Jan S. Hogendorn. 1993. *Slow death for slavery: The course of abolition in northern Nigeria, 1897–1936.* Cambridge: Cambridge University Press.

Lugard, Frederick D. 1926. *The dual mandate in British tropical Africa.* Edinburgh: Blackwood.

Makozi, A. O., and G. J. Afolabi Ojo. 1982. *The history of the Catholic Church in Nigeria.* Yaba: Macmillan Nigeria Publishers.

Manning, Patrick. 1979. The slave trade in the Bight of Benin, 1640–1890. In Henry A. Gemerz and Jan S. Hogendorn (eds.), *The uncommon market: Essays in the economic history of the Atlantic slave trade,* 107–141. New York: Academic Press.

Marigadi, Barje S. 2006. *Divisive ethnicity in the church in Africa.* Kaduna, Nigeria: Baraka Press.

Mason, Michael. 1969. Population density and "slave raiding": The case of the Middle Belt of Nigeria. *Journal of African History* 10(4):551–564.

Mbiti, John S. 1969. *African religions and philosophy*. London: Heinemann.

McKinney, Carol V. 1983. A linguistic shift in Kaje, Kagoro, and Katab kinship terminology, *Ethnology* 22:281–293.

McKinney, Carol V. 1985. The Bajju of Central Nigeria: A case study of religious and social change. PhD dissertation. Southern Methodist University, Dallas, TX.

McKinney, Carol V. 1986. Retention of traditional religious beliefs by Bajju Christians. *Notes on Anthropology*, Special Issue No. 1:58–66.

McKinney, Carol V. 1990. Which language: Trade or minority? *Missiology* 18(3):279–290.

McKinney, Carol V. 1992. Wives and sisters: Bajju marital patterns. *Ethnology* 31(1):75–87.

McKinney, Carol V. 1994. Conversion to Christianity: A Bajju case study. *Missiology* 22(2):147–165.

McKinney, Carol V. 2017. John 3, 'being born again' in a culture with reincarnation beliefs. *GIALens* 12(2).

McKinney, Carol V. 2018. "Witchcraft or spiritual power among Bajju Christians." *Anthropological Ethnography and Analysis Through the Eyes of Christian Faith* 2(2).

McKinney, Carol V. 2019. *Baranzan's people: An ethnohistory of the Bajju of the Middle Belt of Nigeria*. Publications in Ethnography 46. Dallas, TX: SIL International.

Meek, Charles K. 1931. *Tribal studies in northern Nigeria*. Vol. 2. London: Kegan Paul, Trench, Trübner.

Minutes of the Conference of Missions in Northern Provinces, Nigeria. 1935.

Morrison, J. H. 1982. Plateau societies' resistance to Jihadist penetration. In Elizabeth Isichei (ed.), *Studies in the history of Plateau State, Nigeria*, 136–150. London: MacMillan.

Nitecki, Andre. 1972. *Nigerian tribes: Preliminary list of headings for use in libraries*. Legon: Department of Library Studies, University of Ghana.

Ohene, Elizabeth. 2011. "False Prophets?" African Viewpoint, BBC.com.uk, June 22, 2011, http://www.bbc.co.uk/news/world-africa-13816050. Accessed 4 August 2017.

Omoyajowo, J. Akinyele. 1982. *Cherubim and Seraphim: The history of an African independent church*. New York: Nok Publishers.

Palmer, Richmond. 1936. *The Bornu Sahara and Sudan*. New York: Negro Universities Press.

Powell, J. Mark. 1981. Cropping system in Abet: Report 1, cropping patterns. Ms.

Quarterly Report, Zonkwa. July 1954. SIM Archives.

Ray, Benjamin C. 1976. *African religions*. Englewood Cliffs, NJ: Prentice-Hall.

Report of the United Conference of Protestant Missionary Societies held at Port Harcourt, 1928.

Sanneh, Lamin. 1983. *West African Christianity: The religious impact.* London: Christopher Hurst, George Allen and Unwin; Maryknoll, NY: Orbis.

Sanneh, Lamin. 1989. *Translating the message: The missionary impact on culture.* Maryknoll, NY: Orbis.

Sanneh, Lamin. 2012. *Summoned from the margin: Homecoming of an African.* Grand Rapids, MI: Eerdmans.

Smith, Mary F. 1954. *Baba of Karo: A woman of the Muslim Hausa.* New Haven, CT: Yale University Press.

Smith, Michael G. 1960. *Government in Zazzau 1800–1950.* London: Oxford University Press.

Smith, Michael G. 1975. *Social organisation and economy of Kagoro.* Occasional Publications 4. Zaria, Nigeria: Sociology Department, Ahmadu Bello University.

Sudan Interior Mission, *Missionary policies.* 1942. Jos, Nigeria: Niger Press.

Swank, Gerold O. 1970. Church growth in Kagoro and adjacent tribes. Ms.

Temple, Charles L. 1918. *Native races and their rulers: Sketches and studies of official life and administrative problems in Nigeria.* Reprint edition. London: Frank Cass.

Temple, Olive Susan Miranda, comp. 1922. *Notes on the tribes, provinces, emirates and states of the northern provinces of Nigeria,* ed. Charles L. Temple. Second edition. Lagos, Nigeria: C.M.S. Bookshop. Reprinted by London: Frank Cass.

The Sudan witness. July–August 1934:10.

The West African yearbook. 1915.

Tibenderana, Peter Kazenga. 1983. The emirs and the spread of western education in Northern Nigeria, 1910–1946. *Journal of African History* 24:517–534.

Tibenderana, Peter Kazenga. 1985. The beginnings of girls' education in the Native Administration Schools in Northern Nigeria, 1930–1945. *Journal of African History* 26:93–109.

Tremearne, A. J. N. 1912. *The tailed headhunters of Nigeria.* London: Seeley, Service.

Turaki, Yusufu. 1982. The institutionalization of the inferior status and socio-political role of the non-Muslim groups in the colonial hierarchical structure of the northern region of Nigeria: A social-ethical analysis of the colonial legacy. PhD dissertation. Boston University, MA.

Turaki, Yusufu. 1993. *The British colonial legacy in Northern Nigeria: A social ethical analysis of the colonial and post-colonial society and politics in Nigeria, Kenya.* Jos, Nigeria: Challenge Press.

Turaki, Yusufu. 2006. *Foundations of African traditional religion and worldview.* Nairobi: Word Alive.

Turaki, Yusufu. 2010. *Tainted legacy: Islam, colonialism and slavery in Northern Nigeria*. McLean, VA: Isaac Publishing.

Tylor, Edward B. 1871. *Primitive culture*. London: J. Murray.

Walsh, Jarlath Paul. 1983. The development and consolidation of the Catholic Church in the Diocese of Jos, 1907–1978. MA thesis. University of Birmingham.

Waters-Bayer, Ann. 1982. History of land use and settlement patterns on the Abet Plains. Zonkwa. Ms.

Winick, Charles. 1977. *Dictionary of anthropology*. Totowa, NJ: Littlefield, Adams.

Yahaya, A. D. 1980. *The native authority system in Northern Nigeria 1950–70: A study in political relations with particular reference to the Zaria native authority*. Zaria, Nigeria: Ahmadu Bello University Press.

Zonkwa. n.d. SIM Archives.

Index

SIL International® Publications
Publications in Ethnography Series
ISSN 0-0895-9897

46. **Baranzan's people: An ethnohistory of the Bajju of the Middle Belt of Nigeria**, by Carol V. McKinney, 2019, 283 pp., ISBN 978-1-55671-399-6.

45. **Acclimated to Africa: Cultural competence for Westerners**, by Debbi DiGennaro, 2017, 163 pp., ISBN 978-1-55671-386-6.

44. **The heart of the matter: Seeking the center in Maya-Mam language and culture**, by Wesley M. Collins, 2015, 205 pp., ISBN 978-1-55671-375-0.

43. **African friends and money matters**. Second edition, by David E. Maranz, 2015, 293 pp., ISBN 978-1-55671-277-7.

42. **Ensnared by AIDS: Cultural contexts of HIV and AIDS in Nepal**, by David K. Beine, 2014, 357 pp., ISBN 978-1-55671-350-7.

41. **The Norsk Høstfest: A celebration of ethnic food and ethnic identity**, by Paul Thomas Emch, 2011, 121 pp., ISBN 978-1-55671-265-4.

40. **Our company increases apace: History, language, and social identity in early colonial Andover, Massachusetts**, by Elinor Abbot, 2007, 279 pp., ISBN 978-1-55671-169-5.

39. **What place for hunters-gatherers in millennium three?** by Thomas N. Headland and Doris E. Blood, eds. 2002, 130 pp., ISBN 978-1-55671-132-9.

38. **A tale of Pudicho's people**, by Richard Montag. 2002, 181 pp., ISBN 978-1-55671-131-2.

SIL International® Publications
7500 W. Camp Wisdom Road
Dallas, Texas 75236-5629 USA

General inquiry: publications_intl@sil.org
Pending order inquiry: sales@sil.org
publications.sil.org

About the Author

Carol McKinney with her husband Norris and their four children (Mark, Eric, Susan, and Christy) worked in Nigeria, West Africa, with the Bajju people who live in southern Kaduna State. Completing her PhD in Anthropology from Southern Methodist University, Dallas, Texas, she taught at the Texas SIL school, then at the Graduate Institute of Applied Linguistics, where she was an Associate Professor of Applied Anthropology.

McKinney previously published *Globe Trotting in Sandals, a Field Guide to Cultural Research* and co-authored, with her husband, *Introduction to Field Phonetics*. She has published many articles which largely focus on the Bajju.

She was involved in language development in Jju, working closely with a local Bajju team translating the New Testament. The Bajju themselves are currently working to complete the Old Testament.

Further publications

www.sil.org/contributor/mckinney-carol-v

www.ingramcontent.com/pod-product-compliance
Lightning Source LLC
Chambersburg PA
CBHW062023270326
41929CB00014B/2294